## Linnie Thomas from clients and colleagues

"Linnie is a gifted healer, mentor, and teacher. She has a calm and reassuring presence as she teaches her classes. I had spent a day and a half trying to master one particularly vital healing technique. On the final day of the weekend class, Linnie came over and just held her hands over mine to help guide me, and reassured me that I could indeed do it. In that moment, everything aligned for me and I felt what I had been spending thirty-six hours trying to learn."

**Jamie Marthaler, RN**

"Linnie is a teacher in our community filled with wisdom, strength, and light. We thank her for gifting all of us with the knowledge from her soul. There are no words in the dictionary to describe how amazing she is."

**Janna Moll, MSN, HTCP/I, LMT**
Founder of **Energy Medicine Specialists**

"Linnie Thomas is a real thought leader in the field of energy medicine and healing and a pioneer in bringing visibility and viability to the field of energy medicine. She is able to view the industry from a higher perspective and share a worldview of the effectiveness and importance of biofield therapies with the public and practitioners.

In her book, *The Encyclopedia of Energy Medicine,* she provides comprehensive descriptions of the most widely used and professional energy modalities, giving people who are seeking alternative therapies a place to explore and understand what is available. In *Laws Governing Energy Medicine Practitioners,* Linnie supports and highlights the importance of practicing legally in the energy medicine field.

Both books are valuable reference manuals that help spread awareness of energy healing therapies and further the care and rights of individuals to be treated and viewed as whole in body, mind, emotions, and spirit. This book promises to be another best-seller."

**Lisa Mentgen-Gordon**
CEO/Visionary, **Healing Touch Program**™

## Books by Linnie Thomas

*The Encyclopedia of Energy Medicine*

*Laws Governing Energy Medicine*

*There Is No Hell*

*Pioneers in Healing Touch*

# Pioneers
# in
# Healing Touch

Compiled by

**Linnie Thomas**

Copyright © 2018 by Linnie Thomas

Cover photo supplied by Cynthia Hutchison
Cover by Billy Courtney

All rights reserved. No part of this publication may be used or reproduced in manner whatsoever without written permission except in the case of brief quotations embodied in critical articles and reviews. For further information, please contact the author.

Published by Ellinwood Publishing

Library of Congress-in-Publication Data

Thomas, Linnie 1946 –

Pioneers in Healing Touch/Linnie Thomas

ISBN: 978-1-72920-609-6

    1. Pioneers

Printed in the United States of America
First Printing

10 9 8 7 6 5 4 3 2 1
For more information about Healing Touch go to www.healingtouchprogram.com

## Dedications

*posthumously to*

### Janet Mentgen

*Our first pioneer to lead the way*

### &

### Lisa Mentgen-Gordon

*Who continues on as a pioneer*

*with vision to lead the way*

*for the rest of us*

# Table of Contents

Foreword ............................................................................................. xi
Acknowledgements ......................................................................... xxii
Introduction ......................................................................................... 1
Janet Mentgen ..................................................................................... 5
Cynthia Aspromonte ............................................................................ 9
Anne Boyd ......................................................................................... 21
Mary Jo Bulbrook .............................................................................. 29
Nancy Burns ...................................................................................... 49
Karen B Chin ..................................................................................... 57
Bernie Clarke .................................................................................... 71
Barbara Dahl ..................................................................................... 81
DEBORAH ........................................................................................ 93
Donna Duff ...................................................................................... 101
Mary Ann Goeffrey .......................................................................... 121
Franny Harcey ................................................................................. 135
Jane Hightower ............................................................................... 147
Ines I. Hoster ................................................................................... 175
Dorothea Hover-Kramer .................................................................. 183
Sue Hovland .................................................................................... 187
Cynthia Hutchison ........................................................................... 201

Rita Kluny .................................................................................. 227

Carol Komitor ............................................................................ 245

Nancy Lester .............................................................................. 263

Renata Maniaci .......................................................................... 273

Tim McConville .......................................................................... 287

Janna Moll ................................................................................. 297

Kathy Moreland ......................................................................... 315

Bonnie Morrow .......................................................................... 331

Monica Nebauer ........................................................................ 337

Reverend Rudy Noel .................................................................. 347

Sally Nyholt ............................................................................... 353

Sharon Robbins ......................................................................... 367

Sharon Scandrett-Hibdon .......................................................... 369

Kathy Sinnett ............................................................................. 383

Linda Smith ............................................................................... 387

Barbara Ann Starke ................................................................... 411

Linnie Thomas .......................................................................... 419

Amelia Vogler ............................................................................ 433

Dawn Warnaca ......................................................................... 451

# Foreword

## by
## Lisa Mentgen Gordon

### Introduction

I felt Lisa Mentgen Gordon should be at the beginning of the book and decided her interview would make a good foreword. Her story is well worth reading.

Lisa is Janet Mentgen's daughter, the CEO of Healing Touch Program, and also is a visionary for the future of the program. Her number one goal is to support Healing Touch practitioners and instructors in sharing Healing Touch with others.

Lisa Gordon is on my top ten most admired people list. She had two very young children when she took over Healing Touch Program, and added a third child a few short years later. She dealt with betrayal by people she thought she would always be able to rely on for help after her mother died. This could have brought an end to the Healing Touch Program that Janet had created. Instead, Lisa sailed through it all with a quiet and determined confidence that has kept the program going through those difficult times and on to many better things. She is an amazing woman and leader.

## Interview

Thank you for the opportunity to tell my story.
*Your story is the most important one.*
I think the Healing Touch story, the story of how we became the kind of program and company we are is a rich interesting story of growth and change reflected in the people within the company, the company itself and most importantly in the ideals of Healing Touch growing and reaching out into the world around us as a result of our actions.

As of 2018, Healing Touch is being integrated into allopathic medical communities worldwide as well as being utilized in homes and communities. This program has empowered over 130,000 individuals to learn about and use their own natural ability to use energy to support health and well-being for themselves and others. There are over 100 U.S. based hospitals that have integrated this modality for their staff and patient care. Healing Touch has been recognized by the U.S. National Institutes of Health as a form of complementary and alternative medicine and Healing Touch Program's educational program is accredited through the American Nurses Credentialing Center (ANCC), and the practitioner certification, Healing Touch Certified Practitioner (HTCP) is an accredited credential by the National Commission for Certifying Agencies (NCCA).

The story of Healing Touch really starts much earlier, with Janet Mentgen. As a child, Janet had gifts that let her to see, feel and sense people's energy. She grew up in a holistic home and following her mother's footsteps, Janet became a registered nurse. As her energetic abilities grew, and her interest escalated, she took courses from other gifted mentors and teachers like Barbara Brennan, Rosalyn

Bruyere and many others. As a nurse, she saw a way to put an energetic education program together for nurses that would be beneficial to their professional practice, personal growth and self-care.

The point at which Janet decided to take all of her knowledge, practice, and nursing education and make this hands-on healing program everything changed. Her program was endorsed by the American Holistic Nurses Association and began rapid growth and acceptance as health-care professionals and the public began to focus on alternative and complementary approaches for relief of anxiety and pain.

Janet faced many challenges with her program, including skeptical doctors and nurses who thought energy work was unfounded, and lacked specific research to validate the practice. Janet was unyielding and forged forward anyway. Healing Touch became a movement in the medical field because it was a different way to see and treat people – body, mind and spirit.

I think that's our story and it continues on today as we train and support healers in this growing field. I think it is still in its infancy as far as potential.

*I like to say we are on the cutting edge of a brand new, very old science.*

Yes, I love that.

I think that it is vital that we have empathy for people. We need to have empathy for the nurses and other care providers that struggle with seeing patients suffering and struggling with the medical system. A system that is based more on drugs and masking symptoms than on addressing prevention, lifestyle, and wellness. We have specialized medical care so specific that it no longer looks at people as a whole being. I want to see patients empowered to have a say in their care and to know that they have holistic treatment options available, and to have access to the treatments that are right for them.

*A lot of that is in the book, really. The individual stories are pretty fascinating. I am really in love with a lot of the new people in this program. They are not nurses. Their stories are more current and easier for people to grasp. At the same time the elders need to be heard because that's the beginning, and their stories are just as remarkable.*

My experiences are not in the medical field.

*Neither is mine.*

I'm a mom, wife, and CEO who uses Healing Touch all the time.

*Tell me the story of how you came to be where you are.*

Where I am in using Healing Touch or where I am in running Healing Touch Program?

*Both.*

Let's start with how I was first introduced to Healing Touch, or more correctly energy healing. Before my mom developed Healing Touch as a specific program, she was learning, using and teaching methods and techniques in energy medicine. She would share these with me, for personal use and experimentation starting when I was a pre-teen. She was also teaching techniques to other nurses. She would bring home gadgets and biofeedback devices to measure physiological responses. She would use these on me and my friends and explain how they worked. She took great delight in sharing what she learned, and was always able to capture an eager audience. It was pure joy for her.

Healing Touch was frequently used in our home and it became simply normal to me to use energetic interventions all the time.

## Foreword

I began officially working with Janet in 1993. I was the graphic artist and webmaster for Healing Touch. I created the first Healing Touch web site, brochures, and anything that went out about Healing Touch publicly.

I moved from Colorado to California in 1996 and with Janet's guidance, started the Healing Touch West branch office, where I coordinated and organized Healing Touch classes and facilitated the growth of the local community. I loved that I could bring my mom to the area and people were so excited to see her. She had a following already in Southern California and people wanted to take her classes.

I took Healing Touch Level 1 in 1996 with Kathy Allan in San Diego. I clearly remember taking the class and being in awe afterwards. I felt so nurtured and cared for in that class. I called my mom after the class and with tears told her how beautiful this program was. I felt that if everybody had Healing Touch in their home, humanity and our world would be profoundly better. Lives would be more peaceful and the way we would treat our children, spouses and family with care and compassion by using these simple Healing Touch methods and principles. We lack touch in our society and I think when people experience Healing Touch that probably one of the strongest things they experience is being held and touched in a loving and caring way.

After I took Level 1 I had many opportunities to practice Healing Touch. My most profound experience was with a HT instructor in San Diego. She was scheduled to go for surgery for a bowel obstruction. I asked her if I could visit her in the hospital before her surgery to give her a Healing Touch treatment. I was still only a Level 1 student, but I wanted to give her my support. She agreed and I went.

She had been prepped for surgery and had done a barium swallow. They took her away to take x-rays and then brought her back to her room. I did a treatment with the techniques I had learned in Level 1. I did a chakra connection and then cleared her field. They took her back for a second set of x-rays before her surgery and all the adhesions in her bowels were gone! They cancelled the surgery.

I know that it was her body healing and that for whatever reason, it happened at that time. I was shocked! The doctors had no explanation for what happened. They had before and after pictures documenting the changes. That's my most fantastic personal healing story.

Another great story is the time my husband Chris and I were at the beach. We were walking by the tide pools and he fell backwards landing on his hand and wrist. We sat and watched his wrist and palm swell and turn purple and black. It was really bad. I did Healing Touch for twenty minutes, not knowing what I was doing, but thinking this has got to help. We watched it change from black to purple, then to red and pink. He ended up with two little scratches on his hand and he was fine. I think it's because we worked on it immediately.

I've seen other things like that. I've used Healing Touch on my kids, being able to sooth them and heal their scrapes, bumps, bruises, burns, anxieties, fears and everything else. I really use it in our home as a first aid remedy all the time. That's just what we do. My kids know Healing Touch and they do it for each other. I have one child that can actually see colors and auras. I fully encourage his ability and ask him to talk about what he sees. I think it's a great holistic way to raise children to have these skills and try natural healing instead of thinking they have to take a medicine for everything. We would not give our kids medication for anything if we can avoid it. And we haven't had to because we have a different way to care for them. I know they'll pass this on to their children because they're already

## Foreword

using Healing Touch for themselves and their friends. It's a whole new generation with a different way to take care of the body.

Since taking Healing Touch Level 1, I have taken all the classes loving every experience I've had in this program. I have not become a certified practitioner because I don't feel the calling to be a practitioner. I use Healing Touch almost every day and that is what works for me.

My mother's role was to create the standardized curriculum, putting together ideas that people could use in a way that fit into the current paradigm, opening it for something new that could be shared and taught to others, and then reaching others to share it with. She was a Nurse, and an explorer, but also an entrepreneur. She was able to take these exotic ideas and synthesize them into a message that the medical community could understand and embrace.

My job as CEO of Healing Touch Program is to amplify and spread the message about this amazing program, and to give others the tools and inspiration to share it as well. My main interest is marketing and power of connecting with people. The more we can connect, the more people will learn about the benefits of Healing Touch, and will learn to use it and have a positive effect on their lives, and the lives of those around them. I'm proud to be carrying on Janet's vision, and leading it into the future.

Since my mother passed away we have had many achievements and accomplishments in the program. We have continually worked to improve the curriculum, maintain the standardized offering so that the training a person receives in HTP is the same training that Janet created. We have added to the professionalism of practitioners through the Healing Touch Professional Association. We started Healing Touch Certification to provide the best certification for practitioners in Janet's program. We have achieved two national accreditations for the program, and continue to improve the reputation and influence of Healing Touch Program.

I ended up as the CEO because I had worked with my mother for many years. Healing Touch Program is not the first business we worked in together. Janet was very entrepreneurial and shared her passion and knowledge of business with all of her kids. She actively encouraged and supported us to create and follow our passions and endeavors. She was a guide to us on many levels, and we definitely had a unique upbringing.

When she passed away, she gave the program to her three children, my brother, sister and me. I was the one who worked directly in the program and had the greatest familiarity with the program and community. It made the most sense that I would be the one to run the company. My sister and brother both worked to help stabilize the company in that early time, contributing their own experience and expertise. I am grateful for the help and support they gave. They have both moved on to focus on their own businesses and have not been involved in the company for several years now.

Our mission is to spread Healing Touch so people can utilize this work in their homes. That's our goal, a healer in every home and it's my mantra. This comes from my experience in my very first class and saying, "My gosh, if everybody did this, what a different world we would live in."

Our goal is to have a healer in every home and the way we will achieve it is to continue to offer our standardized classes. We are currently working on making our program more available through on-line education, and by developing more introductory programs for using Healing Touch in the home. We want to develop new and better ways to reach more people online so they can start learning Healing Touch, and then we can encourage them to take a Level 1 class. That may be as far as they go in the program, but it is a great foundation to begin getting Healing Touch used in every home. We understand that not everyone wants to be an energy practitioner, and it is okay. That is the beauty of Healing Touch, it is many things to many people.

And at the same time, we are dedicated to keeping a strong accredited, credentialed path for those want to be a professional healer or energy practitioner, establishing Healing Touch and Energy Medicine as a valid respected healthcare practice.

One of the pieces that has helped people open doors and give this modality validity is the research that has been done in the field of energy medicine, not only for Healing Touch, but other biofield therapies that are similar. The NCCA accredited credential, Healing Touch Certified Practitioner (HTCP) validates that an individual has the knowledge and proficiency needed to be a safe effective practitioner. We understood the importance of adding this additional validation to our credentials, and that it is recognized and backed by an accrediting body. We did not want to be viewed as just a certification body claiming some kind of meaningless made up "gold standard."

I know that the professional accreditations have helped open doors in healthcare facilities and VA medical centers. Nurses get credit because the HTCP credential is NCCA accredited.

As we move forward, we want to see more research taking place, especially in efficiency and effectiveness of Healing Touch and how it relieves pain and helps patients recover and heal faster.

*There are few stories in this book where people are critical of Janet and I'm thinking that brings balance to the book. We don't all have her on some pedestal or as something better than everybody else. It makes for a real person. Almost all of that criticism has to do with administration, the nuts and bolts of things. It has nothing to do with her healing ability or the program or any of that kind of thing.*

*But as a financial whiz, some of the instructors, especially the early instructors, mentioned that that's not her forte.*

It is interesting how easy it is to look at something from the outside and criticize, without having practical experience or real knowledge of what it really takes, what a person is actually doing, and what it takes to achieve or accomplish anything. People tend to see the result and think it comes without effort, and don't realize the work and sacrifice that goes into creating what they are seeing. The world is full of armchair quarterbacks.

If you can imagine this, Janet would teach forty weekends a year. Her routine was to leave on Wednesday night or Thursday morning, depending upon the length of the class. She would come home on Monday, and empty her suitcase into the washer and put it right next to the dryer. Once her clothes were clean she would put them right back in the suitcase and she was ready to leave again. She was running her entire business home and office in two days a week. That included managing around one hundred instructors. Her heart and love was in the teaching.

Honestly, the fact that this program has been sustained for all of these years is amazing. Business is difficult and complex. There are a lot of moving parts that need constant attention. It's a true testimonial to the love that people have for this work that the program continues to endure and thrive.

*That shows all through the book. A couple of people even mentioned the guidance that helped keep the program going through difficult times. especially in the beginning.*

Yes. We have received great guidance at many times when needed, and still seek guidance in our regular business. I think that helps set HTP apart from many businesses. We have also received real on the ground support and caring from people who have made the effort to selflessly give of themselves to help Healing Touch. There

## Foreword

are many angels out there who have supported us, and continue to support us in many ways and we are truly grateful for them.

I'm grateful that you would let me be a part of your book, helping to share people's stories about Healing Touch and helping to spread Healing Touch. The healing stories we have to share give so much inspiration to people. Thank you for bringing this together and making it happen.

You are truly one of the angels supporting Healing Touch and I am grateful for all that you do Linnie. Thank you!

Pioneers in Healing Touch

# Acknowledgements

I have so many people to thank. This book wouldn't have been made possible without their help, support, and encouragement. To top the list is Cynthia Hutchison. She has been beside me during the whole process with words of encouragement. Bless you Cynthia.

Also at the top of the list (they tie) is Dawn Warnaca. Dawn connected me to people when I needed contact. She helped with some of the editing. I couldn't have completed this book without her. Thank you so much Dawn.

Other important people include Lisa Gordon for giving me the idea in the first place, and Leslie Gifford who kicked me in the butt whenever I'd think of quitting.

Billy Courtney: the best proof reader, and for a great job on the cover.

Every person interviewed in this book taught me something. These are truly amazing people gifted with great wisdom and courage. Without them, you would not be doing Healing Touch. They are the reasons you are able to enjoy the benefits of this wonderful program. Thank you all very much.

Pioneers in Healing Touch

# Introduction

I am a Level 1 Instructor. I certified as an instructor in 2001. Because there have been so many changes in recent years to the Healing Touch Program curriculum, I decided it would be a good idea to audit a Level 6 class. I am very glad I did. I learned a lot. I have incorporated the new material in my classes and passed it on to my mentees. That was four years ago. I need to do it again.

At one point in the class, Cynthia Hutchison, our Education Program Director, passed out hard boiled eggs with the names of prominent people in Healing Touch written on the eggs. Quite a few of the students didn't know who some of the people were. Lisa Gordon, our CEO was also auditing the class and happened to be sitting next to me. I mentioned in passing that we ought to have a Who's Who for Healing Touch. Somehow, I got the job of writing one.

I meditated on the project for about three months. My first thought was a small booklet with a paragraph or two about each person. However, just to have a few nuts and bolts about a person's contributions to Healing Touch sounded a bit boring to me. Stories are so much more fun to read.

Several people suggested I include the elders in the booklet. I thought of a few ways to do that and finally decided I would interview each person, and transcribe the interview. I came up with a list of some twenty-three questions, all in very logical order. I got approval from both Lisa and Cynthia.

I began to think of the elders and leaders in the Healing Touch community as pioneers, whether they have been around for a long time, or newly arrived.

I made my first call. Half way through the interview I took my list of questions and threw them up into the air. Most Healing Touch instructors like to talk. A lot. There are a few of us who are not quite so verbose, but even then, the stories that rose are delicious and full of history, techniques, laughter, disappointments and downright fun to read.

My original plan was to include a special chapter devoted to Janet Mentgen, our founder. That isn't necessary. I did include a memorial to her by Franny Harcey. Almost all the elders I interviewed had at least one Janet Mentgen story. Some people loved her, some admired her. A few were critical of her. I included the critical comments as well as the lavish praise. As dear as Janet is to most of us who knew her, she was human. She made mistakes, got angry at times and other totally normal actions we all do. I wanted to show all sides of her.

You will find as you read through the book that some of the stories contradict other stories. It shows how many of us see things through our own filter and that there are different points of view. I love the differences. They add the spice to our lives.

Because the interviews are transcribed, you will probably notice not all the wording is not perfect. The grammar can be off. Even the punctuation can be considered, well, ahem. It is what makes them so personal. You can read the voice of the person talking. So if you notice glaring errors, don't judge them. They are all part of the story

The elders often told similar stories about the origins of Healing Touch, and how they personally got started with Healing

## Introduction

Touch. Even so, there are golden nuggets in each one's version and you will learn a little more with each reading.

Four years later I am still working on this book. It has grown and changed each time I sit down to work on it. The people interviewed in this book are amazing. I feel very humble to be part of the program. I have said and will probably continue to say, "Healing Touch is the best introductory program available." These people are the ones who have made it possible.

Enjoy the reading. Find out about some of your favorite instructors. Learn about their instructors. Learn about what hooked them on Healing Touch. I found the variety of reasons quite fascinating.

A couple of people wrote their own interviews. You'll notice a change in style. I think it makes for easier reading to have a little difference here and there and adds a little more spice.

After I interviewed several elders, I found many of them came into Healing Touch through the American Holistic Nurses Association. This made their stories similar. As a result I didn't interview all the elders on my list. Instead I chose to add a few people somewhat new to the program. They are pioneers too. We have some young people who are contributing to the program in ways in ways I would not have thought possible when I started twenty-one years ago.

As a result this book is a compilation of many authors. I compiled it, but each chapter belongs to the person interviewed. If you want to quote someone, I suggest you ask them personally.

I would like to bless and thank each of the people included in this book and the many that aren't. Each one of you is a blessing, providing comfort and healing to those who need it. Thank you!

For more information about Healing Touch go to
www.healingtouchprogram.com

# Janet Mentgen
## BSN, RN, HNC, HTCP/I
### Senior Elder

**In Memorial**

I spent four days with Janet. I felt like I had known her all my life and then some. To my delight I learned she had read *Relieve Tension the Autogenic Way* by Hannes Lindemann, MD, one of my favorites. That got us going, and the conversations didn't stop until we were on the way to the airport. The book has been long out of print and is a bit spendy now. However, Janet uses one of his techniques as part of the Advanced Practices classes.

Shortly after she died I was tidying up the healing room in my house. I felt a presence and there was Janet standing beside me. She said, "Please don't let go of Healing Touch."

I assured her I had no intention of doing so and would do what I can to support the program. She smiled and left. I have kept my promise.

There really isn't a need for a chapter on Janet. She is mentioned in almost every other chapter in the book. However, I thought Franny Harcey's touching memorial would set the stage for what is to follow.

**From Franny Harcey November 2006**
Janet was such a gift to humanity, and lived from her heart-space, bringing the Christ Consciousness to the planet. I believe there are many of us that continue to work with her in helping to evolve raising the collective frequency to aid the ascension of the human consciousness, always working from the heart as Janet did.

Entering Level 4, I knew I would require a mentor to complete the program. Janet Mentgen agreed to be my mentor. This truly was a blessing for me as I had the profound opportunity to spend a year with Janet, at her side at least one day a week, treating her and learning from her. I was in Janet's presence and learned more than you could imagine.

Those I have spoken with in the Healing Touch community have told me what an honor it must have been to be with her. I can only tell you how profound the work we shared was. As one would embark on a great journey, so I would get in my car at least one day a week, and make the almost two hour drive from my home to Janet's. Every time I made this drive, excitement would well up inside of me, as I never took for granted the pure wisdom and gift I would receive in the hours to come.

When I arrived, usually the Mentgen furry friends would greet me at the front door. One with a ball, wanting to play, and the other as a great sentinel keeping watch. Janet loved those dogs! It was an honor for me to be so freely allowed into the Mentgen home and be so embraced with love. Janet was always ready for a treatment and eagerly found her place on the table after we caught up on the week.

I will be the first to tell you that in the beginning of our year together, the thought of me "treating Janet, the master of Healing Touch" scared the heck out of me. But Janet in her non-assuming way would be so eager to receive that it just really was not about "me" but about divine will, and releasing the outcome! For this was Janet's time to receive and just "be".

This time together became such sacred time, not only for me, but my sense, for Janet as well, allowing and just "to be", making no judgments. Janet's wisdom would overflow in her energy field. As she would be on the table, we would discuss what I was feeling, what she was feeling, and how the energy would shift and why it wouldn't shift if I held my hands in a position for an extended period of time.

We discussed numerous topics from hand positions, releasing attachment, guided work, to how different medications "felt" in the energy field. Working in this manner has made me understand that once you experience something in your hands, they remember "photographically" how it should feel and bring that knowledge to your consciousness. My work with Janet was truly that of student/teacher, and yet as our time grew together, that of friend. Her infinite knowledge of energy, her kindness and non-judgment was deeply imbedded within me.

She often talked of how important it was to her "to read at least 10 pages of a book a day". She always seemed to be going deeper within herself and finding more answers and more questions.

We studied together the work of Torkom Saraydarian. For those of you who have studied Alice Bailey, he writes as intensely as she does (not an easy study if I might add). Janet was very fond of both Alice's and Torkom's work. Both about raising your consciousness and the consciousness of humanity.

I had the profound privilege of being with her the day before she transitioned, and was blessed to be allowed into her energy field one last time. As every other time with Janet, she was still teaching me, still bringing every question I had back to me, as she always did in her gentle way of helping me understand that I already knew the answer! Her gentle wisdom and firm beliefs in the work have been an inspiration for me. Her guidance has only expounded my learning tremendously. I am once again thankful for the quiet wisdom of such a leader on this journey.

If you can imagine it, learning through osmosis is how I would define my year with Janet. Her messages ring in my ears whenever I am "doing the work", or working on myself. As she told me, "Continue to work on yourself and become clear. The clearer you are and the higher your vibration, so, you raise the vibration of all humanity."

I am once again thankful for the quiet wisdom of such a leader on this journey. So, each day I "do the work" I have the great joy of "knowing", to think of how my vibration affects not only my clients on the table, but each person I cross paths with or exchange a smile. In concluding this wonderful little story, I will tell you that my journey, life changing as it has so far been, is only the beginning.

# Cynthia Aspromonte
## RN, NP, AHN-BC, HTCP
### Elder

**Introduction**

Cindy is one of the earliest pioneers in our history. Other elders spoke highly of her and wanted to make sure she was included in this book. She rewrote the interview and did a splendid job. I had very little to edit, for which I am very grateful.

Cindy worked hard in the early years to help bring Healing Touch forward. We owe her a debt of gratitude for her persistence, patience, and love of Healing Touch. It's people like her that make this organization great.

**Interview**

*Have you, or do you now hold any positions in Healing Touch or served on any committees?*

I met Janet Mentgen in 1984. That was the beginning of a very auspicious journey, for which I am forever grateful. Janet introduced me to new ideas, philosophies, and teachings, which in turn led me to 3holistic nursing, Healing Touch, and all of the other certifications that are woven through my life and make me who I am today.

In 1984 I took my first Therapeutic Touch Class with Delores Krieger at Orcas Island, Washington. I knew immediately, that this was my passion. Serendipitously, as soon as I returned to Denver from that course in the autumn of 1984, I was led to Janet Mentgen. I discovered that she had a center in Denver called Health Control Centers, where she offered an abundance of classes. I began taking as many classes as I could, to study with Janet, as I knew right away that she was a highly gifted individual. I sometimes took two or three classes per week. This went on for over twenty years. In those early years, from 1984 through the 1990s, I was very involved with Healing Touch. I helped on many committees bringing speakers to Denver, helping with the Shadowcliff retreats, helping with our conferences, etc.

Janet's center was changed to the Colorado Center for Healing Touch, in the 1990s.

*What got you started in energy medicine to begin with?*

While I was getting my Women's Healthcare Nurse Practitioner degree from the University of Colorado, in 1983-1984, we were introduced to Therapeutic Touch as one of our classes. My program was highly innovative and visionary for that time. There were five nurses in my program and we had three instructors. Our instructors introduced us students to cutting-edge ideas- holistic healthcare being part of that. I graduated in 1984 and that summer, I traveled to the San Juan Islands in Washington state to study with Delores Krieger- the founder of Therapeutic Touch. While there, I learned about energy medicine. That started me on a life-long journey to continue studying in this field. I bought every book on the subject and read voraciously.

The day I returned to Denver from that course, I called a friend to share my excitement about discovering a whole new way of looking at life. I expressed dismay: "Now what... I want to learn more... how can I do that?"

She said, "I know this nurse Janet Mentgen- you should call her."

As soon as I hung up the phone, I called Janet. Much to my surprise, she answered the phone. We had a lovely conversation and she said, "Why don't you come on over?" (to Health Control Centers). Of course, once you are on the path of learning about energy theory, you know there are no accidents. The center just happened to be located in my neighborhood! I went right over. I noticed that she had on her bookshelf, all of the books I had just purchased on Orca's Island. I immediately signed up for her classes and that's how my journey began.

*Are you certified as an instructor?*

Yes, I became certified as an instructor in 1994, I believe. I taught many classes over the years. In the past ten years, I became a certified instructor in the Arvigo Techniques of Maya Abdominal Therapy® and began focusing more on that work, as far as my teaching goes, yet also incorporating Healing Touch into the Maya Therapy treatments.

*What levels do you teach in Healing Touch?*
Level 1.

*What is Arvigo Techniques of Maya Abdominal Therapy?*

These techniques are founded on the ancient Maya techniques of abdominal massage, and are an external, non-invasive manipulation that increases circulation and flow of blood, nerve, lymph, and chi, to internal organs that may have shifted due to the activities of daily life, thereby restricting the flow in these areas. Dr. Rosita Arvigo, an American woman, developed these techniques based on her extensive apprenticeship with the Maya shaman Don Elijio Panti, and other indigenous traditional elders, midwives, and healers in Central America. Healing Touch and energy medicine, are critical in helping restore the body and spirit towards homeostasis and balance. The Arvigo techniques, for me with my work in women's healthcare, are "the missing link" and add a depth and increased dimension to the energy work. If the uterus is out of position from daily life, lifting, exercise, falling, childbirth, running on hard surfaces, etc, it impedes circulation in the pelvis, thereby causing pelvic congestion and disruption of chi, which then leads to a myriad of symptoms including painful periods, back pain, headaches, fertility challenges, fibroids, and even difficult childbirth. There is also a spiritual component to this work. Combining Healing Touch with this massage is the perfect combination, and I always combine the two with my treatments.

*What happened during Level 1 that hooked you on Healing Touch?*
    After learning Therapeutic Touch from Delores Krieger, I was intrigued by the concept of energy medicine and I wanted to learn more. After returning from that workshop, the next day I discovered Janet Mentgen and her classes. This was before she developed Healing Touch and the Levels. Her classes were called Therapeutic Touch Beginner, Intermediate and Advanced. I started with the Intermediate class. Upon entering Janet's classroom space, I immediately felt the positive healing vibrations emanating from the space. She had set up an altar in the classroom and her presence, integrity, sincerity, and level of knowledge was welcoming, impressive, and inspiring. I knew I wanted to study with Janet and continue learning from her. It seemed to me that Janet's classes were

geared towards practically applying the Therapeutic Touch or Healing Touch techniques, into our care of patients as a nursing technique. As Janet's classes developed and she created the Healing Touch levels, they made sense to me and they took Therapeutic Touch to a more advanced level, and this called to me. Janet's teaching ability, dedication, compassion, and healing techniques gave me more in depth knowledge and I just loved taking class after class! Throughout all of the Healing Touch levels, Janet always gave much deference and respect to the foundation of the Therapeutic Touch techniques and to the knowledge and research of Delores Krieger.

*How has Healing Touch changed your life?*

Meeting Janet Mentgen and learning Healing Touch was a life-changing experience. Healing Touch led me to my soul's longing. I am a Board Certified Holistic Nurse, as well as Healing Touch Practitioner and Arvigo Practitioner. These, along with other healing modalities that I have studied, are woven into my daily life and are part of who I am and how I practice as a nurse and nurse practitioner. Healing Touch should be taught in all nursing schools, and it was taught in my nurse practitioner program, but not in my basic nursing program. Healing Touch offers an invaluable tool that brings a nurse or practitioner from ordinary, to exemplary. Healing Touch taught me about compassion and caring, in deeper ways than what I learned in nursing school. It's not just something I have learned - it's a calling. Healing Touch introduced me to a body of knowledge that is immeasurable in terms of enhancing my life, my philosophy of living, and my experiences. It introduced me to a community of like-minded, kindred souls - really a family. All of our conventions are like family reunions. Janet Mentgen was an important teacher and mentor, and I continue to call on her for guidance.

*Do you have a favorite Healing Touch healing story?*

I have many anecdotal case studies of Healing Touch treatments over the past thirty years, since it has been such a part of my life. I have done many treatments with patients, such as before and after surgery, for fertility support, during labor and delivery, and for acute and chronic illnesses.

Two stories stand out: One is that, when my mother was seventy-five years old, she had open heart surgery to repair a heart valve, damaged by rheumatic fever. There were about a dozen patients who all were having open heart surgery at the same time, in different operating rooms. I did extensive Healing Touch on her prior to surgery. She was the first, out of the twelve patients, to come out of the OR, and the first to be weaned off the ventilator following anesthesia, and the first one back in her room. I was able to continue doing Healing Touch post-op. She did great that first day and had no pain, unlike the others. I went home about eight pm. When I arrived the next morning, early, she was unresponsive. They were about to call for the resuscitation team. I was shocked, as she was fine when I left her the night before. It turned out that they overdosed her on narcotic pain meds. The nurses said that when they asked her if she was having any pain, she said no, but they did not believe her, because that just doesn't happen. So they gave her the pain medication anyway. Since her energy field was so clear from doing Healing Touch, it was too much. It took me all day to clear her field again from the narcotics, and then she was fine. She was discharged home, earlier than expected, and continued to recovery quickly and surely. I taught the nurses that day, about Healing Touch and they could see for themselves how well it worked and how powerful it was.

Another story is about Janet. In 1987 during one of our classes, she had me get on the massage table to demonstrate a technique. As she assessed my energy field, she loudly stated, "You're pregnant!"

I said "What?!"

She said, "Oh yes. I really think you are. I can feel the energy field of the baby and it is very distinct. You definitely are pregnant."

I hadn't even missed a period. Of course, a few days later I got a positive pregnancy test. She was correct. She was able to assess the energy field of the fetus at about four weeks gestation.

We always joked: "Janet, you're the one who got me pregnant!" That was a good learning tool, because it showed all of us that there is a distinct energy field between mom and baby, and it is perceptible. If one was attuned enough, one could distinguish it. We all paid a little bit more attention to that. This helped me in my own work with pregnant women, in learning to distinguish the difference between the mother's energy field and the baby's energy field to help in healing.

*Do you have any comments or advice for new or potential students?*

Janet always said to study with as many people as you can, keeping an open mind, pushing past your comfort zone, yet be discerning. She would encourage us to study different healing modalities from many different healers and healing traditions. She would tell us to listen to our own inner wisdom, always be in integrity and right relationship, and follow our guidance and intuition. She also said to be gentle when we provide healing treatments, follow the energy, and don't bring someone farther than where they are at the time- everything in due time.

Another thing that Janet always imparted to us is that you have to practice, practice, practice. She encouraged us to provide treatments to our family and friends and animals. She taught us that it would take at least a hundred times of practicing a technique, to become proficient, and that we are continually honing our skills. She would advise us to "follow" the energy and "listen" to our hands and "don't do so much talking". She said you could get into trouble with your words, but not with the energy, so just listen to the energy and "just do the work".

*What do you see or what would you like to see in the future of Healing Touch?*

It is paramount that we keep the purity of the vision that Janet bestowed upon us, as our primary focus. Janet was clear about keeping the techniques simple and pure. There were so many participants that came to classes with their own ideas and their own techniques, but Janet felt strongly about not adding a lot of other techniques to our root knowledge. She did not want to dilute the material that she had developed.

*Do you have a favorite Janet Mentgen story?*

Janet was always generous with her time and teaching and I value dearly, the time spent with her. She was a dynamic teacher, visionary, and leader. I did put a notebook together, documenting photos, flyers, and some of the classes we held in the early years and Lisa Gordon now has that. It is remarkable how many classes she taught, sometimes ten or more per week! One time Janet set up a twenty week course to study Alice Bailey. She loved Alice Bailey's work, and referenced it often. She felt Alice described the basis for magnetic clearing. Janet had aspirations in this twenty week-long course, of studying several of her books. We ended up only getting through a few chapters of Esoteric Healing!

Janet also taught us a meditation technique called Yoga Nidra. She had on-going classes in that. I still have her tapes, in which she narrates the meditations.

She also would bring in outside speakers. We learned another technique in the late 1980s, called Mari-el which is based on one of the rays, I think the sixth ray. Many of us received a special attunement. There were two women who developed that technique, who then had a falling out with each other, and we were forbidden to use the name Mari-el, again.

Janet exposed us to many different healers, for which I am again grateful. We learned hypnosis from her close friend and associate.

She brought in a woman by the name of Linda, who was a channeler and we studied with her for several years. She brought in Sun-Day Martinez, a gifted nurse, healer and musician from Las Vegas, New Mexico. I am still in touch with her.

When we would go to Shadowcliff, Janet loved going into town to get ice cream and became a little kid again! She loved doing fun things at our retreats, including wild and zany talent shows (Sue Hovland did a hysterically-funny routine) and such. One time we divided the room in half, made forts out of piled-up chairs, and had a marshmallow-throwing war. We hooted and hollered and laughed for hours!

*Is there anything else you would like to add?*

Janet did support a few individuals, who added to her program: Rudy Noel, who developed mind clearing and the Hopi technique, Catherine Fanslow who developed the Chakra Spread and later asked Janet not to attribute it to her, for reasons which I am not aware, Carol Komitor who developed Healing Touch for Animals, and Linda Smith who developed Healing Touch Spiritual Ministry.

Rudy Noel lived in Denver, and I actually knew him. He was a videographer, as well as an intuitive healer. He videotaped several of my family's events over the years. My husband, children, and I performed in a Rock and Roll band through my children's school, and he videotaped all of our performances in the 1990s. He was wonderful. I am not sure how Janet met him, or how he developed mind clearing - mainly through his intuitive healing abilities and through his studying with Hopi elders.

In that regard, her daughter Lisa Gordon, together with Cynthia Hutchison, have done an exemplary job of keeping Janet's vision and legacy alive. I highly commend them for their dedication, insight, and respect. I hope Healing Touch can continue with that vision, as that is what Janet truly wanted.

When I see Lisa Gordon speaking to our groups, I see Janet's wisdom channeled through her. Some of her mannerisms are the same! It gives me comfort to know that Janet is working through Lisa and Cynthia, and they are doing such a good job. They are growing the program, yet keeping the original purpose in the forefront of their actions.

I would like to add a few thoughts here:

1. All through the 1980s, many of us in Denver attended classes taught by Janet, weekly, for years and years. When one class would end, Janet would add three more classes. There were always more classes to take and we realized early on, that we were life-long learners, and we would never "graduate" as there was always another enticing class on the horizon. We developed a close-knit community. We loved taking classes from Janet and felt blessed that we were fortunate to have that relationship with Janet. We attended yearly retreats at our beloved Shadowcliff Retreat Center and Youth Hostel in Grand Lake, Colorado. Shadowcliff is located in a gorgeous setting in the Rocky Mountains, on sacred land. It was built by Warren and Pat Rempel. Warren was a minister there and Pat was an RN. They were close friends and supporters of Janet and her program. Warren passed last

year, but I am still in touch with Pat, who is now in her 80s. Pat and Warren lived in the same apartment building as my mother, and they were great friends, until my mother passed away in 2012.

There are several women who stand out amongst those early classes, who also taught the beginning level classes. I would like to acknowledge them here. They are Dona Leiper, who along with Susan Greenberg, were Janet's business partners and founding members of Health Control Centers, and also Nancy Burns, Regina Zoglo, Lisa Harris, Vicky Seeburg, Rachel Lord, Pat Berger, Jane Ellinger Snow and several others. I met Janet in the 1980s, but some of these women worked with Janet since the 1970s. In the 1990s, our core group was very involved.

Then, out of the blue, with no communication, Janet held a class up at Shadowcliff with a whole new group of people, and did not tell us, nor invite us. This is when she started the program out of Gainesville with Sharon Scandrett and Dorothea Hover. This was very hurtful to all of us who had studied with Janet for years, by this time. We felt left out. Then she started a certification program and certified these people as instructors. We should have been the first to become certified, as we had studied with her the longest, but we were barely even notified about it. Therefore, this was a shock to us. That caused the above-mentioned people to drop into the background. It caused a lot of hard feelings, and we lost some valuable, skilled, and wise teachers, which is very unfortunate, and which I feel bad about, to this day.

2. In June of 2005, when Janet was ill, she called the Healing Touch instructors together, to go to Shadowcliff for another group gathering and retreat. It was there that she presented her future vision and wishes, as to how Healing Touch would go forward, after her passing. She communicated to us with utmost clarity and vision. Her

family was there. There was no question, as to her wishes, and we were all unified and supportive. Therefore, after her passing, it was astonishing to me that there was a rift in Healing Touch, and that some people, who were present, broke away and acted on things that were in direct opposition to Janet's wishes and vision. These are individuals who were all there that weekend, and who expressed support and acknowledgement to Janet, the same as I did. I still have confusion and disbelief, as to what exactly happened to make them break away. Cynthia Hutchison has reached out to them many times, and they will have no part of communicating with Healing Touch any longer. It is very sad to me, as these individuals were an important and special part of our community. Janet would be devastated.

Again, just profound gratitude to Lisa, and Cynthia, and Franny Harcey who has Janet's journals, for continuing to uphold Janet's vision, spirit, and legacy.

# Anne Boyd
### MDiv, HTCP/I
### Elder

**Introduction**

Anne is an artist. She may not think of herself that way, but she is. She has done some wonderful drawings of angels.

Anne has provided some wonderful, personal insights to the early years of what it was like to struggle through the trainings and to teach it. Most of this chapter she wrote herself instead of using the transcription of our interview. You can sense her energy and her passion in what she writes.

Look out for the grub.


**Interview**

I came into Healing Touch within about its second year. I called us the second wave. There were just a handful of instructors then. My friend, Linda Smith who has been the director of Spiritual Ministry, she and I and Jane Hightower were in Augusta, Georgia at the time. Linda had to go to a Healing Touch presentation in Colorado and returned saying, "I'm bringing it to Augusta." The three of us went through the program. I believe we took all classes in about seven months, including teacher training.

The three of us lived Healing Touch that year. After attending classes, we became helpers catching the instructors who came to the east coast. Janet was there, and other early instructors; we followed wherever they were – like groupies. In between class weekends, we did practice sessions. We were in the energy a lot that year.

We were allowed to take teacher training, but still had to do our year's mentorship. And then qualify to teach. The three of us knew from the beginning that we were going to be instructors. It was our mission. We were treated like instructors-in-training. We hung out with instructors around the class weekends.

We traveled where we needed to go, the three of us sharing expenses. For me, a lot of issues were overcome. It was a joyful and challenging time. Our energy was high. My body had a hard time keeping up with the energy. Janet would say, "Don't you want to take more time between classes?" We said, "No. We can't stop." We pushed on through to teacher training (and did our year's mentorship after that, before becoming instructors).

In those days our mentors challenged us. I remember a Level 4 class in Atlanta, Georgia, the only class that was ever held there, where my mentor told me to keep silent for the whole weekend. Pretty tough for me to do. We did what we were told to do and that's what it was.

We were fortunate to have the early instructors. I took some classes with Janet. I treasure those above all.

In high energy, I found creativity coming out with me. I started spontaneously drawing angels. They were line drawings, drawn in a continuous line, and an angel would appear. If I tried to change any of the design, I'd almost ruin it. I learned to go with it and let it happen. They would appear about five inches square and I'd reduce them down, water color them and cover them with resin, put a pin on the back, and make pins that I sold around classes when we also sold books. My mentor saw the designs and encourages me to put angels on T-shirts, sweatshirts, and cards. We then had them for sale.

(Even in recent years, when I see someone wearing one of my angel pins, it gives me a thrill.)

For one of the first Healing Touch notebooks to be released, photographs were needed of sessions' etc. When photographs were taken, I happened to be there as helper and was a client, with Janet as healer. Janet was wearing a sweatshirt with my angel design on it. So I feel my angel was meant to be in that early notebook.

In the early days, I was known as Peggy Boyd. But as my energy changed, I took my middle name Anne as Peggy no longer fit. And, as previously said, we three friends were often helpers treated at workshops, including the one where the hara alignment was introduced. The gal from Barbara Brennan's school demonstrated the hara at a Level 3 at Emory University in Atlanta. Many instructors attended that class and we were thrilled to be part of it.

About the same period of time, I accompanied a Healing Touch group that traveled to Australia and New Zealand, in three consecutive years, for two to three weeks at a time. There were just a few of us the first time, including Janet, Mary Jo Bulbrook, Donna Duff, and perhaps one or two others. I was a helper in those classes, and also interacted with the Aborigine and Maori natives and had amazing experiences with them. The second time, there were more and by the third journey there, we had a busload of Healing Touch people.

Before Healing Touch, I had been first a spiritual study group leader, and then doing shaman work. I was able to hold a Shaman Journey Workshop the first time over to help defray my plane fare over. The Australians were excited about it, and it went very well.

The groups in Australia and New Zealand were wonderful. The second trip over, Janet gave a keynote address to the Australian Holistic Nurses Association. The story goes that we never saw Janet in a dress. She always wore pants. But her mother said that if she was going to give this address, she ought to wear a dress. So she bought one for Janet, and Janet wore it at the keynote. I was there. That keynote address is found in one of our Healing Touch notebooks.

In those days I was known as Peggy Boyd. As I moved the through the first year of energy work, my energy had changed significantly and I took my middle name of Anne. I knew Janet better in those early days when she came to teach on the east coast. Thereafter, I'd see her at conferences and an occasional advanced class. These were times I treasure and when I traveled to with her to Australia and New Zealand. We had some great interaction with the indigenous people.

*Do you have a favorite story about her?*

I have a few. The most significant was riding to a tract of land belonging to the Aborigines that we had been given permission to use as a camping ground. It was the first time non-aborigines had been given use of land like that. I was with Janet and Mary Jo Bulbrook to see the tract and bless it. I went on top of a ridge of the land and drummed to thank the ancestors for that permission. I stayed there for a while sensing intuitively that some ancestors were less than happy about that arrangement and got soothed through the drumming I did.

You have to be careful what you ask for. Talking about that, years ago when I was pretty young I did the treasure map. You may call it a vision board. I just happened to see a picture of Australia. And I thought to myself, how can I get to Australia? That's the other side of the world. It just intrigued me, so I cut out the picture of Australia, never dreaming that ten, fifteen years later, I'd be in Australia and have the experiences that I had.

We were, or at least one of our leaders, was on the bus. Actually it was before the year before that. We were in a van. Robert, our driver and guide, was an aborigine who was one of the lost boys, part aborigine, and part white. He was taken from his mother at a young age. To find his own tribe, it took many, many years. He was helped to get through school and the university. He was a wonderful tour guide for us and brought us to the center of Australia to root around that area, the center of Australia, and took us to what he called his playground of yellow sand, all desert. It was pretty interesting to me there. It was the first time I had ever seen, not yellow, but orange sand.

Anyway, he led us into interesting, mystical experiences around that. It was a fun way to travel because the van was air conditioned. We would get out into this blazing sun overhead, well over a hundred degrees, look around for a period of time and then get back into our air conditioned vehicle and drive away. That was a good way to see the interior of Australia. There were a lot of experiences around that.

Another incident, this time on the Healing Touch tour bus in Australia, Janet was with us in a busload. The bus driver had been keeping a live grub in a bag. A grub is a yellow caterpillar looking creature about as wide as a thumb and twice as long. This one was active. The driver carried it on a stick in a plastic sack for a few days and dared someone to eat the grub.

Once he took it outside the bus and held the stick. Janet took it and held it over her head. We took photos of it, but she didn't bite into it.

Finally one of the gals on the trip said she would eat the grub. Halfway down the bus, I watched her. The grub was still alive.

The driver said, "Make sure you take a bite with the head down or it will try to come back up on you."

With mouths hung open, we watched the girl take a bite. Her mouth filled with yellow butter-like juice. She said it tasted like butter. She gulped it down and kind of urped, but didn't throw up. We could hardly believe it.

Later I am home from Australia and at a yard sale I spied the figure of a fat caterpillar. I grabbed it, wrapped it in tissue, boxed it, and mailed it to Janet's office. I heard later that she got the box and opened it up. I had included a note reading that I thought of her and just had to send it. I heard later that she started laughing and folks ran to see what was so funny. They say it stayed in her office for quite a while.

*Out of curiosity, what first attracted you to energy medicine?*

It' a favorite true story that I tell my Level 1 classes. Friend Linda Smith had come back to Augusta, where I was, from Colorado where she had attended a Healing Touch workshop. In excitement, she told me that she was bringing it to Augusta. "Janet Mentgen is bringing it here, and you have to go."

I kept saying, "I'm really not into that. No."

But she never gave up. After hearing about it several times, I finally said, "If you will shut up, if I don't have to hear the words Healing Touch again, I will go." I grouched about spending all that money for something I didn't even really want, etc. What I didn't tell my classes for a long time was that she offered me half a scholarship to get me to attend. Now I am sure there was no half scholarship. She probably paid for half of my class.

It was a life changer. I wasn't in that class half an hour when I knew, I wasn't sure what it all was, but I had to know all about it.

In my case, the teacher appeared as student me was definitely ready. That class, Healing Touch, changed my life forever.

*In what way did it change your life?*

My personality changed. I became softer, gentler, over time. Emotional issues got cleared. And physical issues too. One recurring kidney infection that had been treated twice with antibiotics and came back a third time – that worried me. Like it never completely cleared. Well, soon into Healing Touch, I had no more problems with kidney infections.

I also had an issue with ulcers in my mouth. No one knew what it was exactly. I was given a paste to keep it under control. Healing Touch cleared it permanently.

Energetically, there was tremendous change. I became a different person. I remember asking one of the instructors, "Do you believe it is possible to be so changed that you are an entirely different person? That you really feel different energetically speaking?"

She said she didn't know if you could be entirely different, but pretty much so. You could be quite changed through being in higher frequency for a period of time, like we had been, That was a revelation to me, a long way within a year's time.

Also during that time, I found myself saying, "I'll do anything to get clear. Whatever it takes." Well, I was getting challenges – many at the same time! I felt overwhelmed. And though, "Well, I asked for it."

I happened to go to a new practitioner who took my history and I told her of this dilemma of getting clear. And she said, "Did you ever ask to be clear with grace and ease?"

I said, "Oh. What a thought." So I asked and challenges came one at a time and were easier to work through.

*Did you become certified as an instructor first and then as a practitioner?*

No. I became certified as a practitioner first, after completing mentorship for a year. Although I took teacher training early, I still had those steps to complete first. Then went through steps to become a certified instructor, in the early 1990's.

*Do you have any comments or advice for new or potential students?*
Be true to yourself and devoted to The Work. Give and receive Healing Touch often. The energy is amazing. The experiences can be sublime. Energy medicine creates change. That's a given, and that's the hope for us. It does help you clear as well and makes you a much better healer.

*What do you see as the future for Healing Touch?*
A great future! We are now accredited. It is being used in hospitals. Two of those in our own neighborhood of Asheville, North Carolina – including the V.A. for pain control. It's exciting to be in the work now, as it is becoming more known. It's meant to be in this period of time. I feel that Janet guides The Work, still. I feel her often.

I feel she was a remarkable person. While a student in her lasses, and whenever I was with her, I never felt her judge anyone. She always kept the faith. I feel she would see our foibles and know that if we stayed in the energy, we'd change. And so many of us did.

Janet was a very dedicated instructor on a mission. I feel she watches us now. I know it's up to me, as instructor, to do best to live up to the kind of healer-teacher she personified; and to be a role model for those coming after. It's as important for me to inspire students to Do The Work (as Janet would put it) as it is to teach techniques. By keeping that my mission inspired by Janet Mentgen, I do my small part to foster this Work, this amazing Healing Touch Program.

The sky's the limit.

# Mary Jo Bulbrook
### RN, EdD, CEMP/S/I, HTCP/I, HTI
### Elder

## Introduction

I met Mary Jo many years ago at a conference. She impressed me as being a very intelligent and knowledgeable lady. I put her on my list of people to go to with questions above and beyond Healing Touch. I was surprised to learn she was awarded Canadian Holistic Nurse of the Year in 1989. She is also Dean of the Division of Continuing Education and Director of the Complementary and Alternative Medicine Graduate Programs at Akamai University located in Hilo, Hawaii.

Mary Jo wrote the first Level 1 Notebook. Until 2004, she was the primary author of the Healing Touch notebooks. She served on the board of directors for many years. She was instrumental in bringing Healing Touch to Australia, New Zealand, Peru, and South Africa.

Currently, Mary Jo is president and developer of Energy Medicine Partnerships International, a non-profit organization. I have taken many of her classes and found them truly inspiring.

## Interview

*What attracted you to energy medicine in the first place?*

I had been working with energy medicine, first starting with Therapeutic Touch when Delores Krieger introduced it. I watched the evolvement and development of that. I had workshops with Delores. I even created my own training work. It was called the Bulbrook Method of Therapeutic Touch. I wasn't the one who coined it. It was the Canadian Nurses Association that came up with that. No, I take that back, it actually it was the Canadian Nurse Journal. I was living in Canada and a professor in nursing at Memorial University of St. John's, Canada. I had started teaching Therapeutic Touch and presented at the International Nursing Diagnosis Conference the work of a theory I had put together called "Healing from Within and Without". It was from that start that I began to follow the thread with energy work.

When I moved back to the United States, or was starting to, Charlene McGuire contacted me because they were getting ready to start the Holistic Nurses Association in the United States. I was up in Canada at the time. I helped them kick start it off in the organization up in Canada. I've been interested in energy medicine for a very long time. When I was helping the Canadians to develop their holistic nursing program, it was at the same time that Janet had started the program with AHNA or was starting it. I said to my Canadian colleagues, "I had better check out to see what my American colleagues are doing in America."

Parallel to that, I went to my first class. It must have been about the third class that Janet offered, here in North Carolina, and John Seskovitch was the one who sponsored it here.

We had a pretty large class. I want to say like maybe close to 40 people came. I was there for the sole purpose of, for my intent, working with the Canadians and helping them with their holistic nursing, I just wanted to see what Janet was doing at the time. When we did the introductions of who we were, I remember Janet looked at me and she said, "Are you the Mary Jo Bulbrook who wrote in the Canadian Nurse about Therapeutic Touch? Are you that person?"

I said, "Yes, I am." And so into that she and I started talking together. During that class I heard a voice that said to me, "I need to help Janet do her work." From that spiritual inspiration, that's when I made a commitment to assist Janet with what she was doing. I spent the next year then, as Janet was starting to teach, going around to all of the different courses that I could get to that were on the east coast of the United States. Also I went up for Canadian classes.

It was at the same time that Susan Mayor was working with Janet. Her goal was to create a teaching book with Janet. My goal was to just learn the material and to begin teaching it. After while, Susan hadn't followed through with creating a book. I am not sure if I was the one who suggested to Janet that we start recording, writing the materials down, and creating a book. I think it was me, because Janet was using handouts for the classes and had used them for, I want to say, at least two to three years before we wrote the text book together.

That was my original connection with the work. I was through helping develop the Canadians with their holistic nursing program, the certificate program. The certificate wasn't called that. It was, I don't remember what the official words were at the time. I would have to go back and recheck my notes. But it was the first thing they did with the AHNA. We kind of like all grew up together at the same time. We were touching base. Janet was working with Sharon Scandrett-Hibdon, Dorothea Kramer, and Myra Tovey and using them as consultants to help build the base, because Janet was not an academic, nor a writer and I am not saying this disrespectfully. She would gladly describe that. She did the work and followed spirit. The rest of us, and many other people helped; provided, I would say, the academic aspect connected to the growth of Healing Touch.

It was about the same time that I had accepted a position in Australia, that I was learning Healing Touch. When I went over there to teach, I think it was 1990, in Australia, I started talking about how I was doing Therapeutic Touch and really doing my own energy based training at the same time. One thing that happened, was when I came back to the United States. I was only there for a year as a teaching professor. It was a couple of years later that I brought Healing Touch, leaving the United States, and in Canada, as the first international course. I took it on my own, first starting with Australia, and then I brought it to New Zealand.

How we got to Peru, this was with Sister Barbara Cavanau, who was a missionary sister in Peru for many years. She had practiced Healing Touch there. She learned it in the states, at home on vacation, and then took it to her center in Peru. When she came back to the United States one time I met her in San Francisco. I had started teaching my own work which was "Transform Your Life through Energy Medicine". That's what it was called back then, but it was a parallel program to Healing Touch. Sister Barbara said to me she wanted to take Healing Touch to Peru. I went to her and I said, "Well, I would be happy to assist you with the process."

She made the original arrangements, that was through Stella Maras Hospital in Peru, and I invited Donna Duff to join me. We taught the first class in Peru. There were a 100 people who came to the class. Most of them were Catholic, either priests or sisters representing a variety of different orders, and a number of nurses. They were the population of the group who sponsored it and who they sent it to. That was through the, I think they were called the Congregation of Religious Orders. It included both the priests and the nuns. I would have to go back to look up the specific historical times, of how many times we went back or within the first year, that I continued the development of Healing Touch in that country and started teaching teachers. Right now there is a very established program that continues to today, with the Peruvian sisters that I had started teaching Healing Touch there.

How we got to South Africa, I went to teach in Australia and one of the women in my class was a South African. Her name was Janna Ross. She was living in Australia for a number of years, and she attended my healing class in Healing Touch while I was in Australia.

Janna, after a while, I invited her to help me take the work with the aborigines, which she did. Then I suggested to her about taking the work to South Africa. She made the original contact there. At the last minute she wasn't able to join me. So I taught the first class, there in Cape Town, for 6 people. One of them was blind. I'll never forget that. I really learned a treatment and how to work with people with special needs. I'd be demonstrating and I would say, "Hold your hands here." She had no idea of where I was holding my hands when I was saying that. I had to learn how to teach, working with someone with special needs.

That program continued, and is alive there today. I worked both there, and took it to New Zealand as well. It's a separate story how we got to New Zealand, but over the years that I brought Janet over to start teaching the instructors there. We started the Australian Holistic Nurse Association, and held it in combination with Healing Touch, with Janet coming at the same time. Donna Duff joined me as well.

I got them back at my own expense for a number of years. I included both Janet and Donna. They came about once a year. I would travel sometimes three times a year and started teaching in Perth, Western Australia where I was. From there it was taught in Victoria, which may have been the next place and then Sydney, Warhol, of New South Wales and up in Queensland after that, and had a core group of faculty there.

Let's see, how did I get to New Zealand? Oh, I know how I got to New Zealand. I was at one of the American Holistic Association meetings, and there was a woman from New Zealand there, who was a nurse. We met. Either she suggested it, or I suggested it, about teaching Healing Touch in New Zealand. She said that before she came to that meeting she had a premonition, or an awareness, that she would meet someone and invite them to come, and she would host setting up a Healing Touch class, which she did. After that we worked together, I don't know if it was the first trip or more than one, I don't remember, but eventually, I worked with a woman from both Australia and New Zealand who helped me, because it was becoming too much for me to do on my own. I had a business called Healing Touch Australia and New Zealand. After a while, we called it Healing Touch Australasia, which includes both those countries. Then I changed my name to Healing Touch Partnerships. That was so that I could turn the names over to the countries.

At first, I was accused of trying to, what was the word somebody used? What do you call a missionary who comes in and takes over or brings something? That was never my intention. My intent was always to share what I knew, and help create within the country, a framework to carry on the work, which is essentially what I had done in each one of the countries.

Over the years there have been a number of dynamics that have played out, that have affected what I'm describing. That could be a book within itself. I have written up my experiences in a book called "The Roots of Healing Touch." I don't know if you knew that. I did that on one of the anniversaries of Healing Touch. I have a lot of original videos of Janet doing the work in a number of countries, and also from the annual meetings because I used to do a lot of filming for Healing Touch.

Now, if you want to know how Healing Touch International got started? The connection to Healing Touch and the development of the certificate program? This is actually an essential piece. Janet said to me at one point that the AHNA was going to no longer certify non-nurses. I said to her, "Well, Janet. How can that be?" The AHNA grew by leaps and bounds and, as it turned out, a large part of it at that time had to do with Healing Touch. Many people loved Healing Touch, and resonated with it. And since Healing Touch was open to those who were nurses and to those who were not nurses, they could join AHNA. There were a large number of them. Janet confided in me that she was concerned about it, and I said, "Well, something should be done about it." They stood to lose a whole lot of their people.

AHNA had a meeting at, I think it was in Arizona. At the time, that's when the board made the announcement they would no longer certify those who were not nurses. Janet had pre-warned me that they were going to do that, maybe the year before that. I held my hand up and I said to the president then, I should remember her name but I can't recall it right now, "Is it true that you are doing that?"

She said, "Yes, it is." And turned to talk to somebody else.

I said, "I would like to voice an objection to that." I knew that AHNA would not implement this resolution from the board, until they connected to their membership.

Somebody seconded it. I tell you, they were not happy with me, the AHNA board. It got passed at that meeting was that it be tabled until they contacted their membership. Sharon Scandrett told me later, that with the leaders my name was mud for over a year because I took that stand.

I want to say that it was either '95 or '96, I would have to look back at my notes, when AHNA met. Their headquarters were here in Raleigh North Carolina. They were meeting here to discuss it. Janet was here and I went with her to the board meeting. At the board meeting, I can remember that day as clear as if it was yesterday, Charlotte McGuire was there, Janet and I. They discussed in depth the possibility of the position of AHNA, which was that they were going to stick to their decision to no longer certify those who were not in nursing. After they made that statement Janet stood up and she said, "I'm going to withdraw my program now from AHNA, because I cannot accept this. I believe that those who take Healing Touch should be able to be certified as well." So she made that decision at that meeting.

We came back to my house. Janet was staying with me. In my living room, we drafted the guide lines for what and how the certification would go. We created a membership organization which became Healing Touch International to house the, I think it was called the certificate program then, before certification. But that's what happened. In 1996 Janet filed the papers to make that official.

In the meantime, the notebook had been out for a while. I updated the notebook when all of those changes were made. That's sort of the core basis of the essential elements that happened over a period of years.

*When did you become certified? Did you become certified as a practitioner first, an instructor first, or both or what?*

I didn't make the first class that they had, because I was in Australia. I think the first course was in 1989 in Tennessee, and then it went to Florida, and the third class was in Durham, North Carolina. I was in that class. Then I attended many classes after that, but because in '90, it's when I moved to Australia, I wasn't able to do the instructor's training or even certification as a practitioner. And I'm not sure if all steps were laid out anyway. I was the number one person in Healing Touch International, because I was first to put my money. I was number one and I even beat out Janet, who was number two. We used to laugh about many of those things that happened with it.

I actually lived my spiritual mandate that was told to me in my first class with Janet, where I was told to help her do her work. I kept my commitment and served on the founding board of HTI, and worked with the journal. I was the one who set up the ethics committee that worked through the membership board of that organization and that's the role that HTI was. The program was built by Janet that we now know.

One of the things in the early days was that nobody was in this for a business. Everyone was doing what they loved to do and interacting with other people who obviously did the same thing. Each person brought their own expertise. I was amazed how many people with advanced degrees in nursing became an instrumental part in helping develop the additional, I would say the scholarly, aspects related to Healing Touch.

That's where the research came in. Research was not Janet's forte. I used to challenge her on that in some of the – because I sat in many, many classes with her throughout the years and in many countries. She was always focused on the practitioner part of it. There were others who were really the ones behind doing the academic pieces with it. I am not saying that in a disrespectful way. We each have gifts and we are all called to do different kinds of things with it.

It's probably the reason why Healing Touch spread the way it did, is it caught the people's hearts in a deep way. It called to them, not as a nurse, but it called to them because it rang true. We needed people from all walks of life. I was astounded at how we drew people who were lawyers and hospital administrators, business people, real estate agents, and house wives. People from all walks of life.

One of my favorite stories I used to tell, because I developed work with the poorest of the poor in Peru. A number of these women didn't have any educational background. I had just graduated a class of Healing Touch and the next month I was teaching in South Africa in Durban. I was at the Nelson Mandela School of Medicine. The dean of the school of public health was in my class. He came up to me and said, "Oh, this is so wonderful. I can just see how the docs would love it." Hearing him describe it, I realized that he was starting in the class that I had just graduated people who did not have an academic background, or even have a high school education. They were very gifted healers in Healing Touch.

I had a similar ah hah moment when I was in Australia. I was teaching the practitioner level of Healing Touch in Victoria, Australia. There were three people in that class: two men and one woman. I often laugh and say this is probably the first Healing Touch class that the men outnumbered the women.

One of the men was a physician. His name was Warry Cain. The other man was a massage therapist. His name was Paul Foreman. The woman was a housewife, who worked and helped her husband. I could see a picture of her. I can't recall her name. She helped her husband in his business. It was in construction or something like that. She did the bookkeeping for it.

When we were doing their documentation and their case study, she went first and shared her case study with her client. I saw the physician sit there with his mouth hanging open. He was a good friend of mine. After she finished presenting, he said to her and the others, "She spends more time, than any physician does, with her patient. And what a good job that she did."

That then said to me, they can do it. It's at a very different level. You're still holding the same standard with doing your case study. Obviously what a physician does, and what a lay person would do, were two different things with a knowledge base of where they come from. What is so unique about it, learning energy work is a skill in a body of knowledge that is different, that is I want to say a different caliber than medical knowledge is. Sometimes our fancy knowledge can get in the way of authentically aiding the clients. This was an example of it, and it more drew more to my experience with it. It was really quite amazing.

*What do you like best about Healing Touch? I know you have explored a number of modalities, and developed a fabulous training of your own.*

Healing Touch, in the early days was a group of committed people from all walks of life, every level within nursing, from beginning levels of staff nurses, to researchers, educators, physicians and everyone was treated equally. Everyone was friends. Everyone was committed to working with their clients with this new knowledge base. We had a wonderful support system of collegial connections of those practice teaching and research. That's piece that I miss with the current dynamic, I won't go into that. I'm highlighting the contrast where people loved being together, loved doing the work together, were friends, and very close in helping each other out.

It wasn't until later on when human nature and egos got in the way, that created some of the difficulties we're experiencing today. It's common with any successful enterprise that there can be things that happen. I watched and witnessed Carol Komitor, with her development of Healing Touch for Animals. I watched Linda Smith and her spiritual ministry course. I had my own training program. In fact, Linda Smith had talked to Janet about how I originally designed it the way I did. Because once people completed Healing Touch they were looking for more, and that it could be a continuing education program. But Janet at the time said, "No, no Mary Jo. You just go do your own thing." But Linda had seen that we would be a good combination, and that this would probably help go into the book.

The reason I took on board the route to Healing Touch, I pulled that together in a hurry. It still could do with a little work and I hadn't even begun to touch, not even all of the experiences or even a large percentage of the experiences.

I was guided to do a healing stories book. I published it through Healing Touch Partnerships. One of the things I used to say to Janet, because I was with her for a lot of the Healing Touch Level 4 and 5's. I said, "Janet, we need to write the stories down." I can't tell you how many times I would say it to her. We would hear what people were doing in the work, and I would say we need to capture this. This is so exciting.

One of the things that occurred was, at one time I said. "Well, if she's not going to do it then I'm going to do it." I couldn't think of how I wanted to do it, and I was getting ready to teach a Level 4 or 5 on my own here in North Carolina. I had just come back from Canada to pick something up there and while I was on the plane (I had just bought one of the new "Chicken Soup for the Soul" books) and I was reading it. I am holding this book in my hand and staring at it and I said, "That's the format I need to use for my healing stories book about Healing Touch." Because, you know, there are paragraphs, short stories. There are different lengths, but they capture the essence of the work in the way that the material is generated.

When I came back and I'm teaching my class I knew that I wanted to use that as my format. There was a man in my class, in fact I actually called him today. His name is Dan Collinger, and he was taking Healing Touch. I don't remember if it was a 4 or 5. Somewhere along the line, I had a conversation with him about wanting to do a healing stories book. Oh I know how it came about. When he introduced himself, he said he worked at Duke University and he was an editor, or did some work around editing books. Something connected to that.

I approached him and told him about my healing stories book and asked him if he would help me do it. He agreed to do it. Later he told me he had a dream about how he would be doing a healing stories book before I approached him. He started exploring some things, and nothing ever came of it, and he thought, I guess, that idea was wrong. And then I approached him to do a healing stories book and eventually we did that. He eventually started working for me.

*Do you have a favorite healing story using Healing Touch?*

I am going to tell you this one story, because that's what they're showing me to tell. It's related to Healing Touch. I had had surgery for breast cancer. In ten days, maybe less than that, I was teaching a Level 5 in North Carolina. I remember Janet was there as well. I think she was, but I don't know for sure. During the class, I had tubes hanging from me, drainage tubes from the surgery. Cause I was – it may have only been 6 days post op. So I had numbness in the surgical area and all down my arm. One of the students came up to me and gave me a crystal. This is taking a different direction. I'll finish the story anyway. It might not be the right one.

Throughout the whole rest of the class I held it on my arm while I was teaching. Of course, I would participate. You're being in the energy of the people doing the work. Afterward, I realized I didn't have any numbness at the spot where I was holding the crystal. I made the decision that if I can have feeling in this part of my arm, that I should be able to regain feeling throughout my whole arm. I had said something to the doctor about that, and he said that that is an after effect of the surgery. You won't get feeling back in that arm. What I always would do, and I would tell my students, is we don't have to take what is. We can look beyond and ask why not. That's what I would do.

Probably another Healing Touch story, my favorite one was with, oh I won't identify who the person was. The person had injured her fingers. They got caught up in a vacuum cleaner. I went with the person to help her. The doctor said that she would never have feeling in her hands again, in the fingers that went up into the vacuum cleaner. She had turned it over and had tried to pull something out and she had hit the button on it and it pulled her fingers into the motor of the vacuum cleaner. I worked on her using Healing Touch. She does have feeling back in those fingers. She is a massage therapist today.

*Do you have a favorite Janet Mentgen story?*

(*She chuckles.*) I have many Janet Mentgen stories. It would take a lot of time. We used to do trades with each other, as instructors, where we were in the back room working on each other. I mean waiting, while the students were doing what they were doing at night, because we would usually share a room. This one time I offered to do the chakra connection on her. I did it on her and she fell asleep during it. When she woke up she said, "Well, you didn't do that right." I started to laugh and I said, "You fell asleep during the technique. I did do it right. I did everything exactly as it was supposed to." But she wasn't aware of what was done because she had fallen asleep with it. We laugh about that.

*Do you have any advice to give new or potential students in Healing Touch?*

Yes I do. Allow yourself to grow with the work. What Healing Touch will do, they will teach you a format that is a tried and true process that is very successful and standardized. Follow the guidance and the mentorship in the process of becoming a practitioner, and/or as an instructor. Once you have achieved that base, you may be invited to go beyond what you have been taught. Don't be afraid to do that, because there are more things that we need to discover. If we just stay in the current box, then that's all there is. I use this as an analogy. When computers first came out, I was an academic, and I'd think I'll never use computers, because they're used for statistics and research in universities. They're not really for general life.

I really didn't get that involved with computers until maybe twenty years after they first came out. Look at what they do now. Look at what is possible now. That's why I am working on creating the specialist program. What I'm calling a CAM (Complimentary and Alternative Medicine) specialist. It's because people are being guided to get their knowledge and their unique flavor of who they are, with populations that they serve. They use the basis of this work. Some people will be guided to go beyond that, like adding music therapy or working with special populations.

I was guided when I started working in Peru. One time I heard a voice that said, "Do a kids helping kids program." I called my colleagues in Peru and I said I think we need to branch out and do a kids program.

Sister Marquiho had said, "Well I want to teach self-care with the kids."

At the time, I think, we had Healing Touch, and branched out. She focused on a self-care program. From that self-care program, she then got money together through donations, and opened a children's center. It snowballed from there. Kids stopped being in gangs. The school system contacted her and asked, "What are you teaching the kids?"

She said, "Well, I'm teaching them this Healing Touch." I doubt if she said energy work.

A priest contacted her and said, "We're noticing the influence in gangs has gone down. What's going on in this community? Would you show us what you're doing?"

So that's my point. She took it beyond the confines. She took it to the children and then there was an active program. Rita Kluny developed a program of Healing Touch for Babies. That's what I'm saying. Take what you learn, and follow your guidance. When you're learning it, stay within the basis of what they are teaching you, because they have a lot to teach you. If you blend it in the beginning, as I used to say to my students all the time, then you'll have not a clear differentiation of what Healing Touch is. You need to have that.

*How has Healing Touch changed your life?*

In a lot of ways. I spent fifteen years totally immersed in Healing Touch in every phase of my life. Going to many countries, teaching people from all different walks of life, all different cultures, learning how to work with that as well as dealing with the administrative and academic issues of it. It was a key in the friendships I developed throughout those years that are essential and how we supported each other to do what was unique to what we did. I wasn't focused on research. I was focused on taking it to different cultures throughout the world. That's what I did best. Now I'm an academic and I teach a CAM program. They can invest in education where people can combine, take their training in Healing Touch and get college degrees with it. They can get a master's degree with their concentration in Healing Touch, or get a doctorate degree with a concentration in Healing Touch. So I took my basis in academics and created a framework for that to happen. That's what I said. I know the purity of Healing Touch and worked with Janet and helped hold the energy for that to be established. That's what my gifts were, my unique orientation, and I also helped to create an organizational base to help spread Healing Touch, not only in the US, but in multiple countries.

*What do you see as the future of Healing Touch?*

The future can become as big as the people who take their visions to new territory. The future will either be limited or expanded by what somebody dreams and visions, and follows through to make happen. That is done through heart-centeredness and let the ego get out of the way. We learn how to work in cooperation and collaboration. Do your own personal work, find the demons within and conquer them, because we all have that and they interfere with both our professional and personal lives. They interfere with the organizational life as well. As each person learns how to conquer those and move forward, they will get to where they need to be. One of the things that I have said, and I'll use it as an example, is that I think energy modalities need to work together.

For example, I was on the board of Energy Psychologies Association for six years. So was Dorothea who helped create Healing Touch. But her orientation was mental health like mine. I am a psych therapist in family therapy. I took that field, and added it with energy work. But this is a small example of it.

Healing Touch Program had been very successful in creating an insurance form for Healing Touch practitioners. That got expanded to include anyone who was doing energy based work. The ACEP board approached Healing Touch Program, and they put their practitioners under that same insurance policy group.

That's an example of how everybody doesn't have to re-invent the wheel. Healing Touch had already worked that out. I am saying we have a lot to benefit from what the individual people are doing. I saw that same concept workout in another organization that had many diverse mental health organizations. That was ACEP (Association for Complimentary Energy Psychology). But what they did, was they had a unifying frame work that then became the Association of Comprehensive Energy Psychology that then was built on many modalities that were separate and even big within their own. It became a universal umbrella for people to work from.

If we take that whole network and add it to the whole Healing Touch network, and add it to the whole Reiki network, the Therapeutic Touch network, the Quantum Touch network, etc. etc. You know, what you have done with your other book, the energy psychology book and the energy medicine framework that's out there. If we all worked together and then we go to Washington DC and say, "See. Look at what your options are with what this industry has done to promote health and save lives." If we did that together, as a body of careers, practitioners, researchers and educators, we would be a lot further ahead on the health care issue.

Voice for Hope is doing some of this. I don't think they have a strong enough base. I have had them on one of my radio shows with Voice America. Their angle is the political angle. I don't think they have enough energy workers helping them to achieve that goal. That's an example of where we can stay lost in our own little political issues and not see the bigger picture. They have a large following of Healing Touch people and other people behind them. I, certainly, have tried to help them to take their vision forward.

When people take their dreams together around this as energy workers, there's new stuff for us to understand. The man who created the first computer had visions that transcended what was needed to win the war. Fifty years passed before it became known what this man did. That's my point.

We don't have all the answers yet. I wasn't sure energy work could be taught without having a live class. I have since found that is not true. My first story related to that, is of one of the Healing Touch people I had taught. I invited him into my healing center when I was in Carlborough, North Carolina. I sent him the date and that day he wasn't there. I asked him where he was and he said, "I was there, where were you?" When I opened his email, I could feel all this energy come off it, and I felt attacked. He said, "I was there, where were you?"

What happened is, he came the wrong day. Not the day of the meeting but either the day before or the day after. What I learned is that emails carry energy. I started signing my emails with blessings, because I thought when somebody opens an email from me, I want them to receive blessings. What I learned is how to control my own anger, when I was angry with someone or angry at something. It becomes like a board. It's a weapon. When people get upset, they need to learn how to control in what state their energy is, their own energy, and that's why I said each person has to do their own work.

*Anything else you would like to say about your life with Healing Touch before we sign off?*

I'm holding a vision we can get back to some of the roots of the founding energy, and cooperation and collaboration in the family. We were a family. In a family you have the ups and downs and all the kind of stuff related to that. And, yes we had that. We can get beyond that. Families can be healed when there are family dynamics that come about. That's what I hold for the future. We can grow up and demonstrate something different. We have to be better than where we are now. We do that by living what the principles are. Living it and finding solutions to some of the problems that are there.

# Nancy Burns
### RN, CMT, HTCP/I
### Elder

**Introduction**

I found Nancy interesting, because she has the longest history with Janet. Hers is one of the shorter interviews. I value it, because it gave me some insights into the very early years I hadn't heard before. She also tells us of some of the early struggles Janet incurred, when she started Healing Touch.

**Interview**

*Have you held any positions with Healing Touch?*
I am a Certified Healing Touch Practitioner and a Certified Healing Touch Instructor. I taught Healing Touch Level 1 at Red Rocks Community College, when Janet could no longer teach there, due to her traveling schedule.

*What attracted you to energy work?*
I was involved with the charismatic renewal and very active in doing "Lay On Of Hands" in the community. Then, in 1979, I took a Therapeutic Touch class and I realized I was already doing energy work. This put me on a quest to continue to learn more about energy work.

*How did you get involved with Healing Touch?*

I told Janet about the Therapeutic Touch class I took. The following year, in 1980, Janet took the same class. Immediately after she took the class, she developed a support group with others that had taken the class. We met weekly, sharing and exchanging treatments. After a while, Janet began inviting interesting people to come and speak to us.

Janet decided there was a lot more to energy work. She started attending numerous classes and studying with experts who were energy workers. She became very interested in holistic health. Janet and I attended a few classes together, to acquire our CEU's for nursing at that time. Janet was working as a home health nurse, and I was working in a long term facility. We did some sharing about our experiences.

*What happened in Level 1 that hooked you on Healing Touch?*

In the summer of 1979 I took a Therapeutic Touch Class in Vail, CO. at a conference. Before that time I was involved in a Prayer Group, and we did "Laying On Of hands" for those in need of healing. I witnessed some healings at that time, thus when I took the TT class, I knew I would pursue further education in energy work. I really felt called to take further classes. In 1981 I took a TT class at Red Rocks College in Denver, Co. At that time Janet Mentgen was teaching. Later on she called the class Healing Touch Level 1. Energy work became the passion in my life.

*Why did you stay with Healing Touch? Was it your friendship with Janet?*

Basically, I stayed with Healing Touch because it became the passion in my life. I worked as an RN until age sixty-five. Then I went to massage school for a year, and also became a Certified Spiritual Director. I started my own business, and worked daily for over ten years. Then I slowed down and now only see two to three people a week doing Healing Touch and Spiritual Direction. However, I still continue to give energy classes at Contemplative Outreach.

*How did Healing Touch change your life?*

I was very involved in energy work from 1979 to now. It is a transformation process. Because of Healing Touch, my concept of God changed. My image of God is energy and love beyond my comprehension. The change transpired very early on with the energy work. My desire is to become fully, the person God has created. My life is based on unconditional love for all people.

*Did you explore any other healing modalities?*

I have constantly taken classes over the years. I've taken all Sue Hovland's classes. I've taken Franny Harcey's classes. I studied with Rosalyn Bruyere, Brugh Joy, Greg Braden, Caroline Myss, Barbara Brennan, Donna Eden and many others that offered information on energy work or holistic health. I have attended numerous conferences and, in the early years, Janet and I attended the American Holistic Nurses Conferences together. The conferences always offered excellent classes on alternative healing. I have studied Reiki, Polarity Therapy, Color and Music Therapy, reflexology, dream classes, and numerous holistic classes.

*Do you have a particularly meaningful Healing Touch story?*

I especially enjoy working with cancer clients. I saw a lovely lady for eighteen months weekly, with multiple myeloma. In the process, I watched her become transformed. She had a very beautiful, easy, peaceful death.

I also worked with a lady who had severe Parkinson's disease. I was in charge of her care 24/7. I trained her staff to do Healing Touch. She received Healing Touch twice a day, because medicines no longer worked for her. I felt Healing Touch helped her cope with the severe tremors. It certainly helped with her anxiety and also helped her to relax.

I worked as a volunteer for Life Spark and had a client with third stage breast cancer. She often told me the weekly sessions of Healing Touch carried her through chemotherapy.

I have had a few clients have spiritual experiences while receiving Healing Touch. I had a Benedictine monk receiving Healing Touch on the table. Suddenly he sat up and stated, "Oh my God, I am seeing a bright blue light." He felt it was the presence of the Blessed Mother Mary. Several of my clients have mentioned that they see bright lights and colors.

I have lots of little stories.

*Do you have any comments or advice for new or potential students?*

I'm always encouraging people to take at least Level 1 in Healing Touch. I feel Level 1 gives a good understanding of the energy system, a way to do self-healing, and a wonderful way to help friends and family. In fact, my daughter and my granddaughter have taken Healing Touch Level 1, because I told them this is something that should be a part of your life. If people share with me that they are interested in energy work, I always encourage them to take several levels of Healing Touch.

In the early years, I mentored several people through to certification. That was a highlight of my life.

*What do you see for the future of Healing Touch?*

    I think it's going to keep growing, because I see more and more people accepting it. You know, when Janet and I took it way back, in '79 and '80, it was terrible when you'd go to the hospital. You didn't dare tell anybody what you were going to do. You'd close the door, pull the curtains and pray nobody would come in. So many people at that time were accusing us of being involved with New Age. We were doing woo-woo. You wouldn't believe the criticism that we would have to listen to concerning Healing Touch.

    I can remember there was a book written at that time, telling people how dangerous Healing Touch is. I shared with Janet about how I laughed, because Abbott Thomas Keating, who developed centering prayer, was in the next chapter after Healing Touch. He was being criticized for centering prayer because that's so "bad" for you. I think people's minds have changed due to the media. There're so many articles about energy work now. For the most part I'm seeing that people are very acceptive and very welcoming towards Healing Touch. Now when I go to hospitals, I always go to the charge nurse at the desk, and tell her who I am and what I'm going to do. Usually when I go to intensive care, they welcome me. They can't wait to see me. "Oh. Yeah. Please go work on that patient."

    It's so different today than when I was doing it in the early '80's. That was not fun. We weren't welcomed. It's a big difference, and I think it's going to continue to grow, because people are seeing that it's helping. It's promoting healing. If nothing else, it gives the patients a sense of peace. When the body can get into that state of peace, and relax, I feel like the body has a greater affinity to heal. I think it's growing by leaps and bounds.

*Do you have a favorite Janet Mentgen story?*

    Shortly after Janet started teaching Therapeutic Touch at Red Rocks Community College, she went to Shadowcliffe at Grand Lake, Colorado for a quiet retreat. One day, as she was hiking to Crystal Falls, she had a spiritual experience. She told me she saw a bright light on the path and heard the words, "I have called you to do healing work." A few weeks later, she and I did the same hike, and she showed me where this occurred. I took a picture of the spot and gave it to her. Janet shared this experience with a very select few.

    I can remember Janet saying, "Just do the work. Just do the work." The other thing she would say was, "Don't be so upset about not getting your hand in the right place, because, with intention, the energy flows."

    I remember when she decided to start her own business. I'll never forget that. She didn't live too far from me, so one evening she walked over. You know Janet never dressed up. She had on kind of worn out jeans, a man's shirt, and broken down shoes. I guess you would call it fisherman's hat. It was in the evening. She came to see Jim and I. She wanted to borrow money to start her own business. She was just gung ho to start that business. Jim and I decided that we really couldn't give her money in order to start a business. We had too many of our own expenses.

    I called her the next day and told her that. The next night she called me and said, "I've got the money, and I'm going to start the business. A gentleman I had supper with last night said he would be happy to give me the money. So she started. Right away.

    I would always say to Janet, "Thanks for always saying, 'give this to God'." I think, of all the people in my life, Janet was the greatest risk taker. In fact I have not met another risk taker like Janet.

She trusted God would bring her people for the energy business. She told me she would sit in the office and say, "Okay, God. Send the people." The people came and the business grew. Initially, the business was known as Whole Body Health.

At that time she was struggling, too, but she quit her job, decided to start her own business. It was a marvelous business when it first started. We'd go down there and have the greatest classes. She would have the greatest meditations. For a time, she told me she would just sit there and say, "Okay, God what's on the table? People will come." And they did.

That's how it started. That's what I remember about Janet. A great risk taker. Whenever I saw her, even though we knew each other a long time, I would say to her, "Thank you for always saying yes to God." That is one person who just heard the message and went for it. That's how I remember Janet. What a wonderful legacy Janet gave to our world!

*Is there anything else you would like to add in your history with Healing Touch?*

No. I'm just very grateful that it's continuing to grow and flourishing, and I think it's a great asset for our world today.

Pioneers in Healing Touch

# Karen B Chin
### RN, MS, HTCP/I, CCAP
www.htwfoundation.org

## Introduction

I got the following from a biography of Karen. She began by serving on the board of Directors for the Healing Touch Worldwide Foundation as the secretary. She was involved with the update of the bylaws and the ongoing development of policies and procedures. She began her role of President in 2012.

Karen's background is varied, having been an operating room nurse both in civilian and military capacities. She served in the U.S. Air Force Reserve for 25 years retiring as a Lieutenant Colonel. Karen teaches RN nursing students, ladies' Sunday school and Level 1 Healing Touch classes. She also enjoys being a HT mentor. Her interests include karate, in which she holds a 2nd degree black belt, as well as learning piano. Her growing Healing Touch business is called Touch of the Phoenix.

## Interview

*What is your position within Healing Touch?*

I am the current president of the Healing Touch Worldwide Foundation.

*Please tell me about the foundation and what it is that you do?*

I would like to start with our mission statement: To receive and distribute funds to assist, encourage and advance the philosophy, objectives and techniques of Healing Touch.

I would also like to include our vision: HTWF is the benchmark for excellence in funding Healing Touch rescarch and outreach programs, spreading Healing Touch to communities throughout the world. Both of these statements can be found at the top of our web site.

We spread Healing Touch worldwide. That's what we really want to do.

We do what all foundations do, that is we raise funds, so that we can support research and service projects that deal with Healing Touch: techniques and modalities, results, effects, and that type of thing. While we support research and service, we also have some separate little funds that are housed within our foundation. One of which is Healing Touch for Animals. Another of which is HTPA, Healing Touch Professional Association, and another that's used specifically for military support, endowments and whatnot.

We have a Janet Mentgen vision fund, which Janet specifically wanted to support instructors from other countries, or practitioners from other countries to become instructors. Since I've been president, which is 2012, we had one from Australia, of course Apana from Nepal, and I can't think of the other one.

*As president, what do you do?*

(She laughs.) I have this term, and it's not - don't take it as derogatory – I was also in the military by the way. I was in the military for twenty five years in the reserves. I've been in command positions. Now, being president – there are a lot of similarities of course – being in a leadership position, and when you're dealing with people, sometimes it's like herding cats. Actually I think it is a lot better with the particular group that we have now. People seem to be a lot more into it.

As president, I do my best to keep everybody on task. I pretty much allow each of the board members, who are each heads of committees, to do their own thing. Now we have monthly meetings, monthly telephone meetings, which doesn't cost much. That's where we have motions and things that we have to vote on. Especially the submissions that come in that go to the grant committee, and once that comes to the board we vote on it, have discussions and see whether or not if this is something we want to support or not. Then we have all the fund raising activities and, things like that, that go along with in a foundation.

Our web site has a – like if you wanted to contact someone – and I get those. I go ahead and send them off to whoever it needs to go to. Sometimes, it is me. Sometimes there are questions that actually belong to Healing Touch Program, you know. I'll divert them there.

Our biggest push right now, our board is smaller now than when I first joined, is instead of trying to create, or recreate, a larger board like we had before. Right now our focus is really to get non-board committee members. People who will help out with committees. And just get the little special projects here and there done, so we can take little bites out here and there without the committee members having to do everything. Getting board members sometimes is difficult. People have the perception, of course, that, oh my gosh, how long am I going to be on it? How much time is this going to take? Those kinds of very valid questions.

We're trying to make the shift and try to find people who are willing to help us. Without having to be on the board, they are not committed to being at the meetings. That kind of thing. We have three or four grant readers who are not on the board. I just brought on one person who will be helping in marketing. i.e. proofreading and making sure things look good before we send them off to newsletters and things like that. Not everyone is a good writer. Our new grant committee person got a friend to come on with her to help her out. That's good. Of course we could use more. I have to make some more phone calls.

*What attracted you to energy medicine in the first place? How did you get started?*

We all have our stories. I am a nurse. I'm a registered nurse. I literally fell in to Healing Touch. Until then I had never heard of energy medicine, never heard of – this is totally out of my radar. I am, by trade, an operating room nurse. Very black and white. Things are either sterile or their not sterile. You had to have a minor in mechanical and electrical engineering to be an O R nurse. I was living in Yuma, Arizona at the time. Yuma is in the very far bottom, left corner, next to Mexico. Three hours to San Diego and 3 hours to Phoenix and 3 minutes to Mexico. To get my continuing education hours, that meant a long drive and having to stay in a hotel and go to seminars. Or do things through journals to get my continuing education.

A Healing Touch class came to our Yuma community hospital that we had there. I had no idea what it was, but it was going to give me hours. I think it was going to give me 18 hours. I said, "I'm goin'. I don't care what it's about. I don't have to leave town. It counts. It's here and I'm goin'." So that is how I fell into it.

I was with a group of people who I don't think knew much more than me. It differs now. I would say almost all the students now, have some kind of experience, or have heard of energy medicine in some way shape or form. I was not in that category.

I was very skeptical. I didn't think I was. But, apparently I really was. It caught. I mean I can, probably one other little story is after I took Level 1 I actually did a pain drain on a nurse friend of mine who had burned herself on a grill. Of course, she was in a lot of pain, and it was all blistered, oozing, and whatnot. I did a pain drain on her. A little bit of hands in motion. The pain stopped right away. I had no idea it would be like that and I told her. "I don't know how long it's going to be like this." She said her hand was no longer swollen. She could move it easier.

I said, "Well, we'll see how long this lasts." That was my reserve weekend. She was in my reserve unit then. That was like a Saturday. By Wednesday I spoke with her on the phone, and I said, "Just let me know. How much longer after I worked on you, did you have to go back to taking extra strength Tylenol?" Which is what she was doing before she saw me.

She said, "Never again." She never had to take another one.

I said, "Really?"

She says, "Yeah."

Now she is an emergency room nurse, and she said to me, "Have you ever seen a burn turn into a callus?"

I said, "No."

She said, "Me either. But that's what it looks like."

I had worked on her Saturday. That was Wednesday. By the next Saturday, just a few days later, in front of her family, she took this dry callused skin off her hand. She peeled it off, scratched the skin underneath it, and it was new. Now the whole burn mark remained for a couple more weeks. The mark itself. She said it never hurt again and it was completely healed.

After that experience I said, "Let's get going. I think this works." So then I went on and took Level 2. And 3. Back then it was 2A and 2B. I did take an Advanced Practice 1. I had done 1 and 2 in

Yuma. I did 3 in San Diego. That's when Lisa Gordon was living there, and was coordinating for her mother. Janet Mentgen did not teach Level 3, but she taught the advanced practice after that Level 3 class. But she was a part of that class. So I took the Advanced Practice 1 with Janet Mentgen at that time. I went on and did Level 4 and 5 and got certified. I got certified in 2001. It took me about three years to get to certification. That was probably about right. I think it took me about three years. That would have been 1997?

I am thinking out loud. In '91 I got deployed to the first Desert Shield/Desert Storm thing. All of this happened after that. So that was '91, '92, '93? Was it really '97? I thought it was earlier than that. I would have to look at my things. I honestly don't remember.

That's right. That's when I got my master's degree and I graduated in – and that was after – everything I separate in my life – before Desert Storm and it's all before or after. (She chuckles.) I got my master's degree in '91, '92. Yeah It had to have been about then.

*How has Healing Touch changed your life?*

Oh my gosh! It totally expanded my spirituality. Totally. Not overnight. Certainly not overnight. It took time. But that is the end result of it. I certainly am, and I like to tell people now, that I live in northeast Texas and stuff like that. I do belong, currently, to a southern Baptist church. That's a different culture, for someone who came from Massachusetts. So, of course, religion is one thing and spirituality is another. I think, not to blame Healing Touch, but I think because of the resulted in growth, that I had with Healing Touch, I think part of that, I'm not sure that my first husband was native with. So we parted ways, after some time.

I have since remarried to a man who actually is into crystals. He's done Healing Touch 1 and 2 already. It's very different. You know what I mean? And my Mom, she's 87, she lives with us. She's done Healing Touch 1 and 2. Has she done 3? I don't think she's done 3. Just 1 and 2. She loves it.

*Do you have a favorite Healing Touch story in all of your different healing experiences?*

There are so many stories. The one I just recounted about my friend, and her burned hand, that's the one I use the most, because that's what brought me into Healing Touch.

Yes. This is a personal Healing Touch story. Let's see. I got certified in 2001. So it was in 2000. I had a cerebral bleed. I had a stroke. I was what, maybe forty-five, then. I was very lucky. It pretty much resolved on its own. But, I was moving from Yuma, Arizona to Marshall, Texas. I had to change doctors and all that kind of thing to be followed by the doctor here. The doctor called me one Friday night, 10 o'clock at night on a Friday. I've got a doctor calling me on the phone saying you've got another aneurism.

I said, "What? What? What do you mean another aneurism?"

I hadn't heard that term before, aneurism. I said, "What do you want me to do? I'm supposed to fly out tomorrow for my reserves, a flight back to Arizona. I'm going to be there a week. Do you want me to not go? What do you want me to do?"

He said, "No, no. You go ahead. You go for the week."

I was going to be doing administrative kind of work for the reserves.

He said, "When you get back, I'm going to have an appointment for you to see a micro neurologist."

I said, "All right."

Then I went to Arizona. That is I where my mentor was. I was between Levels 4 and 5. I would see her once a month, because that was when I had my reserve weekend in the Phoenix area. She lived in Sun City, and that's where we would meet. Here I was down there for that weekend and had to meet with her anyway. I told her what was going on and she worked with me and said, "I just want you to know that, not to worry. Everything will be okay."

I said, "Okay. I had complete faith and that sounds good to me. I'm not going to worry about it."

Do you know, when I got back, flew from Arizona to Texas, I went to that micro neurologist specialist appointment. I had to bring all my MRI's with me and films and all that kind of thing. He's looking at it. He's looking and he's looking. He was saying to himself, "I don't know what they're talking about."

He loved it. Finally he said there was this one little picture on the film and says, "Well, I suppose if it's anything, it might be this." Which was a malformation of the ventral essentially.

I'm thinking to myself, "There must have been something else a week ago, or two weeks ago, for a doctor, who has already had a radiologist look at these pictures, and call me at ten o'clock at night to tell me news that, like you need to be followed up some more."

The micro neurologist simply could find nothing. So I had him, and the other doctor, write a letter to the air force saying that I was fit for worldwide duty, so they wouldn't kick me out. They wrote that letter. In fact the neurologist said that the chances of my getting another incident were the same as anyone else in the population who had never had one.

I said, "Okay. Sounds good to me."

Interestingly enough, the air force kept me, after having had a stroke. But once I got asthma, they kicked me out. At least I had gotten my twenty plus years in by then. I think at that time I had been in, maybe fifteen, so if they did exit me, you know, it was for good reason. Then I would not have gotten any retirement or benefits or anything. It worked out. I think that would be my story. I kept the films by the way, the ones that he circled. But it would be wonderful to know what it looked like two weeks before. Because I know that is not what it looks like now.

*Have you explored other healing modalities?*

Yes. I have a bit of alphabet soup after my name. I took the R. J. Buckle aromatherapy therapy classes/modules. I am a CCAP, Certified Clinical Aromatherapy Practitioner. That was four modules. I had to do a little project. That project turned into a published paper. I am now a published author on tea tree oil. That was less than a year ago, that that got published. That was interesting.

But I kept thinking, "Why is this happening? I am so much into Healing Touch. How come I published something on oils and not Healing Touch?" It was a term paper and I had to it. I was pushed into getting it published. It took a couple of years and to finally get around to it. I needed some help in doing it. It's in a *Journal of Complementary and Alternative Medicine*.

I did that, because when people came to see me for Healing Touch they expected me, and still do, to know about herbs and oils and naturopathic kinds of things. For a while I knew nothing except Healing Touch. Nothing. So I said okay it's time to get into other things.

There's aromatherapy and I also took Kim Seer's medical intuition. It's quantum work. I use that fairly regularly when I do Healing Touch. I had also Energetic Transformation. That's Kathy Sinnett's course. I did that.

Both Kathy Sinnett and Kim Seer were Healing Touch practitioners. They used very similar concepts, especially in Energetic Transformation. It just went off, of course, into different things. I would say those are my other modalities, that I am familiar with, and use.

*Do you have a Facebook page for HT Worldwide Foundation?*
Yes. The Worldwide Foundation does have a web site. We do have a Facebook page.
*I'll look you up on Facebook and "like" you.*
That would be good. Very, very good.
We have this one lady, her name is Melissa Ellie. She always posts stuff on our Facebook page. It's wonderful, because she keeps it active. She really does. And it's great that she does that. So, yes, yes, we do have a Facebook page. And, of course, we have our own web site: www.HTWFoundation.org. If you google it, Healing Touch Worldwide Foundation, it'll certainly go there. I think the Facebook must be the same or similar.

*Do you have any comments or advice for new or potential students?*
Practice, practice, practice.
*Do you know how many people have said that? That's what it's all about.*
It's not being afraid to do it. I think there are a lot of people, after they have done Level 1, they just think that they don't know enough to do anything. If they can just be brave, take that first good solid foot forward, and do something, anything. Whoever they're working on, they don't know the difference. Intention is everything.
I would say the very first time I did a mind clearing. It was a distant one on a teddy bear. I had my book in front of me and I was so intent on figuring out where my fingers had to go for this mind clearing that I had never done before. The girl, woman whom I was working on, had the most awesome experience.
When I talked to my mentor about it she said, "For you, you're going to get more of those kinds of results than otherwise, because you're still learning." She made me back off from doing more distance stuff. She said, "You need to do more hands on stuff.

This distance stuff, it'll take care of itself." So that was really interesting.

I didn't think I was really doing anything. I was just looking at that book trying to figure out where to put my fingers. Yet, that woman had an awesome, awesome experience. I thought that was pretty interesting.

I guess just to be brave. They need to be brave and it's okay. It's okay to make a mistake. It's okay that they're not perfect. Because it is in the work and it really is the intention. I tell people who are not familiar with Healing Touch, if you believe in prayer how can you not believe that this works? Or that it is not going to work? People can pretty much relate to that.

*What do you see for the future of Healing Touch?*

I have different feelings on that. Of Healing Touch itself, it has to spread. I can't see it not spread. Part of that, of course, is that the planet really is waiting for this energy work. If not this energy work, other energy work. It is open to that concept overall, you know what I mean? People just are open to that concept. If we can position ourselves where we are available for people to be clients, or to be students then that, I can really see that. Of course, now that we're seeing Healing Touch Program accredited, that should be opening more doors. Or certainly allow other organizations to see us with different eyes and more validity. At least I would like to believe that.

But I'll tell you, there is a little bit of a down side, if you don't mind my sharing this, is because we're accredited now, it's almost like we have to be really careful that we're not over regulated. That we don't over regulate ourselves. That we really need to keep the intent and spirit of doing the work. I just see that happening with the Qualified Mentor and the different levels of stuff that we have now. I think. And yeah, we're growing. I think we're undergoing some growing pains. And then, of course, with the split, changes are going to be happening with that. We're really not too sure what that's going to show. But, it's still Healing Touch.

I really, really would love to believe that Healing Touch will just take off. I think it is in some places. It needs some help in places and not in others. And again I think, part of it is instructors. You know, we were talking about students need to be brave and just keep doing it. I think we, as instructors, need to do the same thing. I don't have very large classes. As an instructor I have maybe three people, maybe four people. It's not large. I supplement by having helpers. Helpers love to come, because they get to come to another class. That's how I get a nice little group. It helps encourage, I think, the helpers. They get to do it more and whatnot.

*Do you have a favorite Janet Mentgen story?*

I'd say what I do remember about her, since I did do that advanced practice class with her, I saw her as being very well grounded. She loved beanie babies. You know how it is in Healing Touch classes. We have the times to get everybody back to class, chronos time. We'd have to come back after a break. We'd go off for lunch and make sure we'd get back on time so that we could get done on time. And here we were, but Janet Mentgen was late. Here she was the teacher and we're waiting on her. She had found a store with beanie babies in it and she had to buy some beanie babies for her grandchildren. She was not leaving that store until she found the right thing, these beanie babies. That was one of her most favorite things that she had. So here we were. Just waiting.

She showed up, I think. Of course she showed up. But she was late and that was the reason. I thought that was kind of cute actually. That was in San Diego, I believe.

*Is there anything else you would like to add or share?*

I would like to, because I am president of the HT Worldwide Foundation. I had one woman on the board for a little bit. She really felt a little depressed that her business wasn't getting off the way she would like to see it. That she wasn't busier with Healing Touch than she wanted to be. She really wanted, of course, to make a difference in the world. And we do. We do make a difference, whether we know it or not, by doing this work. But I told this woman that by being on the foundation, you are affecting the planet at a different level. You still are doing the work. This may not be the way you are thinking that you want to do it, but you are. She took that to heart. She thanked me. She said, "I didn't think of it that way.'

Sometimes I think just as long as we have Healing Touch in our hearts that we are doing the right thing and that we are in the right place at the right time. Doing what we need to do. It just might not be what we planned on. Certainly I never planned on being president of the foundation, believe you me. (She chuckles.) It was like – I was rejected from the board the first time. Not that it hurt my feelings at all. Finally I was brought on and I was inserted and was the secretary. I helped with bylaws. I thought, "Okay. I'm on the grant committee." And the next thing you know I'm being president.

These things I literally fall into. I had no plans on doing this, these things. And these things just happen. You know, I fell into Healing Touch, became certified. Being president of the foundation was never in my plans. It happened. And here I am. I am doing the best that I can with it. They haven't kicked me out yet, so I guess I'm doing okay.

Healing Touch, for me, is now a part of my life. I can't fathom life without it. I tell people that I'm a Christian, that all of this is through the grace of God, frankly. I believe, truly, truly, I believe in my heart, that this is why I have been put here on this earth. It's to do

Healing Touch. As such, I'll always be doing it in some way, form, or fashion. I don't know that I want to be president of the foundation forever, but I guess I have been in it a little bit longer than I expected. That's okay. That's all good.

It really, really is. I have a knowing, that is why I am here. All of the experiences that I've had, becoming a nurse, and being in the military. Doing this, that, and the other thing. I trained in karate, by the way. I'm second degree black belt now. I'm learning piano and enjoying life, too. I love teaching. I've been told. I've been told by an angel even, that teaching is hard wired in me. I thought, "Okay. If you say so. I believe you." 'Cause I do do a lot of teaching. I teach nursing students.

We have a VA hospital close by, in Treeport, but I don't know how to enter into that. I have to take the time to do that. I talked to the CEO at the hospital here in town. He seemed really interested, and I just never heard back from him. I tried to get another appointment with him, and it's not happening. Even though for as much interest as he really had, maybe he just wasn't ready yet. I don't know. He liked it, but maybe he talked to other people who weren't as interested.

# Bernie Clarke
## RN, MS, HTCP/I, FAAN
### Elder

**Introduction**

Bernie Clarke is a much loved pioneer here in the Pacific Northwest. She taught Levels 1 through 3 in Olympia, Washington. I had the pleasure of working with her as an instructor-in-training. That was the weekend immediately following 9/11. She had us do a lovely candle ceremony after class Saturday night. I'll never forget it.

She had me stay at her house and I was treated to some wonderful, down home, southern hospitality. She has been an outstanding leader in working with the elderly. I would happily sit at her feet for hours and listen to her stories about all the Healing Touch work she has done.

**Interview**

*When did you start in Healing Touch?*

Oh my goodness. I started in back in, I guess about the late '80's. I've got this all written down. Let me see if I've got this. I had taken the beginning courses back in Richmond. But I didn't become an instructor until I came out here to Seattle, which was in 1996. My husband and I moved out here because our three daughters all came out from Virginia. We decided if we wanted to see our grandchildren, that when I retired, which was in '94 from my nursing and teaching job, that that's what we would do. I met Barb Dahl and we got involved in teaching Healing Touch.

*What got you started in energy medicine in the first place?*

I was very interested in it and knew about it during my nursing career, which was up through '94. I was into all kinds of other things. It was about then that I started getting involved. I look at this and some of the people that were involved. I went to teacher's college. We didn't know much about it then. I did meet some of the people that were in the early phases, I am trying to think of who they were. I'll have to look at some of this history I thought I had. That's the problem. It's been so long. I got more involved after I came out here to the west coast.

I had finished up my teaching career in nursing. Right at the end, well I was interested in Janet Quinn and all of the stuff that was out of there. I just needed to find a place and I met some people back in Richmond who knew a little bit about it and lived there. It was what I was looking for in retirement. You know, this business – I'm going through a book called "Creative Aging". One of the things it talks about is what you do when you reach a place in your life where you're aging and you're giving up what your career was. My career was in nursing and teaching and doing all those kinds of things.

I wanted a way to continue, but not in the same area. That's basically what happened. I'm trying to look at the time I was involved with it. Right after I moved out here, I just knew some of the people back in Richmond. I think I had taken one class there before I moved here and then I got very involved, very quickly. I met Janet and she got me into the teaching part of it.

I came in much quicker than most people would because of she wanted someone to teach here in Olympia. We got things started here. It was just amazing how things began to fit in.

I also got involved with Energy Medicine with Mary Jo Bulbrook. At that time Mary Jo was a part of Healing Touch. She was on the board. Energetic Healing came in, with her different things, and I taught that and taught the other. I just had a great time for those first four or five years.

I began to have to look at a new path, because I'm 87. That makes a difference. You look at maybe recreating your life again, if you're going to be living to 90 or a 100, You're not sure exactly where it's going to all end up. That's where I am right now.

I guess when my teaching certificates expired, in 2010, practitioner and teaching, I could not go for any of the classes because that's when my husband was getting sick and I had to be with him.

Then I broke my arm. He broke his arm. I was riding a trike, of all things a trike. While going uphill, I turned my wheel and went over on my left shoulder and broke my arm. He had already broken his, playing one of his sports. We were both taking care of each other. I had to have a middle replacement in the shoulder. That stuff kind of fit in there, as we were going downhill or he was particularly.

He died at home, for which I glad he was able to, and I was able to take care of him with the help of my daughter. I was able to do Healing Touch quite a bit as he came to the end. It was sad, but he had lived a wonderful life. He was 94.

I have been spending my time now trying to recover and seeing where I can go. Fortunately I still have, here, and have had for years, where I've taught a number of classes to the people, when I was still certified. You know, beginning classes. We had a group, until John was sick, that met every week. We did Healing Touch.

Actually, it started out with Mary Jo's thing. Then we did Healing Touch that I had taught them, with each other. That was weekly. While he was dying, and I couldn't go back, one of the women, Janet Partlow, who had taken the Healing Touch for Animals class, was very helpful. She was a neighbor. She kept the group going. I went every time I could. They invited me into all kinds of things..

Janet came in and did her thing. They invited in some other people that had Healing Touch. Now, I'm back with them. Basically, we have this group every two weeks. Anyone here in our retirement community, which has about a 1000 people, is welcome. We have had as many as twenty or so, but usually around twelve to fifteen. They can bring a friend. We spend an hour. It depends upon what's happening. If I'm doing it, then we will go around that circle and find out where they are. We will do some Healing Touch as a group or I will teach them. Usually it's just the basic using your hands, those types of things. It works pretty well.

Of course, we have people here that think it's crazy, but they haven't been mean. They just think that stuff is crazy. We don't do a big thing. We put an advertisement for when it's going to be in our calendar. People know it's Healing Touch. I've called it "energy wellness" sometimes, because I have included other things in it. They know which ones are Healing Touch and which ones are Mary Jo's stuff from Energy Healing. I am very careful trying to make sure we keep it safe. Some people don't know where this is coming from.

That's basically what I've done. Janet approved a book I had developed for it, before she died. That made me feel good. I've got that in there, that we did some of the things involved, and some of the things that came from there, with her approval Everybody here knows, or a lot of people know, what it is.

So that's what I've used my years of retirement for. It's been eighteen years now. I guess about fifteen of them, I've worked with Healing Touch. For at least five or seven of them, I was certified. I'm no longer certified. I think Instructor Emeritus is a good title for us.

I was trying to think, when were they here? Was it 2004? We had somebody out here. Were you here? This was in 2000. I'm looking in my certificates here, for when we had a Healing Touch meeting out here. Regional meeting?

It looks like that was 2005 or 2006. I think I've been to one since then. But we did have one out here

*What is your favorite Healing Touch healing story that you've done with a client?*

Oh my goodness. Let's see. One was with my brother-in-law who was really going downhill. He was dying. I have two, both of them are stories with people who are dying. I have learned to do that. That was something in my early years that I have really had to do.

I was a nurse so many years. I worked with children, and it was so hard for me when death was around. One of the first people that died out here was the husband of a good friend of mine. She was not a nurse, but she and I were very good friends. She was a minister, actually.

I was doing chakra spread. She was there. They were sitting together. It was one of the most peaceful deaths I have ever seen. It was very beautiful. The energy, as I did the chakra spread, came up, began to leave his body, and came through his head until he took his last breath, and then he was gone. It was very, very powerful. For me, it was just the kind of thing that helped me realize that death is a movement into the next wherever. It was so peaceful.

His daughter had left the room. She couldn't be there.

Being with people who are dying is very powerful for me. It doesn't happen every day at all. At that point, and being where I am in my life, I can now go into RC&R, our convalescent and rehab center, which takes people when they're getting close to the end or they stay at home. I can go in and really touch with them, if they want it. I don't just go in and do it up. But anyway, that's basically what I am beginning to do now.

I'm working with people who are dying. I think that is going to be my most powerful thing. There is one other one, but I think that is the one that is most meaningful to me in terms of my own movement into old age and working here. Instead of working with young children, like I did with most of my career, I'm now working with people who are aging.

*Do you have any comments or advice for new students?*

Well. I guess I would say, be open to what you find. Do the very simplest techniques as you begin to work with people, depending upon what you are doing. If you're establishing yourself a practice, I've learned that the very simplest techniques that we have, are ones that seem to work.

I'm sitting here thinking about it. I've also worked with people, using a teddy bear, at a distance. So many of the people I work with are at a distance. I will use this old teddy bear and work with hand over hand, or bringing my hands down, maybe doing a drain of some sort, placing my hands in an area that's very painful.

That's what I do, the very simplest ways. I try to finish the chakra spread, as they get closer to death, and I don't know why. But I've used it several times. It depends on where people are. But those are the things that I will use.

I haven't been going to the RC&R section, that's the convalescent and rehab center. I'm sorry. You'll know when I say that. Our long term care thing. I've had some respiratory stuff myself. I've had to make sure I'm okay when I go in there. I am going more.

I do a lot of distance work with many of the people that I was close to back in Virginia I have no way of connecting with them again except remotely. I find that is very powerful, as well as being right there.

That's kind of where I am with that. It's not all in their head. One of the things that happened here that was really interesting. One of my neighbors came to me one day and she said, "I'm hurting in my eye. There's something in my eye." Her eye was just as red as it can be.

She wasn't sure. She hadn't been here for very long. We were going to call and get someone to come. We have a good system here.

As I stood there waiting, I took my hand and put my fingers together and started working with her eye, listening to her talking, walking down the street to get in my house. She was my neighbor, just a few doors down. As it was, it began to change. She opened her eye and she said, "I think it's okay. I think it's all right."

I said, "Well."

And she said, "Wheeoo. I'm glad I came."

That made a believer out of her in Healing Touch. And she came. I had a group of people here to come. She came for a while. She hasn't recently, but we're still neighbors and good friends. That's the kind of thing that happens.

*What would you like to see for the future of Healing Touch?*

I really can't say. I feel like it's in a good place. I wish that there was more of a way for those of us who are of an age to have a, find a way of being more connected. It's not that I don't feel connected. It's that I know that I can't travel. I haven't figured out what that would be. Maybe it's there and I just have not aware of it.

That would be the thing that I would say. Having people who agree and are willing to get us together and help us. Which I don't do much any more.

We used to have gatherings here in the Northwest and we still do. But I can still drive, but I I'm not driving any large distances any more. So I can't go to all of the things, unless I have someone who wants to do that kind of thing.

And I think they are. I think they're aware of it. I guess that's all I have to say.

*Do you have a favorite Janet Mentgen story?*

For Janet I should. I'm trying to remember the last time she was here. It's not coming, I don't think. I should have thought of something. I'm looking at the pictures. There should be something here, right about Janet and I.

Well, I do have a book that has been very helpful to me. One is called "The Circle of Doves:. A Woman's Journey to Herself." And Janet is one of the people in it. I see her as someone who influenced my life, made it stay as something I could take with me as I age. She was very, very powerful. She's smiling in a picture I have. I look at her and realize that there are many others, going back to my early childhood. But how many there be, maybe ten. Janet is one of the predominant ones. I wasn't with her very much, but I felt like I could share things with her. It was a very powerful time.

*How has Healing Touch changed your life?*

How has it changed my life? It has given my life a purpose. I see my life as ten and fifteen year segments, movements through my whole life. I go back and look at my overall history. I've got a little article here in my book called, "The Way of the Butterfly". The butterfly is kind of the way I see life as a process of cycles of transformation. As you move through them, and Healing Touch was the one that came towards the end of my life, as I moved through with my count, how we kind of transform ourselves. I think it made my retirement something that I feel very positive about.

I feel like I was able to work with my dying husband and go through that. I feel like, because of that, I was able to make a contribution to the retirement community where I've lived now for eighteen years, after having lived in the east for all those years. That's what it's done for me. It's given me the things that tend to help me, so that I can make a contribution to where I am. I mean I know that someday, depending on how long I live, it may be that everybody is giving to me. But I would like to feel that I've been a place where I can give to somebody. Healing Touch has made that possible.

I won't say any more as I'm older, because I didn't get into it until then. I'm so glad there are young people. I loved it, when I was teaching it, and we had young people. I'd liked to go back and find out what happened to them. I look at pictures in my book and see where they were. There were a lot of people that were in classes that I taught. I don't know where they all are or what they've done. I'd like to get to know them again.

Pioneers in Healing touch

# Barbara Dahl
## BSN, RN, HTCP/I Emeritus
## Elder

**Introduction**

Barb Dahl has been a much loved Level 1 through 3 instructor in the Pacific Northwest. Through her efforts, Healing Touch spread from Seattle, Washington, to Vancouver BC, to Portland, Oregon and all through the region. She even taught classes in The Netherlands. Because of her leadership and love of Healing Touch, we now have several instructors in Washington, Oregon, and Idaho. Because of her dedication, over a thousand people have taken Healing Touch, either as her students or as the students of instructors she mentored. Both she and Bernie Clarke built a Healing Touch community that reaches out to many more thousands of people, all receiving Healing Touch.

Barb's interview was the first one I did. It is structured slightly differently than the others. It's also the one where I threw out my list of questions for elders to answer. They weren't needed.

**Interview**

*In your history in Healing Touch Program what positions have you held?*

Certified practitioner and certified instructor for Levels 1, 2, and 3.

*What committees did you serve on?*
Ethics committee and certification review committee.

*What attracted you to energy medicine?*
There was a flyer at the hospital where I worked, for a workshop called "Love, Touch and Healing" in Sedona. I always wanted to go to Sedona and that workshop was my excuse. It was taught by a remarkable healer, Lona Peoples. I didn't know what I was getting into. But I knew, watching her demonstrations, that I was seeing something wonderful and powerful and it scared me, because it was out of my little box of reality. I didn't have anything to explain it.

Initially I was a little afraid of the energy, but I was not allowed to forget what I had seen and experienced. I had just had a breast biopsy done, and the drainage tubes were removed the day before my flight to Arizona. I was partnered with a nurse from the Midwest, whom I hadn't met before, and after moving her hands, as instructed, through my energy field she shared that when she was over my left breast she felt a temperature change. So she, again as instructed, just brushed it away. She was almost embarrassed to tell me this. She was wide-eyed when I told her that I had just had surgery on that breast, and the surgeon was amazed at my healing when I saw him the next week.

A voice kept telling me over maybe the next six months, saying "Therapeutic Touch, Therapeutic Touch. I was aware that a nurse, Janet Mentgen, was teaching Therapeutic Touch at Red Rocks Community College near my home. It took me about a year, but I signed up for that class, and that was where I really got into energy work.

*When did you start Healing Touch?*

After Red Rocks, I stuck to Janet like gum. I attended classes at her private business, Whole Body Health in Denver and booked appointments for private healing treatments. Then my husband and I moved back to Seattle. That was in 1988, the same year Janet was selected as Holistic Nurse of the Year by the American Holistic Nurses Association. Then in 1989 the AHNA adopted Janet's program as their first official certificate program with the name Healing Touch. They had to name it something. It couldn't be called Therapeutic Touch any more.

She taught her first, I think it was three classes that year. She had called me up here in Seattle, when she was selected Holistic Nurse of the Year, and said that the AHNA wanted to teach her program around the country. She was rather stunned by that. She didn't think she had done anything that remarkable. The organization, the American Holistic Nurses Association, thought that she had created something very special, and very pertinent, and very needed. She said, "And we're going to need instructors. You're up there in Washington, so you'll be the instructor for Washington. Or even the Northwest."

I heard that, but I really didn't comprehend what was going to happen. I didn't wait. The opportunity to teach came by invitation from the minister of a Methodist church soon after we moved into our home. It was my rehearsal time for what was to come. The first official workshop up here was in 1991. Level I workshops (there was no Level II yet) were scheduled to alternate between Bellingham, north of Seattle near the Canadian border, and Vancouver, BC. In the spring we did Washington and in the fall we did Vancouver.

I went through the very first workshop with (Janet) in Washington and Vancouver. That qualified me to start teaching it on my own. I started teaching the official Level 1 of Healing Touch, alternating between Vancouver and Bellingham. That went on for several years and then it spread. I taught in areas around the country where I was sent by the office, e.g., Cincinnati, Las Vegas, Marin County, California, Hawaii and of course, Vancouver. I considered Vancouver my second home. Most of us taught through the program then rather than as free agents booking our own workshops.

*As one of the early people, were you certified after you had begun teaching?*
    They didn't have certification until the annual Holistic Nurses Conference in Burlington, Vermont. It was like after I had been teaching it for several years, I now I found out I had to do all of these things to qualify to teach. The rebellious adolescent in me thought "Oh, I'm not going to do that. I've already been doing it. Why do I have to go through all of that hoohaw?" And then I had people calling me, panicked, "Barb, you're scheduled to teach here or there, and you won't be able to if you don't get your certification packet in."
    Guess I thought I'd be grandfathered in, grandmothered in but no, you had to dot your i's and cross your t's to be certified. Believe me, it was a lot easier then than it is today. I finally sat on my ego and put together a packet. It wouldn't impress anybody today for sure.

*So you certified as an instructor before you certified as a practitioner?*
    I believe there was just the one certification in the beginning so by certifying as an instructor, you were automatically certified as a practitioner. Back then, Janet selected her instructors.

*Why did you stay with Healing Touch?*

I loved the work. I was learning so much. I felt it was important. I knew we were ahead of the times, and there wasn't going to be any great demand then, but I knew we were a movement. I really felt that. And it was significant. I thrived on how Healing Touch took me out of the box. Things I hadn't even thought about, now were important. Then I started using Healing Touch, applying it. I was going to say it's magical, but it isn't magical. It's spiritual, it feeds the soul.

*You have answered some of the next question, what do you like best about Healing Touch?*

Well, I got a big charge out of teaching Level 1. Having people come in just as I did, not knowing anything about energy work and watching them get turned on to it. That was fun for me. I was using it in the hospital in the psychiatric setting. It helped people. It was obvious to staff that Healing Touch was helping people. That was exciting too.

*Did you ever have a practice other than in the hospital setting?*

I attempted it. But it wasn't even paying my rent. I gave up that space. I don't know how long I kept it. Just one day a week. I had cards made and so on and so forth, but it wasn't drawing clients in. It was just too new. Seattle is essentially holistic in spirit. Many people are open to complimentary health practices. On the other hand the medical community, certainly at that time, is extremely conservative. Healing Touch was just new. The word hadn't gotten around. I remember a massage therapist telling me about a study done on massage therapy. She said that only nineteen percent of the country understood what therapeutic massage was. That most of them associated massage with sex parlors. And I thought, well gee, massage has been around for a long time and most of the population still thinks of it as the sex trade.

That isn't so long ago. Therapeutic massage, with its license and schools, had more going for it than Healing Touch. We were still trying to get a name out there. Nurses had heard of Therapeutic Touch.

I believe that the first instructors were challenged to be the voice of a new way and often we felt like we were crying in the wilderness. We were. There's been a change, a shift in our awareness and often it is the health care consumer who embraces the change before conventional health care.

Energy work has been picked up by researchers. A lot of doctors are paying attention to it. Not the majority, for sure, but especially the younger doctors. Many enter medical school aware of energy medicine. It's still not taught there. In the beginning there was hardly anything available on energy medicine. I've saved every piece I could find that was written after 1986 on energy work, all of it now cluttering my basement. Now, of course, there are whole sections on holistic health and energy medicine in book stores. And you, Linnie, are writing some of them.

*Do you have one or more favorite techniques?*

I use Level 1 techniques almost exclusively. They do the work. I don't do that much hands-on healing any more. I've grown away from the techniques philosophy but I continue to use them. I often use the chakra connection mentally on myself to enter into a meditative state. Techniques help us to hold our intention. You and I know that techniques are not what does the healing. Using the techniques and "doing the work" took me into spiritual healing and spiritual healing does not require techniques.

One of my Portland, Oregon students called me after she and a few other students had worked on a hospitalized baby that wasn't expected to live. The baby thrived. They were stunned by the outcome, and thrown into disbelief. At one point she stopped midsentence, and said, "You know all this, don't you?" When I agreed that I did, she asked how could I then teach techniques. I replied, "Because I didn't always know, and I learned from using the techniques."

*Have you explored other modalities or have you stayed basically with Healing Touch?*

Janet explored many techniques, and the program is built on the work of various healers. She always encouraged continuous learning, but she said she didn't need to do that anymore. It was just all variations. You have Reconnection. You have Reiki and, of course, Therapeutic Touch, all of the different modalities. They all overlap. I think it is by chance the one you connect with, and I happened to connect with Healing Touch. Indeed, I was "called" to Janet's program.

I have taken Level I Reiki. Other than hand placements, the script was the same as Level I Healing Touch. It's all out there in the Universe and some people experience it in a different form. I didn't take Level 2 Reiki, where they get into distance healing, because I was already doing it. Distance healing is not formally taught in the Healing Touch Program and yet, at some point, we come to realize that "hands-on" aren't required. I always thought being a master, third degree Reiki, was so pretentious. I'm pretty good at some things, better at others, but I've never "mastered" anything, including Healing Touch.

I still experience new modalities. I recently experienced Theta. I met a woman at an all-day lecture. We hit it off. She had a degree in physics and worked for Boeing for years. She had given it up to open a private healing practice using Reiki and Theta. I hope it works for her. She gets into her Theta brain waves. That's what you're taught to do in Theta. It accesses stuff about the client. I really didn't agree with what she was accessing, but I stayed open to it. She was picking up on loneliness. She knew enough about my history of recent losses and I believe she made some assumptions. I told her, "I live alone now, but I don't feel lonely. Yes, I miss my loved ones but I have a full life with friends, family, and many interests."

Since my retirement from nursing, and as a Healing Touch instructor, my explorations have been more on the spiritual end of things, primarily through my blog, www.rosesinjanuary.com; the Aging Adventure, Interfaith, and most recently from the writings of Alastair McIntosh. I've found a church community that is compatible with my "out-of-the-box" liberal way of thinking.

*How did Healing Touch change your life?*

By opening up this vast universe of energy and learning to be with the energy and follow where it leads you. As practiced in Healing Touch, we're aware that we are only the instrument through which the energy moves. Where does the energy come from? You start reading about quantum physics, and you start to get a little more curious and informed about the different spiritual belief systems. They, too, overlap. It's definitely made me more of a spiritual being. That's been my path -- to grow and advance spiritually. That changed my life. For me, that was the blessing of the work and the program.

*Do you have any particularly meaningful stories in your Healing Touch history?*

I was working on an Adolescent Psychiatric unit in Denver. I was still new to Healing Touch and very much in the closet, especially in that psychoanalytic setting. I'd had a three day weekend off, and when I returned on a Monday morning, I was assigned to special a fourteen year old boy in the seclusion room.

I reviewed his chart. He had come in Thursday evening, had not eaten or had anything to drink. He was strapped to the cot, his wrists and ankles in leather restraints, sitting up, speaking nonsensically and nonstop, his eyes darting everywhere. I determined that his priority need was hydration, and I gathered drinks from the unit frig. I spoke to him and told him that I had juice for him to drink. He showed no evidence of even hearing me. I held the back of his head to quiet the continual head movement and raised the juice container to his mouth, afraid that he could aspirate. At first I couldn't even catch his mouth.

And then, without even thinking about what I was doing, my hand at the back of his head began to stroke the field. He immediately stopped his body motions and made eye contact with me. I didn't quite know what to do, but explained that I was smoothing his energy field. He was quiet then, drank the whole container of juice and calmly asked if it would be okay if he went to sleep. I told him that he was safe, that I would stay with him. At that he laid down and went to sleep. He slept the rest of my shift. I told the incoming evening nurse what I had done. I charted the same, and reported off on the tape recorder. I was out of the closet.

Janet had said, "To not use the energy when you knew it could help, would be a sin of omission." I didn't set out to be the voice for HT but I did take an oath as a RN to offer comfort and alleviate distress when I could. In the next hospital after our move to Seattle, and after establishing some credibility as a "regular" nurse, I used my knowledge of HT in acute situations; interrupting full blown panic and anxiety attacks easily and effortlessly.

I always got the patient's permission, but they didn't know what HT was and didn't care. They just said, "I'll try anything." Within five minutes their anxiety would be gone and they were smiling. HT was also effective in interrupting migraine headaches that powerful narcotic cocktails didn't touch. And, of course, balancing the energy allowed even bipolar patients in full blown manic attacks to relax and sleep.

I got into Healing Touch for Animals. I had special experiences with horses. That took me another quantum leap forward in energy work, when I saw the effects on the animals. Especially the horses. It was like we communicated together without words. I don't speak horse. But there was communication. We exchanged love.

*What would you like to see in future for Healing Touch?*

I don't think about it actually but I will always support the program and I speak freely about my history in Healing Touch. Lisa and Cynthia are doing such a good job as program leaders. I don't see beyond today with Healing Touch. Will it survive and be something that all people have heard of, know about, want to learn? No that will never happen, because people don't necessarily want to learn it any more than they want to learn to give injections or learn Chinese. They might be willing, more than willing to receive it. But not everybody will want to learn it and do it. Hopefully, hospitals will see the value in making it available to patients and schedule nurses' time for delivering it. Then they will want to offer the workshops in their institutions.

*Because you are an elder do you have a special story about Janet that you really like? You suggested this question, Barb.*

I did?

*You did.*

I always think of Janet telling me about one of her former students who had gone over to Cypress, and was so excited about the healer, Daskalos, and told Janet she needed to get over there. I said, "Well, are you going?"

She said, "I don't have a passport."

And I said, "Janet, you need to get one. Even if you don't go to Cypress, you've created a program that's going to expand out of this country and you're going to be invited to go and, of course, you know the places she did go -- Australia and New Zealand. Many times.

Anyway, the next year I said, "Well, did you get your passport?"

She said, "I don't have a birth certificate."

So the next year I said, "Did you get your passport?" She said, "No, but I got my birth certificate."

I said, "Well, all you have to do, you live in Denver, is to go downtown with your birth certificate, and get your passport."

And then the next year "Did you get your passport?"

And she said, "Yes."

"Are you going to Cypress?"

"No. I don't need to."

"What do you mean, you don't need to.

"We're working together, already."

On another plane, in another dimension Janet was working with Daskalos, doing their work together around the world at night. Strange that I had no trouble believing that. Back then, I was still a neophyte with energy work and the paranormal.

*As far as I'm concerned you were a real pathfinder here in the Pacific Northwest and if it weren't for you there would be hundreds of, maybe a thousand, people who would not being doing Healing Touch today, and many more thousands having received Healing Touch. We all owe you a word of thanks.*

My gift was that I was called to it. That's another strong feeling. I had never given any thought at all to being a nurse. My family were all teachers. Funny, I started my college years in education, but didn't finish in education because I didn't want to teach. I was called to nursing. Being in nursing, I was called to Healing Touch. It was grace, pure amazing grace. I never thought I would be a teacher, even of adults.

*You still are Barb.*

Thank you.

# DEBORAH
## HTCP/I

## Introduction

An angel in our midst: I have given a lot of thought as to how I want to introduce DEBORAH. I decided to tell you what she means to me. I first met DEBORAH in a Level 3 class. I had recently published *The Encyclopedia of Energy Medicine*. When it came time for introductions, I introduced myself as a Level 1 instructor, but didn't say a word about the book. Deborah interrupted the proceedings to ask me why I hadn't mentioned the book.

My reaction to that is unimportant. What is important is that DEBORAH saw a need in me to let go of my shyness as an author. She lectured me in front of the class and spoke to me several times afterwards. This is our DEBORAH. She can get in our faces and let us know we are important and that the work we do is important.

I see her as a golden star traveling around the country helping to build Healing Touch. I also see her as a supporter of each of us individually. She is right there to help any and everyone who is struggling with techniques, certification, or any of the other myriad of things we encounter as Healing Touch practitioners.

She has practice groups going in Alaska. She has her own practice. She is a mentor. She teaches Levels 1 through 3. And she is a very loving, generous, and kind person.

## Interview

*Thank you for responding. I am so excited to have you as part of this project. You are such a love. In so many ways you keep a lot of us going. You certainly kicked me in the butt when I needed it badly. I have always been grateful to you for it.*

*What got you started in Healing Touch?*
One day it actually fell into my lap when I was approached for a Healing Touch (HT) class space request at my job. I became involved, loved it and kept hosting the classes. Every time there was time for another HT class, the universe opened up for me to attend. It grabbed me. It was like a centrifuge type of reaction that kept sucking me in every time it was time to get sucked in. I gave least resistance. It was something I could not put to the side or on a shelf. It was something I had to put within me. I decided after my first class it was a way to live, not something to do on the side.

*What was it that hooked you on Healing Touch?*
What hooked me on Healing Touch was HT emphasized the importance of being balanced, gave me tools for self-care, as well as being a vessel to help others along their healing journey. It felt natural for me. I actually integrated and continue to enjoy several HT modalities daily for balancing and stress reduction self care needs in my life. I have an accepted awareness and commitment of being the best vessel I am capable of being to help others. I celebrate after each class and know I am gaining an arsenal of tools to help change me, others and the world.

Professionalism was another aspect that encouraged my completion of certification with Healing Touch Program (HTP). The continuing education credits are endorsement by two of my professional organizations (American Nursing Credentialing Center and National Board for Therapeutic Massage Therapy and Bodyworker). HTP has a formal methodology of credentialing including experiential requirements, mentorship and a written testing process reviewing all course levels. Certification was essential to me as a health care professional working in large organizations that require or prefer credentialing and certification for specialization. This removed the stigma of energy medicine being "woo woo" and gave HT credibility as an acceptable professional practice within the health care arena. Now that definitely hooked me.

*That is fabulous. What all do you do for Healing Touch? I know you're an instructor. Which levels?*

I facilitate Level 1, 2, and 3 classes wherever and whenever possible. At the end of every class I say, "This is the best class I've ever had." because each class gives me a new element of being better than I was when I entered the class. Then I'm a ghost for Level 4 and 5 classes. Sometimes I'm a helper and sometimes I've gone on my own merit. Those advanced levels enhance my knowledge and skill needs for facilitation of the three basic courses I teach.

*What did you mean by a ghost?*

I use the term ghost to represent the innocence I seek in my attending those classes. I go to discover what do we need to instill in Level 1, 2, and 3 students to get them to 4 and 5? I have no intent just a spirit of discovery with a baby's mind. I see all of the students as people on the journey for becoming better and helping others with their healing journey. They're picking up big packages of knowledge required in order to go on through the process of becoming independent practitioners in energy medicine. That's why I consider this a ghost element. I have no intent just a spirit of discovery. I show up and get out of the way. It is not about me or the time to consult my ego. I'm wherever they are and whoever I'm meeting at that time. That's the ghost element.

*You are so wonderfully supportive of all of us.*
I am being a help-mate. If they just know how important it is to be balanced and what they're able to give and receive as a result. That's what sparks my fire.

*Do you have any good healing stories?*
Yes there are many stories to share since I'm a nurse and worked in an acute care hospital over five years with physicians' standing orders for me to provide HT consultation and services for the end of life.

However, one story still continues to tickle me because it's not a typical clinical kind of story. I was on an airplane. I've been a responder when someone was ill on the airplane, but this story is related to having HT as an everyday, wherever, whenever, life skill. Keep in mind that DEBORAH is "wherever she is when she is supposed to be and all that I am is with me".

I was traveling across four time zones from Alaska to Georgia after working excessive hours at my job to prevent leaving overwhelming workloads for other staff in the department. I planned good naps for my long trip. Well, I didn't have a napping experience on the first leg of my flight because of a loudly screeching, crying baby on the plane. I gathered insight observing parents' behaviors to quiet the baby were inexperienced. I also overheard discussion that the father was just returning from serving in a war zone overseas. Their approach with the issue was passing the baby back and forth in efforts to stop the screeching. It didn't make any difference at all whether mama or dad held the baby throughout the three hour flight.

When I changed planes in Seattle to Atlanta, my introduction to the fellow in my row began with him telling me how tired and sleepy he was. I quickly told him, "Oh, that's my story too". I let him know that on my last flight a baby sitting a row ahead of me deterred my needed rest. We laughed and talked about how we were going to rest from Seattle to Atlanta for sure.

As I looked up, I could not believe that baby and parents were coming down the aisle of this flight. Anyway, the dad sat down in the empty middle seat next to me, and mother with the baby sat in middle seat in the row in front of us.

I took a deep breath, requested help from all my higher powers, and acknowledged it would be alright. As soon as we take off the screeching hollering started. The nonstop crying continued so when it was safe to remove seat belts the mother got up and passed the baby over to the dad. With hollering baby in his hands, I looked at dad directly in his eyes. I held my hands out to get the baby. He had a brief moment of hesitation, but I noted that we connected and he gave me the baby. I'm glad that my energy was balanced enough with an element of trust in the unspoken message of permission ("You need to give me that baby, please") when he surrendered to my look.

As the infant sat in my lap, I was doing one of HT basics known as hands in motion and the dad is sitting there looking at me. I'd look over at him and give him a smile and he gave me his smile. Dad kept looking and I kept waving my hands over the baby.

After a short while that baby was quietly sleeping. Mom stood up and looked over the seats because she couldn't see between the seat crack. She looked at dad, then me, and the sleeping baby (I smiled), and she sat back down. The fellow sitting in our row peeked around and gave me a 'Thank Goodness' look. He got comfortable quickly drifted to sleep with a gentle snore. The dad also got a nice period. Baby slept the entire time and awakened peacefully just before landing. I gave the Dad the baby when we landed. My row mate started clapping, and everybody else obviously benefited from the silence because they all started clapping as they stood up.

The segment of the flight without that baby's crying noise was profound and restful for my weary spirit. I was refreshed and in awe of the reminder of the impact of HT. It was creation of sacred space for a child needing balance and safety flying on this cross country journey. I'm glad I had this experience because as a grandmother it became my saving grace on many airplane trips with infant and toddler grandchildren.

*That's beautiful. I think it's a great example of using Healing Touch in everyday life, and where it's of value.*

Yeah!! I still believe and support founder of HTP Janet Mentgen's goal to have HT in **every** home, school, organization…..

*Oh you're so beautiful. What are your plans for the future of Healing Touch? What do you see yourself and/or Healing Touch doing? Or what would you like to see?*

HT has a future of demand. I witnessed transformation and transition from a frontline view as a medical professional. Alternative medicine phase meant if you chose this then you are abandoning traditional health care choices. Complementary medicine phase gave us permission to be involved because research demonstrated we were doing no harm and folks did seem to benefit. The integrative phase gives clients chances to have all types of resources to help with their healing journeys with emphasis on being whole. People are actively trying to incorporate holistic practices into their lives. Healing Touch, as an energy medicine program, provides an opportunity to be an effective way to give and share help. That's what it did for me and it serves as a great help mate for folks in the world to become better and to help others.

There is a need for more integration of energy medicine at the student nursing level to promote their self-care and patients' stress reduction battles. I am working with a faculty member to include Healing Touch in their coursework options, and possibly recruit students as volunteers for community wide outreach projects that promote wellness.

I expect continued growth of services offered primarily through the Healing Gatherings components of my practice. Healing Gatherings, caring enough to serve, take volunteer teams to serve vulnerable, homeless and aging persons such as homeless and vulnerable Veterans' Stand Down (participated for last six years), or active duty Warriors in Transition, or Senior Centers, or Women Veteran Health Fairs. Another component of is Healing Gatherings "helping those who are helping others". This service takes volunteer teams to conduct clinics into organizations with high stress profiles, and work on the staff members only, not the clinic's clientele. The concept is based on the help mate role to provide balance and relaxation for staff so clients reap the benefits of holistic staff morale. In the South, my volunteer teams are energy medicine clinics in spiritual settings, as well as visitation of the sick and shut in. There are lots of opportunities to expand any of these options to serve and make a difference in communities, states, our country, and globally. The volunteers work within their HT scope of practice (student, apprentice, or practitioner) and certified healing touch practitioners supervise the clinic. Healing Gatherings provide creation of sacred space while promoting balance and relaxation for being whole. I truly honor and profess HTP's descriptor for the whole person in terms of "physical vitality, emotional balance, mental clarity, and connection with spirit"!!!

As a lifelong learner, I find it exciting to explore many powerful dimensions of energy such as presence, caring, vibration, sound, touch, meditation, essential oils, and more, since everything has energy. However, HT has its special foundational place among my professional practitioner tools. HT has the awesomeness of a credential that warrants its program as the leader in energy medicine and the venue for developing great practitioners. So be it!

# Donna Duff
## LPN, CSEM, MST, HTCP/I
### Elder

**Introduction**

Several people recommended, and a couple even insisted, I interview Donna Duff. I met her once, many years ago at a conference, but had no outstanding memory of her. I do now. What a treasure she is. The following interview proves she is one of our outstanding elders. I could talk with her for hours. And never get tired of the conversation. If you get a chance to take a class from her, I heartily recommend you do so. You'll be glad you did.

This interview doesn't follow the format of the other chapters. I only had to ask Donna two questions. She answered all my traditional questions and then some, with no prompting on my part.

**Interview**

We were here the year that Janet passed on to Cynthia the title Program Director. Before Janet passed it on to Cynthia, we were talking about the old stories. Someone, there at Shadowcliff said we should have some of this recorded. I thought, "Well, it ain't gonna be me." Everybody thought it would be a great idea to have the stories captured. I then, started videotaping Janet at Shadowcliff at the last couple of talks that she gave. I don't think the stories are on it. Janet shared her vision of Healing Touch, and I have found the tape.

It's great that you're doing this. Do you have the time frame to pull it off now?

*Yes.*

I am sure you are putting it out there to Janet and all those other great ancestors to make it happen. I will continue to hold that vision for you to get it done by conference.

*The first question I have for you is how did you get started in energy medicine?*

Way back when, I did Deloris Krieger and Dora Kunz's courses in Therapeutic Touch in the early part of the "80's. I didn't get to meet Janet until 1990, the third class that she did. Do you want me to go back to "82?

*I was curious as to why you took the Deloris Krieger class in the first place.*

I read an article on Therapeutic Touch and I thought, "Wow. Imagine if we could do this as nurses, wave our hands over people, and make people well. I think this is all B.S."

I wasn't sure. But then again I thought, "Well, wait a minute. They are writing about it, so maybe there is some truth. Why don't I find out. "

I actually did a course in '82 or '84. When I was in the class I couldn't feel anything. I went through the whole workshop and I thought, "I don't know what these people are talking about. It's crazy."

But, people were telling me they were getting results from the class and could feel what I was doing. I had no feeling in my hands. I continued on and at the nursing home where I was working, this was back in Canada. I happened to work on what we called the priests' floor where the religious priests were. I decided to work on a Father John who couldn't speak because he had a stroke. I started working on him, just practicing Therapeutic Touch.

One day out in the hallway, he was walking and he started rubbing his leg. I thought, "Oh my God."

I got called into the supervisor's office, because then they thought, because it was in his groin area, they thought I might have been doing something sexual to the man. Crazy to say, it was then I realized, it was because I was helping him with his leg pain that he had, he was getting relief from what I did. He was truly my very first client, but my best teacher, because then I could keep doing the work behind closed curtains. I knew it was making the results for him.

The interesting thing about that story is three months later, on a night I was on duty, I was down by myself in the hallway where he was. He was in bed and he started singing. I thought, "Man, for someone who can't speak, you sure know how to sing, Father John." I went in. He was taking his last breath.

I thought afterwards, wow. Where did all this come from? How did this happen?

I never really knew what the work did. I went back to another workshop after that to understand more about Therapeutic Touch. Again I was getting results, people were feeling it, but I still couldn't feel.

While I was in Newfoundland, I met Mary Jo Bulbrook at university. Her dad got ill, and she asked me come take care of her father in North Carolina, until she found another nurse to take care of him. That never happened. I ended up staying, because Grandpa didn't want me to leave.

I went to the massage school that was close by us in North Carolina. I learned more about massage, because I had also done that in Newfoundland. I got trained as a massage therapist. In the massage school we had to do Reiki. After doing the Reiki class, I thought this is really B.S, stuff. I never got into Reiki at the time. Part of it was because I realized I wasn't feeling. I kept doing the work. The attraction, for me, was trying to understand.

I got a flyer about a workshop in Memphis, Tennessee with Sharon Scandrett and Janet. I thought, "Bah, I'm not doing that stuff." Even though it was for nurses, blah, blah, blah.

A client asked me to go to the class. She thought with my massage practice this would be a good thing, plus she wanted to pay me to go get the training. I thought, "What the hell. I can go to Tennessee from North Carolina."

So I went. That is where I first met Janet. One of the students was a sister who happened to be in the class. Her pen stopped writing. Janet told her to hold up the pen. Janet did laser beam on it. Then the pen kept writing.

I thought, "I believe in this group."

I still didn't feel anything by the end of that class, but there was something about it that I was attracted to. I really enjoyed it. I stayed on then. Back then, we did Level 1, Level 2 back to back. I did the Level 2. It was the Hopi work, and the back work, that sold me.

I went back to North Carolina. I had a chiropractor that I worked with as a massage therapist. I said, "I want three patients. I don't really know what I'm doing, but I want to try this stuff out. It's from nurses, and I think it has potential."

She gave me three clients. All three of them had results. Two of them didn't go back to her. They kept coming to me for Healing Touch and for massage. By then I was off and running.

I thought, "I still don't know what I'm doing."

When Janet was in the area, I would repeat the Level 1 or the Level 2, sometimes with Dorothea Hover. Things were happening.

We had a workshop. I remember where I was. I sitting on a lawn in Durham, just outside Duke Chapel, when Dorothea said to me, "You know, you'd make a great instructor."

I said, "What are you drinking this afternoon?"

She said, "No. We need you in this program. This program is going to grow. I know you can do this. I know that you don't feel and I know you're struggling with that, but I really feel that you would be great for this program."

I never turned my back on it.

Shortly after that I got to go to one of the AHNA conferences. By then, I had met Janet a couple of times within a year. (It was shortly after all this, because these gals came back to North Carolina pretty frequently. Within three months, somebody was back teaching a class. We had a lot of classes at Duke).

We had an AHNA conference in Colorado when a big storm came up. I couldn't get a plane home. I said to Janet, "Any chance you can put me up for the night? I'll come cut your lawn for you."

She looked at me. Her house that she had in Denver was on a big piece of property. She said, "Really?"

I said, "Yeah. I love cutting lawns. I'll cut your lawn for you, if you'll put me up for the night."

She said, "It's a deal."

Her lawn was maybe two acres or it might have been ten acres. It was a lot. I thought, "Oh dear God. I'm here for the day, cutting this lawn."

I went around the side of the house and got the push mower out, and started mowing her lawn. About fifteen, twenty minutes later, Janet runs around to the back side of the house and comes back with a Deere tractor. She was laughing her head off.

"You were going to let me mow this whole lawn with this little push mower?"

We laughed. That was the fun side of Janet. She is up on her balcony looking out checking up on me, making sure I was doing a good job. I get on this Deere tractor. Off I am going, back and forth, back and forth. All of a sudden, near the end of the garden, there's colors coming out. . And more colors. I stopped and I go in the house. I asked her, "Janet, what part of your lawn am I at, because it all of a sudden started to look colorful."

She said, "You're not going through my flower garden are you?

"Oops." The grass was so high, I couldn't tell that there were flowers down underneath. I had made two tracks right through her garden. Oops, and if she wanted to smack me, that was the very time to do it.

She took me out to her balcony while showed me a picture of her garden and sure enough, it's a big, beautiful flower garden. By then I had cut through two rows. That was a great beginning, and the end of me being scared around Janet. She let me stay in the house and our friendship grew from there.

In the early days she kept coming back and forth to North Carolina doing her thing. We'd go to workshops and then we'd traveled, of course, overseas with her. My connection to Janet was that not only was she my mentor, but she was a very dear friend for me. We did a lot of Healing Touch stuff together; my connection for Janet was more time that we played. We did fun things together.

Surely, you have heard about her beanie baby stories.

*A few, yes. Do you have beanie baby stories?*

One year she came. We started talking about them. I said, "How many do you have?"

She said, "Well, I got about twenty."

I said, "Twenty? Hmm. I think I've got twenty-five."

Then we started. Whenever we were out somewhere, she'd pick one up. I'd pick one up. The next time she came, I said, "How many beanie babies do you have?"

"I've got about fifty now."

"Oh, good. I've got about forty-five."

Sometimes, I'd be some ahead of her and sometimes behind. Then we came to a Level 4 and 5 in Durham, NC. Someone brought in a donation of a dozen or so, beanie babies. They were in the gift shop and we didn't know it. Someone came in and said, "They've got beanie babies out in the gift shop."

I don't know who got to the door the fastest, me or Janet. We were beating it to this gift shop. It was on the property. The students are like, "Did we just lose our two teachers?" We weren't during class time. We were eating lunch. We got out there and she grabbed one and said, "I have this one."

I said, "I haven't,"

Honest to God, if it was on video tape, it was that hilarious. Here's the nuns looking at these two healers and saying, "What just happened here?" There we were scrapping over beanie babies. There were some original ones. It was funny. We kept them.

Then the year she found out she had cancer, of course, there was the beanie baby at AHNA conference, where there was the silent auction. They had a beanie baby and the two of us were fighting over it. The money we put into that. I ended up winning it. I had the piece of paper where her name was partly on it, but the deal was, that by time's up, you're name had to be fully on the piece of paper in order to get the article. At the very end, people are saying they want it, but you had had to write your full name and the amount you were going to pay. If your name wasn't fully on the piece of paper, then you couldn't get the article. There was a countdown starting at ten minutes.

The two of us stood over this beanie baby and we looked at some other things. I got to write my name down fully last, but she came back too late and only had written "Janet". So I got it. It's my prized beanie baby. Shortly after, she died of cancer. That beanie baby will never be sold, in my book.

She traveled with me. When she traveled, she had Weasel with her. Weasel came from - I don't know where she picked up Weasel. Weasel used to travel in her backpack. This little tiny weasel wasn't much bigger than a beanie baby.

I was taking my Level 2 up in Asheville, North Carolina. She said, "You can teach this by yourself."

I said, "Really?"

She said, "Yeah. Go ahead and teach it."

Back then, we didn't have to train like we do now. Whenever she thought you were ready to be moved ahead, she moved you ahead.

I began teaching mind clearing and I turned around and she said, "Keep going."

I said, "Okay. I turned back to the class.

I was always turning back and checking, because she was sort of to the back side of me. Finally, I turned around again and she just looked at me as if to say, "What are you doing?"

I looked down, and said, "Are you doing mind clearing on Weasel?" Right in front of the class.

She said, "Are you going to continue to teach?"

I said, "If you don't pass me now, and I can teach this, I'm quitting."

She said. "Will you finish the mind clearing?"

She was so serious. Obviously, which I didn't know, she was treating somebody, using Weasel as her surrogate.

Later, we laughed about it. But, at the time, it wasn't funny, because she was in the middle of a healing rite.

Weasel is now with my beanie baby. They sit together here in my sacred place. They, to this day travel with me to my classes on the alter.

*Somebody I talked to, wondered what happened to Weasel. Now we know.*

Yup. I had Weasel and I can verify it, and send you a picture of him.

I forget the other partner she picked up after Weasel. She figured Weasel was getting lonely, and honest to God, I can't remember what the other little character was. It wasn't a beanie baby.

I don't know who truly ended up with the most beanie babies. I think Lisa might have kept them. Anybody, like in this area, if they came to give Janet a beanie baby, they might as well bring me one too, because that was the thing. I'm sure every time Janet came to North Carolina, she got a gift of a beanie baby for being here.

*What's some advice you would give to new or potential students?*

I guess, for me, I'd just have to go back to my experience. I had my mentors, Dorothea and Sharon and Janet. They were always supportive. I think, no matter if you can feel or not, the work does work. I truly believe Janet's statement, "Just do the work." That's what I did.

Not as often, but there are still some times today when I practice, I still don't feel. But, I know it works. I don't need anybody to tell me if this works or not. Not anymore. I believe it and that's what's important. I just kept doing the work. I didn't give up. I had mentors and people to look up to. I think for new people, that we have so much richness now. I'm not saying we didn't have it back then, but I think we have it now.

I believe Lisa, God love her, has done an awesome job taking over and moving this program forward from her mom. I see parts of Janet in Lisa, when we're together. We have that whole connection, because I was more family to them and to Bill and to Lynn, from that perspective. When I'd be hanging out with Janet, we'd be together and hear the Janet stories from the family side of it. There's always energy. Janet lived and practiced it.

I was with Janet. I got to take her up to conference and come back with her from conference that year. She still believed in the work and she wanted the work to continue.

It's an awesome program. Please God, until the day I die I always support HT. When I got my instructor's badge, I put a picture of the world on the back. I put the picture on the back of my name tag. I am not going to give up teaching it until we had a Healing Touch book in every home, like a telephone book. I need to change that a little, because people don't have telephone books now. That is how important it was for me. I kept doing it.

That's why I say I'll never give up teaching this work. I'll always teach someone how to do it, and how to work with it.

I had a student back in 1994. She said, "I can really make a practice out of this with just Level 1."

I'll guarantee you'll never have to go forward beyond Level 1. You have enough that you can build yourself a practice. It's your choice to want to go and learn more. You can treat enough people with what you've learned. She had a full time practice for about four or five years before she finally came back to do Level 2. She did well with it, for sure.

I think that's why I appreciate Janet. When we initially did the certification part of it, she wanted people to practice for at least six months before they came back to be certified. That way, you really knew that this is what you wanted to do. Now, when they get out of Level 5, they've got to get their certification ASAP. That's okay.

I happened to be at the house with her when the other two gals showed up from Borders. They wanted to take it over. Janet asked them nicely to leave. I know where her dedication was. Program was to stay with her family-not to others.

We just keep doing the work and doing it in her honor. It could be stress for Lisa, because that is income for her family with her mother's inheritance that way.

We're all healing and helping people, no matter who or what you call it. I don't say what Lisa is doing is very easy. You gotta get your personal stuff out of the way. Keep doing the healing, however that can go.

I was lucky to be with Janet. I always did the Level 6's with her. Any chance I could get, I was with Janet. It was her wisdom, it was her quietness.

She would sit in a classroom. She was big about knowing students by their first name. Once, we all came back from a break at Level 6. She wasn't back in the class yet and I gathered the class. I got all the plastic name tags hidden. She walked in and she is sitting down. She said, "There's something wrong here, isn't there?"

Linda Smith was there and Linda said, "Yeah."

Janet kept looking around and said, "Okay. What's going on?"

I am half smirking and finally Janet looked across the room at a woman student. She said, "Stand up for me please."

So she stood up. Janet said, "What's the person's name next to you?"

The student turned, of course and said she didn't know.

Now we'd been together for two days. So Janet had her then stand up and said, "What's the lady's name over here?"

The student said, "I don't know."

Janet said, "Sit down."

The next thing Janet did, was stand up and went right around the class saying everybody's names. She said, "I hope you have all learned a lesson, here, why name tags are important to keep to them on at all times."

She said, "I don't know how this happened, but I think the joke is on somebody."

I was about two inches tall in the class at that time. I was afraid that if she found out I did this, she was really going to kill me. It wasn't until later at dinner, and we were sitting down. Linda said, "Janet, what did you think about the name tag thing today?"

She said, "Well, I tell you what. It was the funniest thing. I just gotta laugh about how it really worked out, because I got everybody's name. I was really surprised at myself for doing it."

I thought, "Great."

Linda pipes up and she said, "Do you know how it got started?"

Janet said, "No. Do you?"

I kicked Linda underneath the table. I said, "If you say another word, it will be the end of our friendship."

Janet looked at me and she said, "You did this?" She said, I hope you never do something like that again."

I said, "Janet, you're still teaching me, girl. You'll be teaching me until the day you leave." And, sure enough, she did.

For me, it's trying to know that part about her being the healer and who she was. She had a quiet, good side about her.

Another time we were at a Level 5 in Durham. Janet was outside and I was registering people for class. Janet was talking to students. They were going back and forth. I could hear what the students were saying.

A student came up and said, "Wow. How many classes have you taken?"

Janet said, "A few."

They went back and forth. The student asked, "How did you meet Janet?"

Janet would say, "Oh well, it's a really long story, how I met her."

She would talk about herself with the student, seriously. It was about a half hour conversation. The student went away and Janet walked back in to see how registration was going.

I said, "What just happened out there? She didn't know you, did she?"

She said, "No."

I said, "Janet, when we do the next book, we have to have your picture in the book, because, you know, we're getting so big now, people don't know who you are. They need to put a face to who you are."

She said, "Will you just finish registering?" And she laughed. That was it.

Later when we redid notebooks I told Mary Jo, "Mary Jo. Janet's picture needs to be in the book. We need to see who she is." Because we were doing the books and Mary Jo was doing most of the work at the time. Sure enough, we got the picture put in. It was because of that experience, talking to that student about who is Janet Mentgen.

You should have been in the class when that student walked in and saw Janet was the teacher. I thought we were going to have to do CPR on the student.

She said, "Really?"

I said, "Yeah."

She said, "I could have died."

I said, "Why would you die? You had a great experience with Janet. A personal one on one."

Janet would never say, "I'm Janet Mentgen, I don't have time for you."

The day I walk out and don't learn something new in class, I am going to give up teaching. That has never, and probably will never happen.

That is what I miss about Janet sometimes, if I am out on the road. We had frappuccinos. We loved Starbuck's frappuccinos. They were the best. When we went up to that last conference, driving up that weekend, she said, "You know where we're going?"

I said, "Starbucks? Really?"

She was still eating some, then, but really feeling great. We went on up. The next thing, I got called out of a meeting at conference and they said, "Janet's looking for you."

I went and I said, "Janet, are you okay?"

She said, "Yeah. You know what I want."

I said, "Are you for real?"

She said, "Yes."

Off I went, downtown, and got a Starbuck's frappuccino and brought it back to her. She was looking for things she could digest without upsetting her stomach.

Sure enough, driving back home from the conference, I said, "Is it Starbucks time?"

She said. "Yeah."

At the end of conference her son, Bill, wanted to drive her back. We got out of the garage and I was saying good-by to her. We had her in the car. She was still alert and keeping track of things. I had given the keys to Bill. She said, "Why are you saying good-by to me?"

I said, "Because Bill is driving you home."

She looked over at Bill. Bill is standing outside the driver's door. She was sitting in the passenger's side in front. She said, "Why did Bill have the keys?"

I said. "Because he's driving you home."

She said, "Did you not drive me up here?"

I said, "Yes. But Bill wants to drive you home."

She said, "Bill, give Donna back the keys."

I knew right there and then, how important my relationship to her was. It was one that was of honor and she was just a great friend. I guess I was just awed at that point to do that for her.

We had a quiet journey home. We didn't say a lot. I think that was good for her to do that. We got back and she got settled in the house. I left on Monday to go back to North Carolina. I said, "I'll be back when the day comes."

She said, "I know. We'll just have to call you."

I said, "That's all you have to do is call." She was weak, but I thought she had a few more weeks to live.

She died that Thursday. They called me Thursday afternoon. They said Janet's asking for you. I said, "I'm on my way." I couldn't get a ticket until Friday morning. They called me that Thursday night to say that she had already passed.

I know as much as I know about the woman. She was very gentle. She was very thoughtful. Like anybody, we all have our different moments. There was definitely a grace and a time to be with herself. She will always be a part of me, there is no question about it. I still miss her, even now.

*What a rich, wonderful blessing you've had.*

There was the time we bet to see who could eat the most fish and chips while in Australia. She said, "Are you giving up yet?"

I said, "I'll be darned. I'm not giving up,"

I had about sixteen orders of fish and chips. I think she had thirteen. We would go over to Australia and New Zealand sometimes for about two to three weeks. Sometimes four weeks we were over there on different trips. She would say, "You're the one who'll end up with a gallbladder attack. Is it worth it?"

That's what she told people. I really didn't have a gallbladder attack, but I never told people different. I just let it ride. I thought that's that fun part of the story. I'm the one with the gallbladder attack. She was good that way.

We were hanging out one evening after a class with the students. There were two tables in front of us and two behind. I ordered a beer. They said, "You shouldn't drink a beer with Janet here,"

I said, "Why not?"

They said, "Really, you will?"

I said, "Yah. What's the problem? It's after class. I'm having a beer."

I started drinking the beer and looked around and I was the only one drinking a beer with dinner. I turned around as Janet was at the table behind me and said, "Here Janet. Taste this beer."

She said, "Great idea."

I said, "This isn't one that we've had yet."

Everybody just looked at us. She drank the beer and she said, "Oh yeah. That's not bad."

A waiter passed by and she said, "I would like one of those."

Before we knew it, everybody was having a drink at my table. Some had mixed drinks, someone had wine. I thought about what a little beer starts.

If she went to your home, as obviously she did with me, she would be courteous. She would have a beer with you. If you had wine, she would have wine with you. Joanne McMutrie, one of our instructors, had what's called cheery wine. It's a soda. She would go with Joanne and have soda. She wouldn't have a beer with her. Janet would drink what the host was drinking.

Back to the first story I told you, when I finished cutting the lawn, I went around the flower bed with the push mower and saved the rest of the flowers. She came back and said, "Well, that was a job well worth it. Would you like something to drink?"

I said, "Do you have cold beer, by any chance?"

She said, "No. But let's go."

We went down near the college to a J and P Store, I think they call it, the name of the beer store there in Denver. She said, "What do you like?"

I went down the whole row and I said, "I like this beer, this beer, this beer. I'm not crazy about this one. Which one's do you like?"

She says, "I don't know. You pick them out."

I picked out two different Canadian beers. We brought them back to the house and we drank one of each one. She decided that she liked this beer better than that beer. That's how I knew that Janet liked to have a beer with me every once in a while. That was the fun part about being in her presence.

*I would like to ask you, what do you see for the future of Healing Touch?*

I think, for me, the future of Healing Touch, if we all stay heart-centered, it will grow and it will continue where it is. My hope would be that, just like you're doing now, is to keep the story of Janet alive, so that we know who she is and not lost.

I think we're going to grow into a very strong program. I think all this stuff with what's happening with International, now H.B.B. (Healing Beyond Borders), they still are our brothers and sisters, no matter how we look at it. We don't like it. At some point, when all that truly heals, I believe Program is going to surpass all that. It will be a hard journey, but we'll look back, just like when I look back now, twenty years ago when we started and all the classes we had. To see how small in numbers they were and how, internationally, we have grown. There is no doubt in my mind that Healing Touch will be the future of energy medicine. People will recognize it at the hospital. They'll be offered Tylenol and they'll ask for Healing Touch instead. I believe we're going to get there.

*I like that idea. It's really easy to picture.*

That's Janet's picture for me. Keep it simple. It doesn't have to be hard. Just do the work.

One time, we were doing a workshop in Durham. We were way up in the mountains at this particular place where we still had the classes. I was driving Janet. I ran out of gas. I looked at her in the car and said." Is this the time when we can unruffle the gas tank?"

I thought she was going to kill me. I thought, "Now this is really not funny right now. I am in deep doodoo here." We didn't have cell phones then. I thought, "I truly hope to God, somebody else is late, coming back from lunch."

I was saved, because that is exactly what happened. Another student came back. I said, "Do you mind taking Janet back to the class?"

She left me there with the car to figure out how to get gas in the car. The joke became, every time she showed up, "Do you have gas, Donna?"

People always wanted to know why Janet would ask me if I had gas. Those moments, you just never know.

I know I haven't been out teaching as much. At one time, I taught every other weekend. It is great being back in the classroom again. I'm a private duty nurse.

The growth that the students are coming in at, is unbelievable. They are asking questions we used to hear at Level 3 classes, and now they are in Level 1's. It tells me how advanced the energy work is getting. We're right there with it.

We've been blessed to start when we did. I think we will integrate when it becomes a good part of when we can all ask for it in the hospital. We can all use it when we want.

I was lucky. I learned from what I call the Three Masters that created this program. I was going to offer to have you come up to Washington to help in the Level 2 class I 'm doing.

*I would love that. I have participated in, maybe twenty-two Level 2's. When I coordinate a class, I in stay in the class. I coordinated a lot of classes for Barb Dahl and others. It's a great way to get involved and it's a great way to learn how to do a class.*

Do you do Healing Touch for yourself full time or is it part time for you?

*It depends. I do a lot of Healing Touch. Of course, I spend a lot of time writing the books. I do have a practice. I keep pretty busy with it. If I don't get involved with it, the next thing I know, a whole bunch of people show up on my doorstep needing it. The angels keep me pretty busy no matter what.*

That's like me. I do it on people. Now this lady I am going to take care of, she knows nothing about it. This lady had a stroke and it is her goal to be able to walk and stuff again. For me, this will be a daily practice of Healing Touch on her. I am thinking of recording this. Taking notes, just to see if it is. I'll probably do massage and other things. We'll never really know, and I don't care what makes the difference, but I am going to consciously take a record, for me so that I can use it. Then I can offer it to people to see how it can make a difference in their health. Especially at the end of life, as I consider myself a hospice nurse. I'm used to people dying and stuff like that.

Someday I would like to do the Senior Wellness Plan. I have already done two pilot classes. It I just a matter of putting it together as a formal program. It's like Healing Touch for Babies only we need Healing Touch for Seniors. HT for Animals, I'm not sure if HT for Babies is still going on. *(It is.)*

People used to tell me you shouldn't work more than half an hour on a senior. I can't get them off the table. If they're going to take forty-five minutes or an hour of work, I am going to give it to them. I don't know when the next time will be for when they are going to be on the table to receive. It can be a five minute treatment. They can work that in, in many ways and being able to work with them that way.

One of the things that happens is that your students will follow you. I once said to Janet that I didn't want students to go through all their classes with just me. That's not okay. It's nice that folks want to do that. You know what, you're going to learn from other people. You want to have a different experience.

I will always welcome other teachers to come teach with me. There are some changes. I learned it from Janet and I knew why she put the program the way she did from the energy flow. I know some people changed the chakra lecture around. Janet's experience was that you do the lectures first and then do magnetic clearing, to feel the chakras. She had a reason why she put the program energetically the way she did and why those techniques go together instead of Level 2 techniques in Level 1. She had an energetic reason for doing it.

# Mary Ann Goeffrey
## RN, HTCP/I, QM
## Elder

### Introduction

I have learned so much about mentoring from Mary Ann. She has patiently guided me through some difficult situations with a couple of mentees. As a result, I am a much better editor of Level 5 and certification homework. I am very grateful to her. Mary Ann is a Level 1 through 5 Healing Touch Certified Instructor, and, in my not so humble opinion, one of the best for Level 5.

### Interview

*How did you get started in energy medicine and Healing Touch, specifically?*

I first started with Therapeutic Touch with Dolores Krieger. I took Beginning and Advanced Therapeutic Touch. I knew there was something to it, but I wasn't feeling any energy like the whole class was, you know, except me. I let it go. I didn't do anything with Therapeutic Touch even though I took both beginning and advanced.

It was in 1989 when Kathy Sinnett told me about Healing Touch Program in Atlanta. Janet was doing it. I think it was the second or third class that she and Dorothea taught. Kathy and I knew we had to be there, so we drove seven hundred and fifty miles to our first class.

At that first class, I just knew it was going to be my life's work. I had that sense. We had no tables. We did all of our Healing Touch with mats on the floor. Try to do the chakra connection on the floor. Good thing we were younger, and we could bend. So we had no tables. Nothing. That was my introduction to Janet and Dorothea.

We had some handouts, so we had to take copious notes on the chakra system. Dorothea taught it after lunch. We were all over age. It went on for hours. I always remember that first class. But, I just love Healing Touch.

After that, we just went and took classes over and over. Both Kathy and I, together, took one class after another. I got to be the fifth practitioner that was certified.

*What year was that?*

Oh my goodness, I would have to look at my certificate at the wall here. You're making me move. Bear with me. The first class was in 1989. So it was, I'm looking at certificate number five. I was certified June 26, 1993. And then became the tenth certified instructor. I just knew I wanted to teach.

Kathy and I kept taking classes over and over again so we could teach. In the beginning Kathy and I had a business together. We put Michigan on the map with Healing Touch. We both had a business and brought Janet in. And Barbara. Everybody. They would come in. We had many, many classes. That's when we both aspired to be a teacher. That's the story of I how got to be an instructor of Level 1.

At that time, at the very beginning, because there weren't many instructors, the Healing Touch Program actually sent you out to teach. They didn't have all the independent practices at the beginning, because it was just getting started. So Healing Touch would actually send us out to teach and pay us for teaching. As you know, now, if you aspire to be a teacher you're also in marketing for your classes. At the beginning we got our start because Healing Touch sent us out to teach.

We were part of the American Holistic Nurses Association (AHNA) and that was when, after I got certification through AHNA, that's when AHNA decided that they could no longer certify people who weren't nurses. They had to look at their mission statement and everything and that's when Janet pulled Healing Touch from the American Holistic Nurses Association, because she wanted certification available for everybody.

That's when Janet created Healing Touch International to house the certification process. Healing Touch, you know, Colorado Center for Healing Touch was always the educational body. HTI was started only to house the certification process. How do I know that? Because I was there. Sharon Scandrett-Hibdon called one day to see if I would serve on the certification board for AHNA, while they were doing certification.

I thought, "Oh my goodness, no. I'm not smart enough. Everybody has PhD's. You know how that goes." I meditated. I was going to say no. When Sharon called me back, my soul said yes. I was going to say no.

I spent one year on the cert board of AHNA. I was there when HTI was created to house certification. I served five years on the certification board with Steve Anderson and Mellie Friel. We designed the first certification application and implemented the certification process throughout the country. We designed the first

HTI certification application and began to train reviewers, so there was reliability in all the whole reviewer process.

I served five years on the HTI cert board, and left the board after I felt it had a pretty good foundation in keeping the certification process going. That's what I did in my early years. We had to get a system for all the applications being sent in and create a cert board. I mean reviewers, and sent all the applications to reviewers. At that time, nothing was by computer. Everything was hard copy. There was a lot of managing things through hard copies.

Those were the days when people had to send four hard copies of their application for certification. They would put one on file in the office and the others would be sent to the reviewers. That's my story.

Then I wanted to teach. I kept teaching and eventually 1, and 2, and then 3. I remember telling Janet I know I can do this. It was like training, more through her at that time. When it came to Level 4, that was the time I debated. Linda Smith at that time, Janet had asked her to pull Healing Touch Spiritual Ministries from the program, because, I am sure when you interviewed Linda, you found out that people could take Level 1, 2 or 3 through Healing Touch Spiritual Ministries or the Healing Touch Program, and go on to Level 4.

There was that connectedness. But then after that, was when I think Janet and Linda decided – I don't know how, what Linda said about that, but I think Linda was freer then to develop her program the way she wanted to.

I watched the program grow from having a documentation sheet that just had a picture of a figure on it. If it was up to Janet, we would probably still have that same blank documentation sheet. The program had to evolve into what it is today.

Back to my story. I took some training with Linda Smith. I was deciding whether I wanted to go teach with Spiritual Ministries or the Healing Touch Program. My soul wanted me to stay with Healing

Touch Program. I went to Janet and told her, "You know, I've been six years on the cert board. I know what needs to be done. I would know how to teach it so people could graduate and pass. I've had all that experience and I want to be a Level 4 instructor and then, eventually, a 5." She took me under her wing

Then one day, I went to co-teach, not co-teach, observe Sharon Scandrett do a Level 4. For some reason her plane was late. It wasn't coming in that day and I thought, "Great. I know I can teach this. It doesn't matter if she's there." So I started teaching that way, because her plane was late. I knew I could do it. I just knew I was capable, that I could teach this class.

*How would you say Healing Touch has changed your life?*

Oh my goodness. My life would be so boring, if it wasn't for Healing Touch. It changes the very essence of who you are. You enter a world that sometimes is mysterious in the healing process, the results, the outcomes you have. Sometimes, you just don't have the logical explanations. It can give you the ability to teach people to do good work. I always feel that. I can work on people, but if you teach people to do this work, and they work on others, the ripple effect is thousands and thousands and thousands of people have a more positive outcome in their lives because of Healing Touch. It's such heart-felt work.

It's the spiritual aspect of this, because way before I got into Healing Touch. I started having out of body experiences. I didn't know what was happening to me and now it helps me to understand the chakra system and everything better, because I went on a spiritual journey in 1985. I started meditating three or four hours a day. I didn't know anything about grounding. This was way before Healing Touch..

I was living in my upper sixth and seventh chakras, three or four hours a day. Pretty soon I didn't realize I was soaring without being grounded. I became so out of balance. I remember the day I laid on the grass, and I could feel my whole aura start to leave my body. I'm trying to pull it back and say, "Come back here." Like I'm on earth. It really taught me how you have to be grounded in the lower chakras because for months, I wasn't.

Then I started having these mystical experiences out of body. I realized I had to get grounded. That's why I preach balance, balance in the chakra system, and the importance of grounding, and the importance of each chakra.

It was on the day I was so out of balance that I felt my aura start to leave, I could just feel that if I started rooting in the ground for about forty-five minutes I'd be okay. I started digging and digging. Something was helping me say, "Hey, I'd be on the earth." I didn't understand the earth. I didn't know anything about grounding. If my neighbors saw me, they probably would have locked me up wondering, "What is she doing?" I was digging in the earth and saying, "I belong on earth. I'm rooting, you see, God. My roots are deep in the earth."

I kept doing that for forty-five minutes and praying, "I need help. I belong here on earth." After about forty-five minutes I felt a rumble like a train, a freight train coming from the earth, that intense, enter my body, and really ground me. I could feel it all the way up to my ears.

I thought, "Oh, the earth, it's like an embryo, when you look at the shape of it. I'm saved." I kept on saying, "You know I'm grounded."

I had help along the way to teach me. I did. I learned the hard way about grounding.

*What is your favorite healing story?*
My favorite healing story?
*Yeah.*
I walked into this auto dealership, here in Tennessee. This man, a salesman, an elderly guy, was limping so bad. I asked, "What is the matter?"

He said he had had surgery on the bottom of his feet, for like a planter's wart. He was in so much pain. He was six weeks, post surgery. He was still in pain.

I said, "Let's go into the office and see what we can do." I worked on him for fifteen minutes, through his shoes. I did magnetic passes and ultra sound. Two days later I go back there and he's walking as normal as can be without pain. He said, "Oh my goodness. I even played with my grandkids yesterday, walking all day and had no pain. I just came from the doctor's office. The doctor said I have to have surgery again, because there was that black seed still there. It still had infection."

I said, "Well, we'll work on it again."

A week later, I bump into him again." He goes, "Oh my God, the doctor couldn't believe it. When I went there, that seed had come to the surface and was gone. He flicked it off. My foot is healed. I have no problems."

I love that story because it was only two fifteen minute treatments. It made me realize how effective the work can be. So I like that story.

*Do you have any advice for new students coming into Healing Touch?*
Yeah. What Janet said. Just do the work. We can show things in books, but Healing Touch is learned by doing and having your own experiences. Also to make yourself the purest vehicle that you can be. Working on your own spiritual evolvement, whatever that means to

the student. Be emotionally, mentally, spiritually, and physically balanced as much as you can be.

I would say, you just have to have your own experiences. We learn from those experiences. Just do it. That is what I would say that they should do. I think they should assess, because of one thing I would say to students. We do this work and we start working in the upper chakras. It is very blissful. We start loving the whole world. We're opening and developing these upper chakras where that incredible spiritual love is. It just feels so great when we're up there and, yet, we have to integrate those upper chakras into the lower chakras, to be a soul-infused personality. It takes some balance to do that.

At the beginning, I thought no one was doing this, makes decisions about their life, or whether they're going to leave a spouse or something because they thought they weren't on the same wavelength.. They didn't give themselves a chance to integrate that new understanding they have. You know, to walk on earth with that for a while, and become that soul infused personality. To make wise choices in your life. That's my speech.

We walk up a mountain, developing new muscles. The journey isn't straight up the mountain. We go and sometimes we slide back, in our development as a practitioner. When we slide back, that's for us to really look it and see what other muscles do I need to develop? Is it more emotional balance, more mental balance. I like to see, are all four parts, are all you walking together, physical, emotional, mental, and spiritual, being an integrated being. Are all your parts integrated, walking together? Or are you trying to strengthen a part of who you are?

These fly backs are used to help you understand. They're here to help you grow, to get more balance. The experiences that knock you over, you're strengthening some muscle, whether it's spiritual, emotional, mental, or physical. They're strengthening a part of you.

*What do you see for the future of Healing Touch?*
I would love to see it continue to grow. Janet would always say, there's a practitioner in every home. I don't think we've reached that goal. I think that would be a foundation, very foundational, to keep that goal in mind and, yet, to get a practitioner in every facility or clinic to have Healing Touch available for people who need it and in clinical hospitals. But not to let go that there should be a practitioner in every home or family hopefully in the future.

I just think it's amazing what Cynthia Hutchison has done. I don't think anybody I know could have taken the program to where she has, because she is so heart-centered. She has her PhD backing her. She's so familiar with the educational process, and has such a great deal of integrity.

In all the times I have worked with Healing Touch, and everything, working closely with her, I have to say she has so much integrity.

Along the way, I became the lead instructor for 4 and 5 and that put me on the curriculum committee. I didn't know what the responsibilities were as Level 4/5 lead instructor. Actually it got my feet wet and I got into it. I totally worked with Cynthia for years and years. I just can't say enough about her integrity. I have never heard her say anything other than a kindness for every single person. I'm really impressed with her.

I don't think anybody could have gotten the program to where it is. That and, of course, along with the Mentgen's and the backing of the office. They're taking it into the twenty-first century, with the computer, with everything, with Facebook. I've heard people say they went to the Healing Touch Program, because they're in the twenty-first century, versus when they made a choice which program they were going to be in. So I give credit to all the work that's been done behind the scenes to get this program where it is today.

There's been so many behind the scenes, I could name so very many. All the work. Everybody at the office. It's the volunteer time that people have put in, instructors, practitioners, in their own way to help the program develop. The volunteer hours are beyond imagination.

I think the program is just like a beacon, a light that people, at the soul level, are attracted to. I love this program. I love Healing Touch.

*Do you have a favorite Janet Mentgen story?*

I remember when the program was really getting busy or starting to develop, I hung around with Janet at Levels 4 and 5. When the program was smaller, like after Level 5, if somebody still had work to do, Janet would tell them to write it on a piece of paper, and give it her to submit it. Then they would get their certificate and I said, "Hey, wait a minute Janet. We've got to do something about this, because this program is going to grow big. We really need to have a tracking system."

That's when I developed that three part form, verification, of course, for completion. It still stands the test of time today. Janet was so resistant. I would say, "Well, think. What if, all of a sudden, there are hundreds of students out there you have to keep track of? The office has to keep track of them. You really have to have a system that can verify their work and follow up."

I remember her finally saying okay. I always had to tell her, "Hey, I'm on your side, Janet. I'm on your side." Because, over the years she had so many challenges with people that challenged the foundation of the program. She really had to sort through who. I had to convince her that I'm on your side. That it would help the program. So that's the story where she finally decided she needed to look at the bigger picture.

Another favorite one, she knew when we were updating workbooks and stuff. There was the full body connection. I don't know if you remember, in one of our earlier workbooks, one of the hand positions or pictures wasn't correct. We were trying to get her to change that. I'm saying, "Come on Janet. Here's the new workbook coming out. Let's fix that."

She looked at me and she said, "Do you want to be out of a job?"

I look at her and I said, "What do you mean, do you want to be out of a job?"

And she said, "Well, if everything was perfect in the book we wouldn't need the teacher."

So I thought, "What? Am I going to get fired because I'm trying to say let's make a change?"

And she says, "If everything were perfect, who would need a teacher?" I loved that. They wouldn't even need a teacher.

I followed her to the ends of the earth. I am so grateful that she was one of my teachers. She was resistant to change, but she knew she had to do it to enable the program to grow. So, she did it. That's my favorite story.

And a favorite healing story. She was over at my house and my sister had a severe migraine. Janet could see this red spike of energy coming from my sister's head going eight feet into the room. She could actually see that red spike of energy.

We worked on my sister's headache together. Janet was really a healer. She did so much for people. To be a Janet, you just have to do the work.

*Is there anything else you would like to say about the program or your life in it?*

Every volunteer hour was worth it. When we rewrote the Level 4/5 book, it almost took a year just to do it, the hours, the stress, the everything behind the scenes. Trying to get the program to where it was standardized. I was just glad I could help make a contribution in the areas that I could. I always wanted to make sure, before I retired, that Levels 4 and 5 were running smoothly and had a good foundation in the way the class was run. We had to make changes based on all the student input we got through the years. Finding out how stressful students felt at Level 5, and how we switched things around, so that they could get their results on day two instead of day three so they could enjoy the rest of the class. We really worked hard to get Level 4 and 5 more helpful to the student. It was like, students weren't paying attention. They were so worried about their homework. Anything we taught on the first day, they really weren't paying attention. We knew we had to fix that and get them to know where they're at by day two. That way they had another day to fix anything. If they had minor changes they still had time to do that during the class. I think that worked out good.

Always making our evenings having healing work at Level 5. We worked hard to find a way to get them to work, to get with the office at Level 5 on a system for having reviewers. How did the coordinators get reviewers? We created letters for the coordinators to send out. There was just so much behind the scenes work, to get all the ducks in a row for 4 and 5 to run smoothly from the office to graduation. I am proud of our accomplishments.

One other thing I'll say on record, so that when I leave Earth plain – it was when I was teaching Healing Touch in Ashville, North Carolina. I was at a very holy center. One morning there was this bright light coming from the window out of the bathroom. I wondered, "What's going on?"

I looked at that window and it was an opaque window. Outside that window was, as I peered through it, I could see could see a beam of light. It had a three hundred and sixty degree circle. In there was this being all in white. It looked like it had a face without character. No eyes, no shapes and an outline of almost all the organ systems in different shades of white.

I was going, "Oh my goodness. What is this? I must be imagining this."

So I walked back to my bedroom, looked out the other window and there was nothing there. I went back in the bathroom and the being was still there. I'm being a doubting Thomas. Pretty soon out of the woods another identical being comes, just like that. I am seeing, it was quite beautiful, another white circle, three hundred and sixty degrees huge circle of light with a being in it. So now there's two.

I'm still doubting what I'm seeing. Pretty soon, two smaller ones come out of the woods with lights flickering all on the outer end, which you could call the outer edge of an aura. I am finally, realizing they are here for a reason. Telepathically I could hear one of the things that would be, was that Healing Touch is under guidance and protection. That always stuck with me, that there truly is that world of spirit there, guiding our program. That was very, very meaningful to me. That was about forty years ago.

I truly wanted to draw an image of what they looked like, but my artistry skills aren't so good.

That did happen. I felt very confident that healing Touch is under spiritual guidance. So I'll have that on record. I couldn't tell anybody about it. Cynthia was there and we were sharing a room together, but I had this vision in the morning while she was sleeping. I don't know why I never woke her to say, "Cynthia, look what's happening." I'll never know. I think it was for me to see this, and hear what had to be said. That was that Healing Touch is under guidance of the spiritual world.

I felt very good about it. That's it. I guess I'll end with that. One day, maybe I'll write that whole story down. Or maybe someday I'll write some chapters of Healing Touch. People shouldn't lose the stories.

# Franny Harcey
## HTCP, QM

**Introduction**

We have a very special gem in our midst. This lady is so full of love, compassion and comfort. I would love to clone several million of her. Whenever I have had a problem, either personal or with a mentee, she has been the first to offer assistance. As head of the mentor program, we couldn't find a better person.

Franny is a Healing Touch Certified Practitioner and Qualified Mentor. She is the Founder/Owner of Golden Shadow Healing Center in Parker, Colorado where she teaches labyrinth and energy awareness workshops. Franny works with individuals interested in personal transformation, physical healing and soul evolution. She has been on a spiritual journey since childhood and embraces the concepts that Alice A. Bailey and Torkom Saraydarian present in their extensive study and brings principles of these teachings to her work. She has developed and teaches work that she was gifted through intuitive guidance.

**Interview**

*First of all, I would like to know what position you hold in Healing Touch Program?*

At the moment, I am mentor lead.

*Mentor lead? What does that mean?*

It means that I communicate with mentors and mentees. My main focus is to be available to all mentors and mentees as a resource for them to have: someone to answer questions. Sometimes instructors aren't available, or the program director. Instead of an instructor to contact, I kind of made myself available as the lead to be able to be a resource.

Also, I take care of the mentor portal and some of the other stuff that we have.

*What other positions have you held in Healing Touch?*

I was assistant to the Healing Touch Program Director. Not assistant program director, but assistant to, for over a year. It rolled into conference coordinator for another year, plus.

*What did you do as an assistant?*

I assisted Cynthia in anything that she needed. I communicated with the instructors quite a bit, with the practitioners. I fielded questions, answered emails. You name it. Secretarial work. Anything that was needed and supported Cynthia at the time. And Lisa and Bill and everyone else.

*What got you started in energy medicine in the first place?*

Actually, I was having panic attacks and was empathically picking up other people's stuff. I wasn't realizing it at that time. I had a friend at that time who was living in Minnesota. I was living in Colorado, back in 2000. I needed some really good drugs to calm me down.

She said, "You're at the home of Healing Touch. Find Healing Touch." She was a certified practitioner at the time.

I took my very first class, I believe, in January of 2001. Within the first hour I felt like I was home. I went full force in it from there.

*When did you become certified?*
I knew you were going to ask me that. I just had a card that had the date on it. I couldn't tell you. It might have been 2006 or 7. It must have been 6, because Janet transitioned in 2005 and she was my mentor.

*A lot of people say Healing Touch has changed their life. How has it changed yours?*
I believe, with the amount of personal and spiritual growth, I have completely changed my focus on how I am in the world, as well as how I treat and want to treat others, and how I am present in the world.

*Do you have a particularly meaningful story in your practice you would like to share?*
I would like to share a story about Janet. When I was at Level 4, I had a group of friends that were going through Level 4 at the same time. They were working as a group mentorship and they wanted me to work with them. I felt like that might be fun, but it just didn't feel quite right. I sat with it over the Level 4 weekend. I got a real strong hit from someone who was there, about mentoring for me.

She referred me. She said, "I think that you and Janet are a lot alike. I think that the two of you would work right together."

At that time, Janet had already been diagnosed with cancer. I did ask her. She agreed. I spent the next year, the last year of her life, with her, one, many times, two days a week. It was about an hour and a half drive for me. I would spend the whole day with her.

She would always get on the treatment table. That was her thing. I was good at being such a self-starter that I was able to really do mentorship, the paper work, and all of that on my own. She really didn't have much to do with that, but she was available if I had any questions. Once she'd get on the treatment table – like, I'd come to her house and I'd have a notepad of questions. I was told, if you don't ask the questions, Janet won't answer them. I didn't understand what that meant until I started working with her. So I'd write my questions out.

I'd get to her house. We would talk a little bit, and then she would get on the treatment table. I would give her a treatment always. We talked while I was working with her. We talked about the energy and tracking it, then working with it. But not a lot. Enough. We'd finish up and probably anywhere after three to eight hours I'd go home. I'm half way home and I'd think, "Oh shoot." This happened many times. I'd totally forget to get out my notebook and ask any of my questions. But when I'd get home, I would open my notebook and look at my questions. Every one of them would have been answered.

It was because I was in her energy field, I was picking up her frequency, and had all my answers. It would happen time and time again. I continued to write questions down, sometimes not as many, but they would always be answered.

*Have you explored any other healing modalities?*
I've dabbled in mind, energy body transformation, which is working positively, somatically, and energetically together. I did training in this as well as was a teacher-in-training for that. I stepped away from it, as it didn't resonate with me any longer. I do

incorporate some of those principles in my practice combining it with my current practice.

*Why do you stay with Healing Touch?*
Because of the structure and because of what it has and also because of what I have to offer. I think Janet is still so much within me that I feel it is important that I share that and carry that down into the program and share that with the people. I like the structure. I think it is a very good base structure.

*Do you have a web site?*
I do. www.goldenshadowhealingcenter.com.

*Do you have a Facebook page?*
I do, but I don't use it very much for marketing. I just check it occasionally and connect with family and friends, but I don't regularly keep up on it.

*Do you have any comments or advice for new or potential students?*
I think it's very important for anyone searching out an energy medicine program to really look at the structure of what Healing Touch has to offer. It's a strong basis. It is not only a starting ground, but a leaping off place. It is a very good learning piece. Instructors are trained in a standard format and in many other modalities they aren't. I've taken classes from other people and every time I do, I come back to the structure and the importance of how Janet set the program up, which is an energetic construct. When I was working for program, Janet's children allowed me to read Janet's journals. She had year upon year upon year of journals. Obviously, I couldn't read them all, but I had the opportunity to and was guided by Janet as to which ones

would be the best ones for me to read. As I started reading, what I found very clearly was that she worked with two main guides.

The program was implemented by her, but it was set up by her guidance. The reason a technique is in Level 1 is that it was guided. It was a necessary template for the techniques in Level 2, and then beyond that, Level 3 and Level 4. It was all set up energetically by Janet and by her guides.

The program is strong, structurally, from an outside view, not only for nurses and a nurse practitioner point of view, but also for the general public, so that there is a consistent structure. It also was set up energetically so people can follow the flow intuitively and be engrained in it.

*What do you see for the future of Healing Touch?*

I see the expansion of Healing Touch, not only in hospitals, but vastly throughout the U.S. and the world. I think that, energetically, it feels that there is a shift that needs to occur. This is just my perspective, as consequence of the planet is shifting. We need to keep a structure, but we need to be more expansive. I am not even sure what expansive means, other than just that word is inclusive of many things.

*Is there anything else you would like to add?*

Well, I had the pleasure, when I was working with program; we reinitiated a relationship with Reverend Rudy Noel. He lived in Denver. Bill and Margaret had asked him to redo the BHS (Basic Healing Touch Sequence) Level 1 techniques. I believe you can get the program on the web site. I don't know if they have that available right now. We did for a long time.

I started working with Rudy with revamping and creating a little memorial Back in the late '80's I guess, or early '90's, Janet did a Level 1 technique DVD and Rudy recorded it, because at that time he had a video production company.

Rudy had the master VHS of that. And since he still did videoing and films for his daughter and that kind of thing for her ballet studio, he had the equipment. Bill had asked him if he would redo it and upgrade it to a DVD instead of the old VHS.

That being said, Margaret and I worked on him a few times. Rudy and I really had a connection and we started working together. Once that process was complete, I continued to see Rudy a couple times a week, sometimes more, sometimes less, extending over the next four years until he transitioned.

I learned a lot from him as a healer. He studied with Rosalyn Bruyere for six years at Healing Light Center in California. He shared the healing with Janet. He did an adaptation of the mind clearing and the Hopi and then it was adapted a little bit by Janet. I feel very honored to be with him.

It was interesting, because I was with Janet one day before she transitioned and did a chakra spread with her. I had the honor to be in her energy field one last time. Then I was with Rudy for most of the day before he transitioned and worked with him energetically as well. I find it interesting I got put in places where I need to learn. The elders share their information with me.

He has a little book called "The Hug and Healer" that he wrote. I helped him write that.

I think one of the things working with Janet, when I worked with her that last year, and when I worked with her for a few years prior to that, she had a class called "The Path of the Healer", that once you had taken a Level 3 class, you were able to take Path of the Healer with her. It was a weekly study and we would meet in the evening once a week for a number of us at the Healing Center of over at her office in Lakewood.

She would talk. The Path of the Healer was about developing the healer and moving beyond the need for attachment to things I guess I would say. It wasn't about letting go of physical attachment, but really becoming the clear vessel, so that we can walk in the world at a higher frequency, and support raising the consciousness of the planet.

She told me one time, it really doesn't matter if you lay your hands on one person. What matters is if you do your own work, because then you'll be changing the frequency of the consciousness and supporting the planet. I think that goes along with why she wanted so many people to be doing Healing Touch: one in every home, school, hospital, church, because as we put our feet on the ground, as we walk, we light the world.

In working with her in the Path of the Healer, we talked about Alice Bailey. We studied Alice Bailey. We talked about Mesmer and energetic construct. We worked with energy at a higher frequency and group consciousness. It was a huge growing process, not only for me, but for everyone in the class. It really was one of Janet's passions, working with Alice Bailey. She really wanted to bring the idea of raising our frequency forward, and becoming a clear vessel.

The reason I feel it's so important right now for me to step into a role of mentor lead is not that I have all the answers, but I've mentored – I think this is my fifth or sixth year of mentoring groups. I've probably mentored thirty people over the course of the last six years. Why I do it is because, I think, Janet instilled, and probably myself from information I came in with, the importance of the development of the practitioner. The homework aspect, all those pieces of classroom work that we teach, is really important. But what I see as the part of growth work of each student. So that's why mentoring is my passion.

I was an instructor in training and I thought I was going to be an instructor. I keep getting what my path is; to hold a different frequency for program, to really help the students when they are at that Level 4 or 5 place, to explore energy on their own, to explore themselves and what their path is on the planet.

I think they are ready at that point, most of them. Some aren't. I think Janet's gift with them was transferred to me on some level, that I feel that I'm able to kind of ignite that place in students and push them to expand themselves beyond just the homework.

Janet always said this is the structure. This is why Healing Touch Program needs to stay strong and in structure. Can we build on it? Yes.

I created the back chakra affirmation workshop. I was always curious as to why we didn't talk about the back and teach the back work. I may be off track a little bit. I think it's important that, as I travel around the United States, I have taught it eighteen times. What I noticed is that people keep saying they always wondered why we never learned about the back.

Quite frankly, there is not a lot written about the back in any of the writings, ancient as well. Not that that's good or bad, we certainly can balance the energy from the front. Absolutely. What I found was that when I would assess, even six or seven years ago, a lot of times that back aspect wouldn't open on the back side.

My guides gave me the workshop to bring it forward. Is that part of program? No, it can't be, because it's not what Janet wanted as program. Can we have adjunct classes to support our growth on the planet? Absolutely. We aren't stale and we aren't stagnant. The job is to keep showing up from a place of higher consciousness.

Healing Touch will change. It has to change energetically. It can still hold the same structure, but it's consciousness raised on the planet. The whole program needs to lift as well.

*Anything else you'd like to share?*

I want to share a concept that Janet shared with me and those of my friends who were in The Path of a Healer. This was way back when.

Janet had, I think it was the '90's, it was maybe even '80's when she was working with Claire Etheridge. Claire was Janet's mentor. Janet helped her, but Claire coined the book *Right Rhythmic Living*. It's listed in the 4/5 Notebook, I believe. Janet studied with Claire in California. There were other HTP people as well.

They had a group called "The Order of Healers". I came across it when I was exploring, through Janet's guidance when I was working for Program in 2008 or 9. Something like that. I came across the bylaws or the write-up of what the Order of Healers was. They were a spiritual group. They always didn't meet in person. They maybe met once a year or twice a year in person, but they would meet on the energetic plane and connect. They would do clear consciousness work. Like I said, I think it was the '80's.

That concept for Janet was very important. In the Path of the Healer, I don't like to say she gave mandate, but she was very strong in saying that she truly believed that it is important that healers come together in groups, in group consciousness, because it supports the planet. What we can do as a group is greater than what we can do individually.

Myself and a couple others that were taking the class at the time, really felt that was important. It will be our eleventh year, tenth year, of meeting as a collective. We began as four. We went to five and we have been at six for the last year and a half. For many years we were at four. We all went through the program together.

We come together religiously, two times a month and we meet for a few hours. What we do is, we're soul sisters, so we support each other. If someone is having a challenge and someone needs support in a certain way, if a parent died or something happened, we listen and we support each other.

Then we go into meditation for twenty minutes. We set a group consciousness of, not even a goal, but what are we coming together to meditate. Sometimes, it's earth healing. Sometimes it's supporting what's going on a given location. Sometimes it's locally. Sometimes it's what's going on, even with one of our clients we are having a challenge with. We don't bring names, but we say, "This is the client and I'm just having a challenge."

That way we get support. We bring whatever it is. We work very universally. We do it in meditation for twenty minutes. Then we come out and we share, if there is anything pertinent that we need to share.

Then we go to the table. We are each on the table for ten minutes, five to ten minutes. When you are in a group consciousness, healing goes really quick. It's emphasized. That's why, in Level 5, we do group healing. The power of group healing is so profound.

We feel we have grown exponentially as a collective consciousness. Our goal is, eventually to create, I don't want to say a cheat sheet, but a seedling sheet, to support any other Healing Touch people that want to start groups.

How did we do it? What did we bring? What is our goal? Why are we together? I think, bringing that forward has been, for our group, very powerful to be able to come together and then be able to share that.

We have shared it with some people, but we have not had anyone commit in the group to that. It is a commitment. It is a way of life, now, for us. When I travel, and I'm gone for a few weeks, I'm missing it. It is really fascinating. We hook up energetically, and even if someone isn't able to be in the group, we still put them on the table and go to work on them so they are part of the group.

You are only on the table five to eight minutes, because of the frequency. When we work together, our frequency has shifted so profoundly, that we are such a great support for each other.

When some people say that practices groups, after a time, aren't working any more, I think the piece that's missing with that, is the depth of why you come together. Practice groups are great. The depth of why we come together is not only to get on the table, but it is really to support the consciousness of the planet.

# Jane Hightower
## BA, HTCP/I
### Elder

**Introduction**

Many of the people in this book talk about Jane Hightower. Her enthusiasm, even after all these years, shows up in conversations with her students and clients, and with all of us who have had the privilege to know her.

She is also a great story teller. Be sure to read the story about using magnetic passes: hands in motion for swelling and bruising. I have used her technique many times now and it has worked every time.

**Interview**

*I would like to start with what attracted you to energy medicine and specifically Healing Touch?*

I was working as a manager for St. Joseph's Hospital and Home Services, managing several programs over the years. Another home services manager was Linda Smith. She was the hospice manager.

My daughter had a horse. We would spend a lot of time out at the barn. I think, probably, I scratched behind my ear and introduced some kind of bacteria. I ended up with cellulitis at the back of my head, which was exceedingly painful.

The hospital was getting ready for joint commission to come and assess us. We were working hard to make sure our policies were in order. I was in pain, but I couldn't go home. I went to Linda and said, "Linda, I have heard that you do this weird stuff with your hands that can help with pain. I have taken pain medication, I've started an anti-biotic. Nothing is helping here, and I'm in trouble."

She put me in a chair. She started doing magnetic passes: hands in motion. She wasn't touching my head. Finally she ended by just laying her hand against my head with hands still. The pain was gone and never returned.

JCO came and went. I went back to her and said. "This stuff is magic."

She said, "Well, no. It's not. It's based on laws of physics, but it does seem like magic doesn't it?"

I told her, I just had to know more. This was back in the end of 1991. She said, "In January, I'm bringing a class, a Level 1 class here to Augusta. Why don't you take it?"

So I did. I actually talked my boss at St. Joseph's Hospital into paying for the class. He said, "Jane. I have no idea of how this has anything to do with your job."

I said, "It doesn't. It has to do with personal development and I have never asked you for anything."

He paid for it. Well, that worked one time. After the Level 1 class, I was caught. Linda Smith, Anne Boyd and I were all here in Augusta. From the very first Level 1 class, we knew that not only would we do this for the rest of our lives, but that we had to share Healing Touch with others.

We were determined to be instructors. Our original teachers, Elaine Mueller and Barbara Latham taught that Level 1 class. Barbara Latham has passed away and Elaine, I believe, is living in Tennessee and practicing as a Sufi. She is no longer active with Healing Touch, but she was for many years, and was a fabulous teacher.

They immediately saw us as teachers, and let Janet know. Linda had already met Janet. That's how this all started. They had become friends. We were treated as teachers-in-training from the very beginning, which was really wonderful.

We would get in the car, once or twice a month, going wherever we could, to be helpers in classes. Plus taking our own classes. We took six Level 1's, several Level 2's, and a couple of Level 3's, then went to Level 4, and then went to Level 6 in six months. It was really a killing pace.

I tell people that we pushed each other, shoved each other, fought each other, and loved each other through that six months. We could not have done it, not any of us could have done it alone. You know the changes that take place in your life, when you say yes to this path. It was just unbelievable. We hadn't even taken Level 5 yet.

In those days we didn't have certification. We were working toward that. Just about everybody there was being trained as an instructor, before even taking Level 5. They had an idea of what our packets would look like,

Something else really wonderful that happened, was that Barbara got permission. There were a group of women, here in Augusta, that were just incredible healers, but had no money. They were really living on the line. Barbara got permission from Janet to do a special class for them. They paid, I think, twenty-five dollars. She came over from the South Carolina coast where she lived. That's quite a long drive. It was an incredible gift that she gave. The money paid for her gas and that was about it.

We started having weekly gatherings then to practice. We would meet at Linda Smith's house. The very first night that we were going to do this, Barbara said she would drive over and be there to support us. She did.

I'll tell you a funny story. I'm not sure whether you want to put this in the book or not. (*I usually do.*) Linda was the only one that had a table. A couple of people were working on the couch, a couple on a pad on the floor. My partner and I were working on the end of Linda's double bed.

My partner's back hurt. I had just had Level 1. I hadn't had the back work yet. But, I'd had pain drain, and I could do hands in motion and hands still. I figured I could relieve her pain at least. I started to work on her back and Linda came in to check on us. She said, "What are you doing? You've never had the back work."

I said, "Oh, I'm not doing that. I'm just gonna do some pain drain and hands in motion."

She said, "Well, I've had back work. Why don't I do that?"

She did the back work on my partner with me watching. When she was done, it was like this hot wind was blowing out of this woman's back, and she could not move. She couldn't move her legs. She couldn't get up. It was as if she were paralyzed. We were terrified. But Barbara was coming.

Finally Barbara came. She was a toughie. In fact she shared with us, one time, that some of the people she worked with, referred to her as "Nurse Cratchet", because she could be so tough. She came in and she looked down at this woman and she said, "What did you do?"

Linda said, "Well, I did the back work."

Barbara said, "Show me."

Linda went through the entire process. Everything was just perfect. She showed her exactly what she did. Barbara looked at her and shook her head. She put her hand about three feet above the woman where this wind was blowing out, and sealed all the way down, still shaking her head. When she got to the body she said, "Get up."

The woman got up.

Linda had forgotten to seal after doing the Hopi technique.

She said, "She had broken the blockage out of the aura, but left that breach. We never forgot that again. All of us used that story to teach Hopi, and how important it was to remember to seal after you did Hopi.

Barbara was just that kind of woman, who would make a three and half hour drive and get permission to leave work early, so she could get over here for our first practice session.

We had so many adventures. The three of us were just hitting the road that first six months. Usually either Anne or I were driving. Linda would be in the back seat. What we saw and what we experienced, in those days is that hospitals were paying for classes. Our classes were big. It was not unusual to have twenty-five to thirty-five in a class. *(We had ten minimum when I started.)* It was amazing. But then things started getting tight and the hospitals stopped paying for advanced education for their nurses. Classes started getting smaller and smaller.

It was exciting times. We referred to it as the Old Wild West of Healing Touch, because it just was phenomenal. There was another class, I think it was a Level 3, in Atlanta. It was the first time Dorothea Hover-Kramer was going to teach that level. There were nine of us instructors there as helpers. We all wanted to see this.

The other thing that was going on was that Janet was there supervising, of course. She had brought a woman named Mary Bell, and was going to introduce her, because Mary was a Barbara Brennan graduate. Mary really loved the way Healing Touch was so accessible financially to people. Brennan, you know, you are talking about thousands of dollars to go to that school. I don't know. I think at this point, with everything that's involved, it's about fifty thousand dollars. Not only are there several trips down to Florida, plus you have to be in counseling the whole entire time. If you have a practice, and you want to use what you're learning, you have to have a paid mentor. Twenty years ago, when I was talking to Mary Bell, that was seventy-five dollars an hour.

She wanted to teach for Healing Touch. Janet brought her in right at the teaching Level 3. She was going to be demonstrating chelation. All of us wanted to see this. There were about thirty students, and nine of us instructors. Spirit was just bouncing off the walls.

One of the women was doing the coning. Janet was running around the room telling all of us to look over there. It was like the woman had a powerful flashlight. The lights were dim. You could see the light coming down from her hands. Janet said, "I have never seen anything so bright."

Another beloved story we have, is when Janet would be teaching and we would all go to dinner afterwards. Usually there was another level being taught at the same time. Janet was doing a Level 2 or 3 and someone else was doing a Level 1. Lots of times Janet would pick up that meal tab. She was really supportive, and unbelievable, to the instructors and the helpers, as well as the students.

Every time we would go some place, there would be tables for us. We would be a group. No problems. But then, every other table in the restaurant would fill up almost immediately. Boy would the people in the restaurant be scurrying around. It usually didn't happen quite so fast. If Janet was there, that restaurant was going to fill up. It was the energy that she brought with her. We took note of that.

One time we were at this place where half of it was a restaurant and then you'd go up one step to the other half which was a used bookstore. Janet and I were over there waiting. We had placed our order. We went to look at the used books. Janet was pulling books off the shelves saying, "You gotta read this. And you gotta read this, gotta read this."

She was filling my arms with these books. She told us that night, "When you go home, you energetically clear these books, as somebody else has read them, and their energy is in here. Books are made out of trees and natural substances. They hold a lot of energy. Likewise, don't just keep books thinking I have such a neat library. Go through your books and, if you think you're going to read it again, or it's still part of an active interest, keep it. If not, pass it on. Get rid of it. Donate it to a library or nursing home or something, because it holds the energy of who you were at the time you read it. You don't want to be held back. You have progressed since that time."

We came home and we all went through our books. In those days they still had those big paper bags that you got at grocery stores. I filled three of those bags full of books. I donated them to the library. Any books that you have read and just put on the shelf, it's time to let them go.

The other thing we learned was that cotton holds energy better than any other substance, including paper or wool. We all had these cotton pads that we would carry around with us in case we'd take a tumble or a joint would hurt or something. We'd imbue that cotton with energy and put it on.

One of our instructors was working. She was a Canadian and she was working with a team, a soccer team in Canada, a hockey team. They all kept cotton pads in their lockers. They would come off the fields and put those cotton pads wherever they had been hit with a hockey puck or a stick or something.

I've done that all these years. I actually make those pads now, because my daughter in California and her husband have a not-for-profit called Apex Protection Project. They save and take care of older wolf dogs that have been captive bred as pets. People get them thinking they're getting a really cool dog. The breeders aren't training the people that buy these animals on how to take care of a wolf or a wolf dog. When they start growing, and people begin to realize they have a wolf on their hands, which is not a really cool dog. The abuse, the neglect, and the abandonment is happening all over the country. Rescues are popping up everywhere.

I make pads out of cotton cloth that have wolves on them. I put a little tuft of wolf hair inside. When people make donations to Apex, I'll send them a little wolf healing pad.

That came right out of Healing Touch Program and what we were taught. It's not curriculum, but was one of the energetic tricks that we were taught, tricks of the trade, if you will, by our earliest teachers.

I went to Level 6 in June or July of 1992. It had to have been July because I did Level 4 in the middle of June. July 12 to 17. We went to Grand Lake, Colorado, up in the mountains above Denver. I don't remember how many of us were there. It was a fair number. Other people had been trained as instructors, but I think this was the first formal class like this. It was just astounding. Things were intense.

Oh, another funny story was at Level 4. A couple of the women were there for some reason. They shouldn't have been there and they didn't really get it. They started doing things. We were in this room with big windows all around. They would go outside and dance on the grass during class. They'd make faces at us through the windows, acting foolish.

Janet got mad. As a result, she didn't teach us one of the techniques you learn in Level 4. She and Linda Smith were rooming together, I believe. She taught it to Linda.

We came back to Augusta, and the next week we were doing one of our weekly trades. Linda, Anne and I would trade every week. I was working on Linda and I was being voice-guided by a guide. I was following what they said to do.

Suddenly Linda said, "Where did you learn that?"

I said, "Where did I learn what?"

She said. "What you're doing."

I said, "Well, I was voice-guided to do it. My guides told me how to do it."

It was the technique. So we taught it to Anne.

Wonderful things were happening. We had such adventures.

At the very end of Level 6, we were in this little chapel that had wooden stairs. We had our closing ceremony. We were given these lovely box lunches. Some people took off immediately for the Denver airport which was a couple hours away. Some were doing other things. I was going to be spending the night with Janet, so I was going to stay and we were going to go to her house. Then I would go home the next day.

As we were leaving the chapel, going down the wooden stairs, one of the participants fell and injured both of her ankles. Mike Tanaka was there, a teacher from Hawaii. He lives in Las Vegas now. He was a nurse, but he had also been an EMT. He grabbed a sheet and tore it into strips. He took magazines and immobilized both of her ankles.

When I ran my hand over her ankles I could feel a break in the right ankle. I felt disruption in the left. I couldn't tell if it were broken or not. A couple of the guys ran to the lodge and got a stretcher. Three men and I carried her down to the parking lot. We put her in the back of Janet's car. She had a SUV kind of thing. She threw me in the back with this gal.

Anne and I were the only two non-nurses in the class. It took us a while. We had to get our belongings, the gal's belongings and Janet's and then go down the mountain to a hospital in Denver. Three hours later, we had her in the emergency room.

Meanwhile I'm bed panning her into a paper cup. That gal had the smallest bladder of anybody I've ever seen. I was throwing it out the window. Janet's driving like a mad woman. The wind is blowing that urine back in. I'm covered with it. I didn't care. It was a wild ride.

We got her to the emergency room. She broke her ankles about noon. It was about seven o'clock when the orthopedic surgeon came in. He's looking at the radiographs and looking at her ankles. He kept looking back and forth at the pictures and at her ankles.

Finally, he said, "These pictures do not match your ankles."

The one ankle, the one I could feel broken, was so badly shattered that it required surgery. The other ankle was also broken, but it was a simpler break.

He said, "I just don't understand. There is no swelling and there is no bruising."

I had been doing Healing Touch on those ankles non-stop. At one point, Janet and Mary Jo Bulbrook came in to the room. Mary Jo, who can see angels, very readily, said, "The room is filled with angels."

I could feel them. But I couldn't see them. I said, "Yes, I know."

She said, "They're telling me to tell you to do hands in motion up her legs."

We were always taught to start at the top and move down.

"It will help with swelling."

I was starting off the feet and moving my hands, hand over hand, up the field of the legs, rather than down. There was no swelling whatsoever. She had the surgery the next afternoon. They didn't have to wait for internal bleeding, or swelling, or anything to go down, to do that surgery. That was another really dramatic lesson.

She did not ask for any pain medication until past midnight about an hour after we left. Luckily, there was a Healing Touch trained nurse on duty that night, who would check in on her frequently and do Healing Touch.

Janet came at eleven and took me home. Janet put me in her bed, and made a pad on the floor next to it, and slept on the floor beside me all night. I felt like I had the protector of the universe by my side that night.

The three of us were then instructors, and it was another year before certification came in. We were at an American Holistic Nurses Association conference, again in the Denver area up in the mountains. We didn't have our own conference in those days. It was all AHNA conferences that we would go to.

In those early days, we were all mentoring each other, because there were no certified people to mentor. When certification came in, there were about six people at that conference who received certification, the very first certification as instructors, and maybe, eight or nine as practitioners. Janet was one of them. That was where she received certification as a Healing Touch Practitioner and as an instructor, herself. That was the summer of '93. The following fall, the rest of us who were ready to do so, turned in our paperwork. I turned out being the eleventh person. My original certification number, both for practitioner and instructor, was eleven. So I was an eleven, eleven.

Those numbers have changed now, because our professional association had to change eventually. Somebody else got my number eleven designation, and you'll never guess who it was: Anne Boyd.

I told Anne, because she'd signed up for all that business. She got in there before I took action, and did it. I said, "If anybody had to get my eleven, I'm so glad it's you."

I redid the Level 6, as you did. I was at conference and talking to Janet. I told her I thought it would be a good idea for me to redo it. I was there, and Carol Komitor was there, and one or two other instructors. Janet actually had us teaching sections of it. We weren't just auditing the course. I don't know what they do now, but she broke the class into smaller groups and assigned each of us a group. We were teaching them different sections. They were doing things and we were watching them, helping and assessing what they were doing.

Carol Komitor, of course, went on to develop the Healing Touch for Animals program that is so fabulous.

At one point, Janet was sitting in a chair. All these students and instructors were sitting on the floor at her feet, like at the floor of the Master. It was a very sweet scene. Janet was very non-directive. Lots of times, if you asked a question, she would say, "Let the energy teach you. The energy will teach you that."

If we would say, "Oh, I can't do this."

She would say, "How many times have you tried?"

"Well, I've tried it a dozen times."

"When you have tried a hundred times, and you can't do it, then come tell me you can't do it."

She knew the energy would teach us.

She knew that the techniques, that she and the other women who helped her put the curriculum together, I call them the Fabulous Four. There was Sharon Scandrett-Hibdon and she's still very active with the program. Myra Tovey is no longer with Healing Touch. Then there was Dorothea Hover-Kramer who wrote that wonderful book on ethics. Dorothea was also a concert pianist. A lot of people didn't know that about her. She was a very creative woman.

They had gone to Janet and said, "You've got to put your work in a form."

Janet was teaching nurses in Denver, what is about like our Level 1. She demonstrated this at an AHNA meeting. She was designated Holistic Nurse of the Year.

These women went to her and said, "You have got to put this in a form that can travel."

The multi-tiered program was born out of that. I guess back in '86 they had two or three classes In '87 they had 26 classes. It just exploded after that. The certification program has certainly developed. It's a little tougher now than it was then. We still had to have the one year mentorship.

At Level 4, there was this woman. She was very tall and older than I. She introduced herself as a retired teacher. Her name was Ruth Johnston. She was a crusty old broad. I liked her. In the introductions, Janet had said that, when introducing yourselves, and you think someone has something you think you can help or that can help you, that might be the person you want to ask to work with for the class and partner with.

I was going to ask this woman, but somebody else got up real fast and ran over to me and asked me if I would partner with them. I said yes. The next morning, we're walking through the rain to breakfast. Ruth fell in beside me on the path. We were in Delonica, Georgia, up in the mountains. It was just beautiful. She asked me to work with her that weekend and I said, "Oh no. Someone has already asked me and I was going ask you."

My mentor, who was one of my first teachers, Barbara Latham, was there. I told Barbara about this. I said. "I so wanted to work with her."

She said, "Do you know who she is?"

I said, "No. I have no idea."

She said, "That is Dr. Ruth Johnston. She was the dean of the nursing school at Rutgers University. That's where she retired from, and now she is coming out of retirement for Healing Touch. She was a personal friend of Martha Rogers, who developed Rosarian Nursing Theory, which was the theory that we had for Healing Touch. In Rosarian Nursing Theory, Rogers talked about body, mind, and spirit: the unitarian human being that you couldn't separate one from the other. She actually described the aura, saying we are not a being surrounded by energy. We are the entire body of energy, the center of which is a form that we can see, touch, manipulate. It's the gross energy and the rest is subtle energy.

Now with Rosarian Nursing Theory, we also have Jean Watson's Caratoss theory, that takes us even farther, and explains what we do even more.

I remember another time with Ruth. We did a lot of co-teaching early in Florida and Georgia. We co-taught in Asheville. We did our first classes together in Savanah, Georgia. We became very close friends. Here I was one of the non-nurses, one of the lay healers. It was a really beautiful friendship until she passed away.

We were out in Denver again, in the mountains, and were in this little town doing some shopping on our free time. I told her I had mentioned to Barbara Latham, that she was a crusty old broad. She looked down at me and said, "Jane, you're probably the only person in the universe who could get away with that."

I really loved that lady.

I pulled out my professional profile notebook to help me remember some of these stories. I see a picture of Steve Anderson, who was also being trained as an instructor in that class of July of '92. We've been close friends ever since.

We forged friendships back then that have lasted through the years. I spent last weekend with Anne Boyd. We were teaching a shaman journey class up in Asheville. She was trained through the Michael Harner view of shamanism, before she came to Healing Touch.

*What advice would you give to new or potential students?*

What advice I would give to new students is to really revel in the glory of Healing Touch. They will experience things that they never thought possible. They will experience miracles. We all experience miracles all the time. We don't pay attention to them. In Healing Touch, you start paying attention to what is going on energetically all around you, and you start seeing these things that can blow you away, and really change your thinking and change you as a person.

One thing that will happen is a little uncomfortable. Some of your present friends are going to draw away from you, because they just don't understand who you're becoming. That's okay, because what they have to talk about, isn't so much of interest to you any more anyway. You find that new people, who are on this path with you, who understand, been there, done that, and understand who you're becoming, are now being attracted by you. They are coming into your life.

If you notice some old friends are moving away, let that happen with love. Don't get in fights. Don't try to force them to come on this path with you. See them less and less, lovingly. You will still love them, and you'll still see them now and again, and love getting together occasionally, but it's not every week, the way it was before. That's one of the changes that you will see as you're doing this work.

Sometimes, we're challenged by people that, "Only Jesus can do this kind of healing." I generally don't get into arguments with people about that, but I do have a file that I made on my computer, of all the places in the Bible where healing is talked about. I am glad to give that to students, so they can bone up, because I don't know what other Bible those folks are reading that says only Jesus can do this. He did it everywhere he went, didn't matter what was going on personally, emotionally, or politically with him. He did healings. He told his disciples to do healings. And then he sent out, I think it was a group of seventy regular folks, like you and me, and told them to scatter and go to all the towns and offer healings. Not to force it on anybody. If people weren't interested, just pick up your stuff and go to the next town. That we were to do this for each other, those were his instructions.

I have no problem, as a Christian, doing this work. The other thing is that he never asked anybody his religion when he did the healing for them. He did healings for Roman soldiers. He did healings for people that were outcasts. It didn't matter what their job was, their religion was, or their background was. He didn't even ask. He just offered.

There's another energy modality that I do and also teach, that the man who developed it, who's a retired dentist, Dr. Donald Engleheart, said one time as he was training us, "Healing happens in the mere presence of the healer." Again, biblically, that was demonstrated on the woman who didn't feel worthy and came up behind Jesus and just touched his robe. And received healing.

I encourage people to understand that this can be an adjunct to any religious belief and it certainly is a spiritual act. It's not a religious act, but it's a spiritual act.

If you decide you want to go for certification, take the whole year of your mentorship and divide all the tasks, because there's a lot you do in that year. People say, "I have to do a hundred healings in one year!"

"Give me a break. " There's fifty-two weeks in a year. Anyone can do one or two sessions a week. Right?

If you do that, and you keep up with it, and you make it a part of your life, rather than waiting for the last three months where you have to give up your entire life in order to get all this work done. Do it little by little. You have to receive ten different modalities and write about them. Do one a month.

I get a Healing Touch a month. I get a massage a month. And I see a chiropractor. A lot us are doing that sort of thing anyway. This fits right in with that. Divide the tasks up, and do your paperwork as you are doing the work. Do your session notes and take a few extra minutes to make them legible so you don't have to rewrite them. I don't believe in doing work twice.

The biggest thing of all, is to be kind to yourself and love yourself. Know that you were a healer before you ever walked into a Level 1 class. That's how we're made. What we're training you to do, is to be a Healing Touch practitioner. You're already a healer.

Apply that healing and that unconditional love to yourself. Then you'll have everything you need to give to other people.

*What do you see for the future of Healing Touch or what would you like to see in the future for Healing Touch?*

First of all, Healing Touch is life changing. One of the really important places I see that this has taken, and has influence, is in the world of allopathic medicine. Doctors, nurses, PT's, OT's, drugs, hospitals, I saw and I see a lot of discouragement, because as Medicare gets more and more vehement with their rules and regulations. Insurance companies follow the Medicare guideline. Nurses have to do more and more paperwork. They're spending more time with paperwork than they are with their patients. A lot of discouragement has come in. Physicians are impacted in the same way. They're given by Medicare, fifteen minutes to see geriatric patients. Excuse me, but we need more time than that when we're old.

I just turned sixty-nine. What does sixty-nine mean? I look in the mirror and I don't see a sixty-nine year old. I see Jane.

I think Healing Touch has brought a lot of hope back to people who are – because we have lots and lots of nurses, of course, because it's a nursing modality. We also have PT's and OT's, a lot of whom have left allopathic medicine to become massage therapists due to discouragement. This is a way to get their hands lovingly back on people. We also have quite a few physicians.

It was in Level 3, my first Level 3, we went to a convent for retired nuns in Kentucky. There were two hundred retired nuns living there. This was one of the huge adventures. They were praying for us the whole weekend, so you can imagine what Level 3 was like.

On Saturday night, they threw a party for us. These gals were pretty much cloistered. There wasn't a lot of interaction with them. We only saw them when they served us meals. We would go through the line and they would be serving.

On Saturday, we went into this room and here is this table with beautiful greenery all the way down the table, laden with food, and nobody in sight. We felt like we were in the castle of the beast when he did that beautiful meal for the beauty. He wasn't there. She had never seen him. The next morning, the whole room was cleared out. We never saw a person.

I think there were two physicians at that weekend. I know one of them was going through the program with his wife, who was a nurse. They were from Atlanta.

We also have attorneys, and artists, and housewives, and househusbands. And car salesmen, people from all walks of life are drawn to this work. That tells me that there is a commonality there of communion with each other. There's a commonality of conversation, of sharing, of loving. It's something that brings people of all backgrounds, all walks of life, together. We have people who are agnostics and atheists, pagans and Christians, Muslims and Jews. All religious backgrounds. It's that spiritual thread, that golden thread, that winds through all of man's religions that Healing Touch seems to cement. I see it as very helpful in bringing peace to many very different types of people in showing us how we can respond to one another.

I see it bringing love and loving touch back into medicine. I see it bringing peace and communication between peoples. This is powerful. This is not just some little workshop you've taken because it sounded like fun. You are changing the world when you become involved in this. You're throwing that rock into the still pond and the waters are moving and reaching out.

That's what I see happening in the future and the fact the we are now an accredited school, the very first energy school ever to be so accredited, and at this time still the only one. The respect that people have for what we do is also growing. That's drawing more people to Healing Touch.

The other thing I really love about Healing Touch is you don't have to intend to hang out a shingle and use it as a profession. You can learn Healing Touch and go through the classes, even going through class 1, 2, and 3, where you get almost all of the techniques. I think there is one more technique that you learn in Level 4. You learn a deeper version of another one. Those are the only techniques you learn in Level 4. You learn none in Level 5. If you want to go to Levels 1, 2, and 3 and not do all that work for practitionership and certification, you still can have a very active practice with family and friends. And to help people, help people not to hurt, help them when they are hurting emotionally as well as physically. That is as revered a practice as those of us who are hanging out a shingle and doing it professionally. I love that about the program. That practice is just as respected as any other practice.

I have a mentee right now, who is an artist. She sees Healing Touch blending with her art to heal.

That's the vision I have for the future. Healing Touch will bring love, understanding, peace to those who practice it, so that we can bring those gifts to those we practice it on in any walk of life.

*Is there anything in particular that you would like to talk about?*

Oh gosh. You have let me talk about all the things I love to talk about.

Like I said, there are friendships forged, miracles seen, adventures lived. This has been a hell of a ride and I have loved every minute of it, even the hard times. The dark night of the soul where I had to affect changes within myself. I had to look in that mirror and see something that I didn't like, and know that I had to change it. I was the only person who could change it. You have those moments of reality at times. But, even that has been good, because the outcome was a better person.

The ability to meet people like Jean Watson.

I'll tell you another funny story. We're at a Healing Touch conference, several years ago. Anne Boyd and I had a table. Anne had made these unbelievably beautiful healing pillows, like pads or thin pillows. I had the book that I wrote on the healing properties of stones, a stone empowerment book. I forgot to tell you about that.

They gave us the table right at the entrance. When you walked into the sales room, you walked straight into our table. Off to the left was another table and there was a woman there. I went over and I was talking to her. She was really cool. She had made these little stones, manmade stones, that had the St. Francis prayer on them. She traded me a box of her stones for my book. Then I went back to my table.

This gal walks in. She's petite, her hair psyched. She's wearing all these bright colors and flowing outfits. The whole room lit up. She saw this gal I had been talking to. They greeted each other warmly. They were talking and chatting, hugging and kissing each other. Old friends who hadn't seen each other. I thought, "Isn't that beautiful."

This colorful gal starts to walk by my table. I came out from behind the table and said, "Hold on a minute. When you walked in this room, the whole room lit up. I've got to know who you are,"

She stuck out her hand and said, "Hi. I'm Jean Watson."

I wouldn't have been more shocked. I just died. I'm marching up to Jean Watson, probably the most revered and famous nurse on the face of the earth at this moment, and asking her who she is. I covered it very well. I stuck out my hand and said, "Well, I'm Jane Hightower and delighted to meet you, Jean."

Inside, I'm just dying. Then I find out that this other woman that I've been talking to, is one of Deloris Krieger's, from Therapeutic Touch, one of her original Krieger's Crazy's. One of her original students.

At the nursing school, Therapeutic Touch came out in the early '70's from New York University, NYU's nursing school. Martha Rogers was the dean. Deloris Krieger was one of her instructors. She developed Therapeutic Touch, an energy modality, for the nurses. They could learn it. It wasn't mandatory. But if they took the class, they would have to do research. A whole lot of research came out of that. This gal was Janet Quinn. I had no idea who I was talking to. I would say, I was really drawn to her and she was a very cool woman. These gals are down to earth,

Later I had an opportunity, Anne Boyd and I, as we continue our adventures together. She now lives in Asheville and I am still in Augusta, Georgia. We went on a cruise a couple years ago, where they had classes in integrative medicine. Jean Watson was on the cruise. She was one of the teachers. The physician who started the American Physicians Holistic Association was one of the presenters. Healing Touch allows you to meet people like that. It brings people to the conferences.

Start your piggy bank for conference, all you students, to be in a room with three to four hundred like-minded people. Sometimes you feel like you're all alone out there. That is so powerful. The people they bring to conference: meeting Brugh Joy, having dinner with Rudy Noel.

He was sitting beside me one night and I said to him, "When I think of what you have given us, just with mind clearing, I can't imagine what you have given with the whole rest of your life."

That big, grizzly bear of a man started to cry. I thought, "If I wasn't in love before, I am now."

Just being able to meet people like that, because you're moving in their universe now. It's amazing. I am just really, really lucky.

I will tell you one thing about Linda Smith. We did all that traveling together. Then Linda left Augusta. Anne and I would want to stop at all of these antique malls. Linda would just want to get there, or she would just want to get home. She'd be irritated that we wanted to stop. She always found the best stuff. If there was a bargain in there, Linda would find it.

Another thing that I want people to really know, is that when you do one of these weekends, at the end of the weekend, I don't care how much you ground, you had better be really careful when you get in that car. You're just not totally grounded. We had some hilarious things happen.

One time, Linda was staying up there, because she had gone in her own car to North Carolina. She was going to stay with a friend she had known from college. Anne and I were in the car together. We could not find the entrance to the highway. We would pass it and say, "There it is." We'd go down, turn around, "There it is." We did that four or five times.

Finally I said, "There's a Pizza Hut. We are going to stop and eat pizza. That will ground us."

You need to be real careful when you are driving home after a Healing Touch class.

Another thing, you feel really off base at first. I tell my students, we all operate from an energetic platform. During our life, that platform gets higher and higher, as we evolve as people. When you go to a class like this, or where you participate in some religious something, such as marriage, that sort of thing. Or you go to one of those women's weekends where you drum and chant all weekend, you're energetic platform takes a giant leap up. When you go back into what you consider the real world, your real life, you feel a little out of balance. It's like you're standing on a pedestal seeing the world from a different place. It's not that you let go of that, it's that you get comfortable at that new level of energy.

I had an experience. I was teaching and the class had gone to lunch. I wanted to stay in the room and just rest. I got on one of the tables. My two helpers decided to stay with me and work on me. I really didn't want that. I wanted to be alone. I asked them to do magnetic clearing. That way they wouldn't be touching me. I could feel alone.

I was taken out of my body and taken to a place for three days, and then put back in my body as the class was coming back from lunch. For the next month, if I would walk into a store, or a bank, or one post office we have here, that have those things at the door with an alarm if you're stealing something, I would set them off. It took me a month to get in control the new level of energy after that experience.

When you sit down at the computer, the first thing you do is ground yourself before you turn it on. Anne had an RV. We went for a weekend up to north Georgia. We blew the microwave, the television, and we blew the air conditioning. I got the microwave to finally work again. I pulled it out and unplugged it and then put it back in. It came back on, so we had the microwave. The television had to be replaced.

The next morning – there was a double bed on one side and a single cot on the other side. I was in the single cot. Anne and Linda were in the double. I woke up and I looked over at them. Linda was still sound asleep. Anne was lying there with the sheet pulled up under her chin. I could just see the knuckles of her hand holding that sheet and she was glaring at the air conditioner. This was Georgia, and it was hot out there. She took one hand and she threw her finger, like lasering the air conditioner and said, "I'm going to heal that air conditioner." It came on.

*Jane and I got to talking about other things. She began to talk about her certification and so I turned the recorder back on.*

From the very beginning, the program was working towards certification. Anne Boyd, Linda Smith, and I all went to the teacher training in July of 1992. Certification was not a reality until summer of '93. The first people certified were those very early teachers and then Janet, herself, received certification as practitioner and instructor the summer of 1993. Linda, Anne, and I turned in our paperwork, along with a lot of other people, in the fall of '93. That was the first time they officially took packets. I went for practitioner and instructor at the same time. I'd taught enough classes. Anne got her practitioner, and then it took a little while, I think the next round was when she got her instructor certification. She could still teach, because she was one of the early teachers. I'm not sure how it worked for Linda.

We had been teaching for a year and a half, before we were certified, because certification wasn't there.

*Who served on the certification board?*

There was Janet and Dr. Ruth Johnston. It would have also been probably Sharon Scandrett, Dorothea Hover, and Myra Tovey, because they were like the four original teachers and founders of Healing Touch. Janet was the founder, yes, but they were the three that went to her and said, "You've gotta put your class in a form that can travel." That is when the multi-levels came out. Most of the teachers on the east coast were trained by Dorothea Hover.

An example of some of the little differences that were in the early program – you see, we didn't even have books. We had a few handouts. We had the scudder technique. Sharon had gone to a workshop and got a hand out on the scudder technique and brought it back. She showed it to Janet and said that this would be great for the program. We popped it into Level 1. It doesn't have to be taught. It's an extra, if you have time to teach it. It's wonderful. It's as close as we get to working with the meridians. I think it's really important.

When you work with someone with a migraine, all the people here on the east coast were taught that you work the pain spike into the head and then you seal the breach. Back in '09, they had talked to me about teaching Level 4. In '09 I went to four Level 4's to observe and then I thought, I really love doing what I'm doing: 1, 2, and 3. I don't want to teach Level 4. I never turned in the paperwork. I said, "No. I'm not going to do this."

At one of those Level 4's, I was talking to Sharon about migraines. I mentioned sealing. She said, "You don't seal."

I said, "Well, sure you do, Of course you do."

She said, "Jane, we don't seal when we get to the head with a migraine. It's not in the book."

When I got home, I got out all my old information. I got out the original book that Janet and Mary Jo Bulbrook put together. It wasn't there. I called Anne and said, "Don't we seal?"

She said, "Of course we do. We were taught that all along."

That was one of the differences, because most of the teachers here in our neck of the woods came from Dorothea Hover. She eventually moved to the west coast, but at the time she was living in Florida and she was the one teaching all the instructors here on the east coast. There was no paperwork. It was all oral tradition. For some reason, it didn't make it in the book and the other teachers weren't teaching it that way. Now, it's in the book as something you can do.

I know that Sharon thought about it and thought it was a good idea. She told them about it when they were redoing the Level 1 book.

If that energetic pain spike blows – I see it as an energetic aneurism. If it blows out, there's gotta be a breach there. In fact once, Anne Boyd had someone on her couch and was working on her headache. That spike moved from almost the forehead down over the ear to the back of the head. As she worked it in, it was like it was trying to get away from her. She had to follow it. When she sealed, she sealed along that entire track, hand over hand. I thought that was brilliant and I teach that. I tell that story as one of the variations that you can have with a migraine.

It has been a journey and an adventure and so much fun! Life is so incredibly rich because of Healing Touch. It really changed things. I had gone through a divorce. In fact, this was '87. I got a part time job at the hospital and at the end of the year, I made it a full time job. That was in February. In June, I graduated from college. In August I turned forty years old and the following March my divorce was final. In thirteen months, my entire life changed.

I had learned I could support myself and take care of my girls. Then five years later Healing Touch came into my life. All of a sudden, everything was light again.

# Ines I. Hoster
## MS, HTCP/I, QM, CTACC
### Elder

### Introduction

**Ines Hoster** thinks that Healing Touch is one of the best kept secrets in the healing arts and that it has a very bright future. Therefore, she is very dedicated to spreading the word about Healing Touch and has spent uncountable hours giving introductions to Healing Touch in the US and Germany. She is enthusiastic about the many applications of Healing Touch, its integration as a therapy into mainstream healthcare, and the healing it can bring into every family. Ines teaches all levels of Healing Touch classes and brought Healing Touch to Germany. She is the founder and director of Healing Touch Deutschland and is teaching students from other German speaking countries as well (Austria, Switzerland, and Northern Italy). She is very excited about the growth of her Healing Touch family in Europe and the many benefits Healing Touch has brought them and their clients.

    She is very much loved by both her students and her clients. Some of our prominent Healing Touch instructors and practitioners would not be doing this wonderful work if it were not for Ines.

## Interview

*What positions have you held in Healing Touch?*

I teach 1 through 6 and Advanced Practices 1 and 2. I have also co-edited the Level 3 book, the technique cards, and written an article in the Level 3 book as well.

*What got you started in energy work?*

I had been on a vision quest. I knew that what I was doing was not fulfilling my soul. It took me two years. I'd been telling all my friends that I was looking for something, but I didn't know what it was. Finally, one of my friends said to me, "I met this woman and she teaches a class called Healing Touch. I think that that is something you would like to do."

That is how I came across Healing Touch. It wasn't one of Janet's classes. It was with a woman who did not stay with us for a long time. It was in '92, I want to say.

*What made you stay with Healing Touch?*

In the beginning, from the first half hour, it was like the curtains came up and I saw the whole scene in front of me: becoming certified as a practitioner as well as becoming an instructor. It was clear as a bell, that that was what I was looking for all along.

*What happened during Level 1 that hooked you on Healing Touch?*

I realized that I had been doing energy work all of my life and did not know it. The other part was that I had been on the vision quest to see what to do with the rest of my life that would fulfill me professionally and I had the vision immediately ( in the first hour) that I would become certified and teach it in the US and Germany – I saw the big picture for me right away and that got me hooked.

Thanks for asking that question.

*Do you have a favorite Healing Touch story?*

I have gotten used to not telling any stories, especially during class as we have such a tight curriculum. I can tell you one story.

I was working on a client. She was telling me about being in a very precarious situation where she felt that somebody was coming behind her and wanting to shoot her. In that very moment when she said that, I had cold shudders coming up my whole back. It was as if there was this evil force standing right behind me.

I turned to the client. In my mind I invoked all the possible bright light I could muster up to surround myself and my client with that. I didn't say anything to the client. I think I used etheric clearing on her. I continued to do that and until that dark force was gone.

She opened her eyes and said to me, "What was that? You got rid of something nasty, didn't you?"

That's when I really became in awe of how many different levels we are working and we don't always know. Nor do we want to know. How important it is to stay grounded, to stay calm and not get into fear. That's what that experience taught me.

*I am nodding my head. I have had similar experiences. I think things like this appear for those who are ready for them, whether they know it or not. For others, such events will never occur.*

Yes. I use this as an example to let people know that they don't need to be afraid of anything. They will be guided and be protected in the work that they do, if they do it with a pure heart. Nothing can hurt them, keeping foremost in thought that they need to stay well grounded.

That was one of those moments where I was grateful for that careful teaching that we do in regard to staying grounded. It was a very good lesson to me. Any one of my students will tell you. "Yeah. She talks a lot about being grounded."

It is so important. Whatever you are ready for, that's what will show up. You are never really over your head.

*I don't think the guides would put us in a position we couldn't handle. I think we are pretty protected.*

I think so. I agree with you. That's partially due to the intentions that we set in the beginning because it's so powerful. Being willing to trust. Trust, that was an awfully huge lesson for me. To be able to trust the energy, because until then I was so much into my head and be the doer. To let the energy do its thing and not necessarily being in control of where it goes and what it will do. That was at the beginning rather awkward. At the beginning I was not there yet. I wanted to make the decision as to where the energy goes. I was doing the treatments, by golly.

*What advice would you give new or potential students of Healing Touch?*

That's a good question. I would have to come back to Janet's favorite saying, "Practice, practice, practice." It is so true. Because when you don't practice, you lose it. We forget about it, and a lot of the insights that you have gained just get lost. That's too bad.

Life happens to people. They allow things to get in the way, and then they sort of sloop it.

I think that is something that contributes to our attrition, too, among other things. It saddens me that we have so few people speaking with a Level 4 apprenticeship program and then doing 5 and certification.

I immersed myself in it. I went through 4 and 5 as fast as I could, also with the urgency of wanting to teach this whole program in Germany. I had to keep running after myself. That's how it felt.

I remember when I started to teach it in Germany, I was just certified for instructor. I immediately wanted to go for Level 2, so then I had to fast apprentice to teach Level 2. We offered 3 and I had Maureen McCracken come over and teach that level. I was apprenticing with her. It always felt like I was catching up with myself. That's how urgent I felt about it taking the program into Germany.

I paid a price for it, but I think one of the things I want to say is a precaution, especially to early instructors, to not get into burn out. Our enthusiasm can take us a long way, but it can also hurt us if we don't keep a good balance. I know of other instructors who have been suffering from burn out. It's something I think we need to be careful about, more careful than we have been.

That's the advice I would give to young instructors.

To the young students, you need to immerse yourself, take the classes, and doing the practicing as much as you can. Reading. Just immersing yourself in it.

The other piece of advice is I know that there are a lot of people who become kinesthetically or who are from the very beginning kinesthetically sensitive. I was not at the very beginning. I just trusted that one of these days it would come. And now, the sensitivity that I have developed. Sometimes I was really in awe of what some of my students were sensing and experiencing. It would go through my mind that I wish I could do that.

There is so much learning, It is such a rich, rich program on so many different levels. When I got into it, I wanted to learn to do it, but I didn't think about the enrichment that I would get would get out of it for myself. I think that is also how it was presented at the beginning. I think we're presenting it now differently.

It's like we have to develop the courage to know the times have changed. At the beginning, when I took my first Level 3 class I heard this woman start to talk about angels and I thought, "Oh my God. Now she is going crazy. What the hell is she talking about?" I would say, "Okay. I'm just taking it in." That's pretty much how I looked at it in the beginning.

*What do you see for the future of Healing Touch? Or what would you like to see for the future of Healing Touch?*

I am in full alignment with what Janet said and that is to see Healing Touch being offered everywhere. That it is a part of everybody's household care kit. The other part, and we may be getting there, is for all of us to be able to be at peace with each other and work with each other again.

*Do you have a favorite Janet Mentgen story?*

I have not always seen eye to eye with Janet. We had our little differences. Sometimes the idolization gets on my nerves. I heard her talk one time with her son. I couldn't believe the way she was putting him down. Totally without any kind of respect. I don't know what that was all about.

There's a story. I was in a board meeting, I forgot who it was, but somebody said something that she didn't care for, that she didn't appreciate. She put that person down so fast, so bad. That was the first time I had seen her in that capacity. I thought, "What in the world?" There was such a disconnect between what she was teaching, and how she was doing in that person. That person was totally befuddled. I felt awful. I couldn't believe what I had been witnessing.

I think she had her teaching demeanor, her public face in that way and there was the other side of Janet. That was not a very nice side. I had talked to other people and they told me, yes, there is that side to Janet and that you have to be very careful.

Part of it was about her showing favors and also who she was giving level classes to. That was also a time when most of the Level 1, 2, and 3 classes were still being assigned rather than people teaching them on their own. People were trying to almost being subservient to her.

I remember when I was at that meeting. I was just blown away. I didn't realize it was a part of who she was.

*I think it is important that people realize she was human.*

Exactly. That is really an important point. She had her frailties, just like each one of us has. If you had disagreements with her, and you wanted to discuss something. I remember sending emails to her, or letters, and she just wouldn't respond. We cannot have good leadership in that way.

I think that's one of the reasons why I'm so happy, honestly. Her role was to get the whole program going and to start it. It was time for her to go, because of who she was and what she could and could not do. For Cynthia to step in, she is so much better a communicator. You feel safe with her. You never had the feeling of being safe with Janet. A lot of people suffered because of the way she could turn around so quickly.

*We loved her just the same.*

I had great respect for her. I cannot say that I loved her. She told me one time she loved me. I didn't think so. I was really amazed. She said to me, "You're going to take this to Germany and I'm proud of you. You're doing a great thing there." I was amazed because we had had our disagreements. You had to walk very carefully and not be blown out of the water.

Innocent people were crying after those meetings. That is how much she had put them into shreds. I'm not trying to throw dirt on her. I feel that she had done a tremendous job. It was creating the program, getting it going, and then it was time for her to step aside.

Maybe she was even aware of that, herself. I don't know if she had that kind of an awareness. I wouldn't be surprised if she did.

She was quite sensitive. I always thought that she, on some level, knew that her time was up. I think it was very smart of her to put Cynthia into the position that she's in. In that way, she gave us another gift, because she was not a good communicator. People, generally, feel much more safe with Cynthia. She doesn't take that kind of stuff personally. She is also a good listener. I appreciate that.

*Is there something you would like to say without my agenda prompting you?*

I feel extremely grateful to the program, to the work, to having come across this incredible community. It literally has changed so many people's lives. I know how I have changed many people's lives. I have seen it change my life for the better. It's an incredible gift that we, as instructors, can participate in giving. Then people who want to continue to practice it, it improves people's quality of life. That is worth so much. Of being able to relieve pain and suffering. The whole program is ingenious. It speaks so much to heart-centeredness and as a spirituality. For me, it was not there at the beginning. It is something that Cynthia has brought in and quality. Maybe that is a perception of my own growth.

I think, at the beginning we were much more intent on focusing on techniques. That is the way I seem to remember it. That is the way I also taught it at the beginning. We had classes every half year, so that was the speed at which I was able to go. What was really true, from the beginning of my very first class were the very strong bonds we made with each other. We were practicing and practicing. That is one of the gifts that we never publicly speak to when we talk about the Healing Touch Program.

# Dorothea Hover-Kramer
## Ed.D. C.N.S., RN, HTCP/I, DCEP
### Elder

**In Memorial**

My first impression of Dorothea was that of a stern, no nonsense person. That didn't last long. She turned out to be a very warm and compassionate person. Her accomplishments are many. Her devotion to Healing Touch from the very beginning helped to form it into the professional organization it is today. We have much to be grateful for because of her efforts.

We have Dorothea to thank for her pioneering work in both energy medicine and energy psychology. Her efforts and enthusiasm for both greatly helped in the process of them becoming more widely accepted over the years. She was a much sought after presenter at various conferences, where she brought enthusiasm and belief into the field.

You will read a lot more about her as you read comments made by other people in this book. So many people spoke about her work with Healing Touch, I thought it would be more fun to include things not so well known and a few things that are.

Dorothea was one of the original group of four elders that helped Janet found the Colorado Center for Healing Touch which later became Healing Touch Program.

Dorothea wrote many books on energy medicine therapies including: *Creating Healing Relationships: Professional Standards for Energy Therapy Practitioners* (required reading for certification); *Healing Touch: A Guide Book for Practitioners, 2nd Edition*, and *Healing Touch: Essential Energy Medicine for Yourself and Others*. Her Healing Touch books have sold more than a hundred thousand copies.

I didn't know Dorothea was a pianist who played chamber music with small ensemble groups. She was also an artist specializing in pastel and acrylic media, with a focus on Western landscapes and the oceans. Many of her works were of professional quality and have been featured in public buildings and galleries.

She was born in Berlin, Germany and given the name Dorothea Antonie Elsa Adelaide Christine Eitel. Her family moved to the United States after World War Two as part of Operation Paperclip which was an American program that brought over German scientists.

With her first husband George Hover, she traveled through Southeast Asia where they worked as missionaries. I couldn't find any mention of what happened to her first husband. Years later while living in Tampa, Florida she met and married Dr Charles Kramer (known as Chuck). Eventually they settled in Port Angeles, Washington.

Dorothea co-founded the Association for Comprehensive Psychology along with David Gruder in 1999. While serving as their second president she was instrumental in implementing its certification program.

A few other tidbits came to light as I did research on her. I would think she was busy enough writing books, teaching and supporting Healing Touch, and all she did with ACEP. I also found out she was a board member of the North Olympic Land Trust and on the Clallam County MoveOn Council. On top of that she chaired the

Dungeness Valley Health and Wellness Clinic's wellness committee. And, of course, she supported the arts in her home town, specifically the Port Angeles Symphony. She was one busy lady.

And I miss her.

# Sue Hovland
## BSN, RMT, CHTP
### Elder

**Introduction**

Sue Hovland is the founder of Anatomy for Healers®. Sue has been studying energy medicine since 1982, and has been a Healing Touch Certified Practitioner and Instructor since 1993 with a private practice. She has studied massage, cranial-sacral therapy, and many other healing and energy modalities. Using her background in nursing, massage, and energy, she developed her own multilevel program Anatomy for Healers in 1997. Her web page is www.antomanyforhealers.com. Her wit makes a dry subject both entertaining as well as informative. She was the Keynote presenter at the HTP conference in 2008, the California symposium in 2011, and the HTP Midwest Regional Conference in 2012. She has directed an ongoing Healing Touch group at her church for 20 years, and mentored several groups of HT apprentices. She served on the Board of Directors of Healing Touch International from 2001-2004.

Even though Sue doesn't teach very often any more, her trained instructors are just as fabulous as she is.

### Interview

*Tell me the name of your organization and a little description of it.*

It's called Anatomy for Healers and it's trademarked. It's the basics of anatomy. More than that, it integrates anatomy into energy treatments. It lets people feel the energy inside the physical body, and get acquainted with what's happening underneath their hands when they're doing energy work.

I don't know if this explains it well. We learn to feel all the organs in the body, and then learn something about how the organs function. When they have clients come in with physical problems, they have some clue of where to work in the body and what's happening in the body. Along with that learning, they learn advanced energy treatments in eleven different systems of the body.

*How did you get started in energy medicine and why did you choose Healing Touch?*

I got started, because I was taking classes at Red Rocks Community College in a nurse refresher course. I had been away from nursing while I raised a family. One of my classmates said, "You have to take a class from Janet Mentgen." It was called Therapeutic Touch. I had the time and the money. So I thought, "What the hay?" I did and I was instantly hooked.

Janet was co-teaching with somebody from Fort Collins at that point. I can't say I grew up knowing about energy and I felt resistant at first, but I loved the people in the class. It just felt like a group of people I wanted to be with.

I practiced at home. I met resistance from my husband about all of this stuff. The kids loved it.

I was in Janet Mentgen's first class, what she called Advanced Therapeutic Touch, where we did more weird stuff. It was in '82. Throughout the 80''s I kept taking classes from Janet. They were all day time classes during the week at her clinic that was over a couple miles from my house on Holly and in the Florida area, which is in southeast Denver. She was in that clinic for several years. I'd take one class and then I'd say, "Hey Janet. What's next?"

She was teaching what she called Therapeutic Touch and Meditation, Therapeutic Touch and Hypnosis, Advanced Therapeutic, and so on. She was traveling around the country and studying with Barbara Brennan, Brugh Joy, and Rosalyn Bruyere and, oh what was that guy that did the meditation stuff?

She had all kinds of classes that she was offering, integrating healing work with different things. I never thought about being a practitioner. You know, one thing led to another. I started seeing some clients and more family and friends.

Then in 1990, she gave a weekend class that was on teaching what she still called Therapeutic Touch. In'87, I think, was when she started becoming a national program through her friends in the Holistic Nurses Association.

It was very confusing in Denver because Janet Quinn was teaching Deloris Krieger's Therapeutic Touch at the nursing school to nurses and in the hospitals. Then people were taking Janet Mentgen's course, and running around using pendulums in the hospitals and causing a lot of ruckus. Janet introduced chakras and what not, that weren't classic Therapeutic Touch.

It was really a relief, when Janet came up with another name and called it Healing Touch. Then we couldn't have that confusion, because it was a big problem in Denver for Janet Quinn. She handled it diplomatically. We were not classic Therapeutic Touch at all. Janet had learned a lot of other things, and taught a lot of other things like chakras. The foundation came from Therapeutic Touch.

After this weekend class on teaching Therapeutic Touch, Janet said, "Just go out and teach it. It needs to be in every home and school and hospital."

I would have groups of four or five people in my home and teach the curriculum. At that time the curriculum was pages of handouts. I kept going out to Red Rocks Community College, where Janet Mentgen was. She had taught there for twenty years and that was her foundation. She taught Therapeutic Touch. She called it Level 1 and 2 out there, before it was called Healing Touch.

I went out there trying to figure out what the heck the curriculum was. We did have chakra connection. We had magnetic clearing and some of the basic techniques. It would depend upon what questions people would ask in the class. She was taught very much like Rosalyn Bruyere and she would respond to the questions. I was always learning different things depending upon the questions asked.

We would cover a basic curriculum. It wasn't until Mary Jo Bulbrook finally helped Janet write a book that we had a standardized curriculum which made it a lot easier. We needed that, because after '93, it became a certification program. There was great demand for the class. It was growing by leaps and bounds, a third or doubling every year, so we needed lots of teachers.

The quality of the teacher training wasn't as good as it is nowadays. We would meet at Shadowcliff, and go over a curriculum and then practice teaching to our classmates a certain part of the curriculum. Then they would slap us on the back and shake our hand saying, "Go out and teach it." It was a lot less standardized. I think it is much better now. But it was a good beginning. The spirit was the same and the energy was the same. It is good to have it standardized now.

*When did you become certified?*

We became certified in '93, using a certification program through the American Holistic Nursing Association. They were the certifying body. Some people got certified in the spring, and I thought, "Oh, gee. Maybe I had better get certified." I talked to Janet. Janet was my mentor. She was everybody's mentor in Denver here.

I said, "Would you sign me up as being – should I be certified?"

She said, "Well, sure." So she signed me off as being a certified practitioner and instructor for Levels 1 and 2. That was in '93. I think my certificate number is 8 or something. I'll check that. I realized that I wanted to get grandmothered in real quick before they changed things and made stiffer requirements. Sure enough, in several years you had to jump through a lot more hoops.

Nancy Burns, who had been with Janet throughout this, didn't do that, and she had to take some of the courses over again to be an instructor.

We had a joint meeting with American Holistic Nurses, until we sat at that meeting in Phoenix. I forget which one. That was when the Holistic Nurses decided we couldn't do certification through them, because we wanted to certify people who were outside of nursing. They said, "We're just a nursing body for certifying nurses."

They had a valid point. That's when Janet Mentgen started Healing Touch International, as an independent certifying body. It was quite a contentious meeting in a Phoenix suburb. At that time, too, Janet's teachers were all through her organization. Kathy Sinnett was starting to teach independently in Detroit and hiring Janet to come teach the upper levels. Janet decided, I think, that we would all be some kind of independent instructors who would be teaching independently and not hired by her association which was still called

Colorado Center for Healing Touch, which sounded very local, even though it was a national and international organization. That name was very confusing, so praise the Lord, it's called Healing Touch Program now. But it took a while.

It came up, when Dorothea Hover-Kramer wanted to teach independently, because she felt her time was worth more than what she had been paid by the Colorado Center for Healing Touch teaching program. We all thought, "Boy, she's really after money." But she had a real good point.

Janet's theory was that she didn't expect anybody to make a real living at this. We were trying to get the word out and change the world. She wasn't into people making a big living out this. Now, the organization has business classes, and they're saying this is a way we can make a legitimate living and still change the world. It is a different idea than Janet's original concept. We were charging for our treatments and charging for the classes. Although Janet was making a living out of it, it was not an incredibly luxurious living.

In fact, she wasn't truly making a living. I assume you've heard, that when she died, she left an enormous debt. She was supporting her business with all the teaching that she was doing. She would run around the world and teach classes of 50 people or so because everybody wanted to take from the originator of the program. Then she would reinvest a lot of that in keeping her business going. I'm sure Healing Touch International folk don't realize that. I'd tell them, if it comes up diplomatically.

*How has Healing Touch changed your life?*

It's changed my perspective on healing, on what is health and on what is wellness. It's given me a whole new group of friends. It's given me a different focus in life. It's given me, I guess, a career. Sort of a supplementary career. I'm married to somebody where I don't have to support myself. It's given me my own direction, and my own program, and a chance to help people. And help family, which in a way I would never have done in nursing. I'm much better at a one-on-one person, than a work the floor type of nursing.

This was during my parent time. I wanted to find something worthwhile to do when the kids left home. Ken was still so busy, I hardly ever saw him. I wanted to work one-on-one with people, which fitted in to my paradigm. I could teach classes, which I loved. It was something I loved to do, and it was a very worthwhile thing. It's given me a whole direction and a community. It really connected me with more spiritual life.

I guess one of the things too, I've always been involved with a church, but I think I really didn't know how to pray and connect with the Divine, until I encountered Healing Touch. Doing the healing work, you're really connected with something that's beyond you. When I learned to do healing work with my hands, it's how I really learned the power of prayer and the connection with the Divine, and being more than your ordinary self.

I wouldn't have met all the wonderful people, and had the mentors I have, without this. The whole Healing Touch community, what a wonderful group of people, amazing people. I think it's more than my church. Most of my friends were from the church group, but I feel like I'm closer to my Healing Touch friends than the church friends. Ken and I do more couple things with the church friends.

Ken was very dubious for a while. He saw an article in the Post about bored middle aged women running off and joining cults, at the time I was getting started. I was just going to a workshop with Rosalyn Bruyere in California at the time. He was really scared. He thought this was a cult or something. I convinced him. I said, "This is an electrical engineer by training, who teaches at UCLA at the med school. She is not a cult, and it's at a Catholic retreat center." He got over it.

What convinced him is that he met all the wonderful people who do this, professional, wonderful people. We're not kooks at all, and not flakes, not religious fanatics.

In fact it's interesting, most of the people – wasn't there a survey where eighty percent, or the majority of the people doing Healing Touch, are not so much allied with specific religious beliefs, as much as they are a more universal spiritual belief? I mean several of them of are connected with churches, and certainly Linda Smith's association is very much church oriented. It's much more a feeling of there's a universality of beliefs, and functions.

About the anatomy, I think in '97, when I started to do this, I was teaching and whatnot. I realized I needed to review my anatomy, because I think I had a client with a kidney problem. Where are the kidneys? The two of them are sort of in the back of the body but I didn't know exactly where they are. I had to read up more about them, and find out where they were, to work on them. I thought, well, I need to review my anatomy. I went to the massage school (I thought rather than take a college course) where Janet Mentgen had started teaching Healing Touch as part of the required massage curriculum. Anatomy was a required part of the curriculum. It was the Colorado School for Healing Arts. Janet taught there for several years and then Ann Day took over. Later, Carol Komitor took over from Ann Day teaching Healing Touch there.

When Carol Komitor's mother was ill and Carol was staying with her, I taught three quarters while she was helping with her mom. Then she continued teaching there. And after Carol, somebody else took over. It's no longer required at the school. They still offer Healing Touch as an elective and we can take it a couple times a year.

Once I took the anatomy course, I was interested in more of what they had to offer. So I ended up graduating from massage school in '93. I realized that there were other people, other older nurses who had forgotten anatomy, plus people who had never had anatomy. I thought there was a real need to have anatomy in the program. Most of the schools of healing had anatomy included in their curriculum, like Barbara Brennan. But Janet had never done it, because it was nursing continuing ed and had been focused, at first, on nurses who had already had anatomy.

Once I started to make a little money, I recycled it into taking classes from other people that influenced Healing Touch Program, like Rosalyn Bruyere. I took a class from Rudy Noel, too. I took a three day class from Barbara Brennan and decided taking her whole program was not what worked in my life. Rosalyn Bruyere, I really liked her. I've taken six or seven classes from her, and several classes from other people that taught with her, primarily Shelby Hammond.

I started teaching a one day class in Denver about useful things that I had learned that applied to the Healing Touch work. I asked Janet one time, about teaching anatomy to people who wanted to review it or people who hadn't had it. What did she think about that? She said, "That's terrific. I'd be glad to support you with doing that. Write an article about it and I'll put it in the Healing Touch Newsletter, and let you advertise for free."

I said, "Well, we need to have an energy exchange here, that's equal."

She said, "I wanted to pay you something. When you start making money, we'll talk about that."

When the program got going, I did pay for my ads. For a while, I gave her ten bucks for each student I taught, as kind of an energy exchange for her support of my anatomy class. Now I just buy certificates from Healing Touch Program. I am very much energetically associated with Program.

*Do you have any comments for new students coming into Healing Touch?*

Do the work. I think it's life changing. I haven't quite run with it as hard and fast as a lot of other people, because I've been married to who I've been married to, a guy who still can't understand it, can't understand the science behind it. Or doesn't think there's science behind it. He's one of the most caring people I have ever met. He thinks of himself as a scientist. He's been so successful, because he brings his caring into it. He doesn't believe in spirit or afterlife. Boy, is he in for a pleasant surprise someday.

I'm a little hesitant to push it on friends. Clients have really noticed a difference. I feel like I have to walk between the two worlds. Other people seem to do that easier in the hospitals. I'm not one for walking into a hospital and really starting a program like others have. Like Joan Stofer. Some people have that magic in that area. I think everybody does it in their own way. We don't all have to be alike, fortunately. I'm glad we have a lot of people breaking it into the hospitals. That's not me. And into the academics. I've worked on Ken sometimes. I think it's helped. I think it helps me, more than it helps him. I feel better, because I've offered him this. The thing is, if it helps, he doesn't really fess up to it. He's the world's greatest guy. It just we're not philosophically on the same page.

If I try and make a science out of it, it steps on his toes. If we talk about making people feel better, making the world a better place, that's fine. He's taught - well, he helps me on the teaching part, because he's taught retinal surgery in over thirty different countries, and a lot of volunteers abroad. He volunteered with the residents here, since he got out of residency. He understands volunteering and teaching very much, and helping the world.

Very early, when I was starting out, I saw a lot of people that did energy work, and got divorced because of it. Maybe they would have divorced anyway. Their life changed, and it didn't fit into their marriage. I thought, "This is not going to happen here. I'm married to a winner." Everybody likes him. He can get along with people very well. We have a strong relationship. I think it can work. Well, it's obvious it can work. I think it's just deciding, philosophically, on the same path of helping people. We're each doing good work in our own way. Everybody's path is slightly different.

Linda Smith's path is slightly different. She's done a brilliant job with what she's created. I don't always agree with Linda Smith. She certainly is brilliant, and has put together a very worthwhile organization.

*What do you see for the future of Healing Touch?*

I think it's going to continue. It's going to keep on making a difference in the world. I think we're realizing there's more to medicine. There's the mind, body, spirit thing that is becoming a stronger thing in medicine. I think it's going to continue to be strong. We still have to work at it. It's a paradigm changing thing. Thank goodness we have PhD's, and science people, and that Cynthia got started in Healing Touch.

She's the one that got Janet to bring research into Healing Touch. It's a harder area to get research on, because it's qualitative rather than quantitative. That's helping us a lot, because we have to speak the language of medicines, and the scientific community as well.

Dorothea Hover-Kramer did a lot of that as well. I was so glad that she came back in the fold. We got back with her. I was able to take one of her breakout sessions, post conference things. I took it a couple of years before she died. I'm so glad I did. I really admired that woman.

*Do you have a Janet Mentgen story?*

I may have to get back with you on that. I think when she traveled, and hung out with people before and after class and whatnot, people had more stories on her. When she was here in town she was so busy. She wasn't the kind of person you called up, and said, "Let's go out to lunch."

Other people did more than I did, too. Every year on her birthday, which was December 18, and I'm a half year older than she was. My birthday is in July the same year. She would have a birthday party, an instructor gathering. Her favorite restaurant was the Olive Garden. Sometimes, she would take the local instructors. One time, there were fifteen or sixteen of us. People have dropped by the wayside for one reason or another.

One year she decided to have a slumber party at her house. She had a house up in Arvada with property, and it had a remodeled kitchen, and whatnot. I think there must have been seven or eight of us. We came for an evening, and a potluck dinner, and the slumber party. That was one of the few occasions where I visited casually.

The Holistic Nurses had regional meetings. There was one in the Santa Fe area. We drove down, and Janet happened to drive back in my car. Along the way, we stopped at Las Vegas, New Mexico which is not Las Vegas, Nevada. There was a hot springs area there. It was kind of dilapidated and whatnot, but we did the hot springs. We traveled on home. She drove my car some and we visited.

She wasn't the kind of person I could kick back and kid with, and relax with, the same way I can do with you, and most of the people in Healing Touch. I don't know how much of it was just me, or how much in general. Sometimes we connected and had fun. She just wasn't, didn't feel like a buddy, the same way that Nancy Burns, or you, and all my other coordinators felt like. I don't know if we're both were a little more introvert, or something. We got along fine but it just wasn't like, well chit chat. I don't know if other people felt that. We were friends, but it just didn't feel like we were buds.

She supported me, and I supported her. I admired her greatly.

*Is there anything else you would like to add?*

Oh gosh, I don't know. I admire her greatly. But she wasn't much of a business woman either. Which everybody knows. Many doctors and healers aren't business people. Some people can't be everything. She got into some trouble with that, obviously, as you know.

The fact that she started Healing Touch International, and was president of both her own business and Healing Touch International at the same time. I mean there was a lot of things that she could have, in retrospect, clarified or stuff that went to a lot of trouble here.

She was a teacher more than she was a business person. She was a teacher that would teach inherently. She was a little like Rosalyn, where it would depend upon what questions were asked, that would determine the content to a large extent. She had a basic content that was set. But until the notebook came out, it wasn't cast in iron.

I think I went out to Red Rocks Community College, and sat in Level 1 and 2, oh five, six, seven, or eight times, trying to figure out what the curriculum was. That was before we had the notebook come out and I said, "Praise the Lord. Now we have a curriculum instead of handouts."

I don't think I was a natural born healer, the way Franny Harcey is. And a lot of others. I didn't grow up being aware that I saw auras, or anything like a lot of people. It was the community I loved. I still don't see auras. I wish to heck I would. Maybe it's not my path in life. But I can feel energy. I guess that's enough. If I could see auras, maybe people would say, "Well, if you can see auras within the body, how are we to know anatomy." You can still know anatomy even if you can't do that. Not everybody does. Maybe someday I'll see auras. Or maybe that's not supposed to be.

# Cynthia Hutchison
## RN, MSN, CNS, HTCP/I

### Introduction

I first met Cynthia at my Level 6 training. I was having lunch with Janna Moll and she invited Cynthia to join us. When I first saw her my thought was that she is absolutely beautiful, both physically and energetically. As I listened to her talk, I knew she was a rising star in Healing Touch. Little did I know how right I was.

Currently she is our Educational Program Director for Healing Touch Program and shining star she is. She has described herself and what she does so well, I think I'll let her do the rest.

### Interview and Cynthia's Writing

The theme of my sharing for this chapter will be two-fold: 1) highlights of Janet Mentgen and the early years of HTP up through now, and 2) how HT came into my life and why Healing Touch continues to be my life's vocational path.

**Part 1**
**Introduction and Reflections on the Past - 2018**
*"...it turns me on to think of growing old."* – John Denver
John Denver is one of my favorite recording artists whose music and lyrics have inspired me a great deal. I remember happily singing along with him back in the 1970s, including his song "Poems and Prayers and Promises" to which I make reference above.

At this writing in 2018, I am 64 years old which feels mind-blowing to me. I remember when my parents turned 50 (I was 10) - I thought they were "ancient". How our perceptions change as we mature and grow into our precious lives! Now, 64 still feels relatively young as I'm in good health, and I'm feeling like I'm getting closer to a level of wisdom where I can be of solace and support to others. I'm thrilled with seeing members from the younger generations taking on leadership roles with HTP as I near the age Janet Mentgen was when she left this world. I look back in awe and wonder at my whole life, and especially my years with Healing Touch.

I started writing this chapter in 2016 and have embellished it since then.

During this part of my writing (June 2016), I happen to be sitting at a desk in Room 5 at Shadowcliff Retreat Center in Grand Lake, Colorado, right now. This is the same corner bedroom that Janet Mentgen used to stay in for over ten years during her annual retreats and classes with her students.

Yesterday I hiked up to Cascade Falls for my annual trek in this holy place, barefoot (my preference when hiking). It is a seven-mile round trip and spectacularly majestic journey with cascading waterfalls as one ascends toward the upper levels of the trail. I have been coming to Shadowcliff every summer for years to reconnect with Janet, and for what I gratefully refer to as "renewing my vows" to her and to the vision and mission of Healing Touch Program. As of this year, 2018, it has been thirteen years that I have served as HTP's Educational Program Director and fifteen years in leadership.

## About Janet Mentgen and the Origins of Healing Touch and Healing Touch Program

Shadowcliff Retreat Center is the place where in the mid-1980s, Janet Mentgen was on a personal retreat, during which time she experienced a vision from a spiritual being while walking alone on a path to Cascade Falls. This being appeared to her next to an immense boulder (perhaps twenty feet tall) and told her that she would be creating an educational program of healing that would reach around the world and touch many lives. The appearance was during a very painful time in her life when everything was turned upside down and she was close to despondent. She was mystified and in a state of awe, and returned a week or two later to show her friend, Nancy Burns, the place the being appeared. (Nancy was also the friend who introduced Janet to the modality of Therapeutic Touch several years before.)

A few years later, through Janet's continual faith in and dedication to fulfilling the vision, the seeds of Healing Touch Program took fruition. Janet was a woman of faith and devoted to a spiritual life, which included belonging to an Episcopalian community (having been a former Catholic). She was prayerful and dedicated to holistic healing and knew that the field of energy medicine was an important key to the future of health care. Along with a dedicated group of friends who helped her contemplate and meditate through the development of what would later become our standardized worldwide education program, the manifestation of the Spirit Being's prophetic statement came true.

**Janet's Last Two Years**

In 2003, Janet was diagnosed with breast cancer. In September that year, she called me to come over to her house for a conversation. Janet wanted me to work for HTP, but was not specific about any particular role. I was thrilled and honored. I would love to participate in any way.

Janet's call was just a couple of months after I went on four day and night Native American Vision Quest in Wyoming. I had just gone through a divorce and bankruptcy and had full time custody of three young children. Life was scary and full of anxiety and uncertainty (a similar scenario to what happened in Janet's life). I was asking God to show me the next chapter of my life. I fasted and prayed within a ten-foot circle out in a remote area of nature with only water, a sleeping bag, and clothes. No journal, no books, no tent (and it was before cell phones). While I felt hopeful that the Vision Quest would lead me to my next step in life, I had no idea it would be what actually manifested about two months later. I was honored that Janet saw me as someone who could carry on in her place. She expressed confidence in me and we began spending three days a week together as I mentored with her.

She made me her assistant program director in the fall of 2003 and later the new program director in May 2005, a few months before she died. In various ways, she communicated to me that the path of HTP leadership would not be easy. There would be challenges and heartbreaks. She hoped that I would be loyal and true with the ups and downs.

In June of 2005, Janet held a three day meeting with forty-four HTP instructors at Shadowcliff Retreat Center to educate them on the history and direction of Healing Touch, including the specific roles of the three organizations she created: Healing Touch Program (core curriculum and overall education program leading toward HT practitionership); Healing Touch International (certification administration body); and the Healing Touch Worldwide Foundation (non-profit fundraiser for research and humanitarian projects). The presentations were videotaped and photographed. She surprised me on the last evening with a beautiful ceremony in the chapel to honor me in the presence of forty-four HT instructors. Her son, Bill Mentgen, was also there.

Janet attended her final Healing Touch Worldwide Conference three months later in September 2005 in Breckenridge, Colorado. She was in a wheelchair and on oxygen, but she was in good spirits and very happy to see everyone. While her chemotherapy treatments resulted in fatigue, she was always in her right mind and remained clear (and sometimes bossy!) until the day she died. She granted several minutes each to everyone who wanted to have a little meeting with her. She was very gracious to all.

Sharing a hotel room with her at conference, I could see her joy in being there with friends/colleagues and seeing the growth of HT, as there were about six hundred attendees! At the banquet, she ceremonially placed a garland of flowers over the heads of each of her three children, Lisa, Lynn and Bill. In her will, she gave legal ownership of Healing Touch Program to them for operating the

Healing Touch Program. (Lisa Mentgen Gordon eventually became the sole owner of HTP and serves as our CEO). I remained in place as HTP's Program Director (As of 2014, the role title was changed to Educational Program Director, a more accurate title).

## Part 2
## How Healing Touch Came in to My Life

*WHY DID I TAKE A LEVEL 1 HEALING TOUCH CLASS? WHAT HOOKED ME?*

**Beginnings with Therapeutic Touch**

As an idealistic young woman, I hoped to impact the lives and health of people as a fresh out-of-college, 22-year old, psychiatric nurse. After a few years of working on both closed and open psychiatric units, administering pharmaceuticals, documenting patient behaviors, and dealing with the bureaucracy of a hospital in inner city Chicago, I realized I was unfulfilled...something was missing. Administering all those medications and being on the electro-shock therapy team didn't seem to create or support any true healing in the people I witnessed being admitted and discharged over those few years.

I began to think that I could feel more fulfilled and helpful if I had more education, so I pursued a master's degree as a clinical specialist in mental health nursing and graduated in 1979. The next few years I found myself teaching in two university hospitals with

BSN nursing programs, first in Chicago and then in West Virginia. There I was, now teaching nursing students how to administer pharmaceuticals, document patient behaviors, and deal with a hospital system, and continuing to not feel fulfilled. Ha! Go figure!

But.... I did notice that I loved the teaching role and educating those motivated to learn. I honed more communication skills, developed more of an understanding and compassion for "the human condition", and started to feel more self-confident as I delved into the growing numbers of psychology and spirituality books and seminars that were being published and presented. I was in awe and wonder at how much there was to learn!

In 1980, I found myself traveling with my husband-to-be (twenty years later to become my *was*-band), living and working for the next two years in Bogota, Colombia, where we had a psychotherapy private practice for English speaking Europeans and Americans living there. I learned Spanish, traveled the country, and learned how to navigate in a very different culture, which was a fabulous and maturing life experience. Teaching part-time at the Universidad Nacional's nursing program, (nursing theory and nursing diagnosis), I now had great compassion for all teachers who were required to teach in a new, second language, and I had great sympathy for my students who were so gracious with striving to understand my poor Spanish!

I continued to feel called to something more, and realized it was yet more education, so I next pursued a doctoral degree in nursing at the Catholic University of America (CUA) in Washington, D.C. Thinking I would specialize in a path related to health care reform, I found I did not resonate with how the political system worked, and changed my focus to studying caring science, founded through a nursing lens by Jean Watson, R.N. Ph.D.

Jean Watson's work on the theory of "caring" became the theoretical framework for my dissertation. Little did I know at the time that she would, twenty years later, become a colleague and friend who just lives ten minutes away from me in Boulder, Colorado, and that caring theory would later become one of two Healing Touch Program's theoretical frameworks. Life is so interesting! [Note: Barbara Brennan's theoretical framework on the human energy system is the other theory we teach in HTP's standardized curriculum).

During my twenty-ninth year (1982), I found my life's vocational path, the field of energy medicine hands-on-healing through Therapeutic Touch. Those of you who study astrology know this was the year of Saturn Return, when, if you have not yet met your destiny for this life, you will have the opportunity to recognize it and embrace it.

At the time, I was a doctoral student at CUA, one of our professors took our class to a one day presentation at Walter Reed Army Medical Center, where Dr. Dolores Krieger was teaching two hundred army nurses, Therapeutic Touch (TT). Destiny arranged for me to sit next to Dolores at lunchtime! I went home that day knowing that I wanted to focus my dissertation on TT. However, the next week at class, I sadly discovered that our professor was adamantly against TT because she felt it was quackery and she warned us to not become associated with it. (Little did she know…and little did I know at the time, that this would be my vocational path.)

While feeling disheartened that my plan could not be manifested for my studies at CUA, another destiny encounter occurred in the CUA hallway a few weeks later, when I met Irene Morelli, a nursing faculty member from OB-GYN. It turned out that she was a clandestine practitioner of TT and was willing to take me under her wing and mentor me. YAY! For ten years, I practiced TT and studied three times with both Dolores Krieger and Dora Kunz, founders of TT. Irene later became an instructor for Healing Touch Program and was a beloved teacher for many in the Virginia/Maryland/Washington, D.C. area until she died.

Motherhood years arrived starting in 1986, just before finishing the doctoral degree. The responsibility of raising three daughters (born within four years) made me turn to learning as much as I could about holistic health care, good nutrition, home birth, and natural healing, as I was already turned off by mainstream nutrition, and our western medical system's focus on pharmaceuticals, vaccinations, and lack of acknowledgement of the importance of our mind and spirit. I studied homeopathy, flower essences, essential oils, various forms of energy healing, nutrition and continued my studies of world religions and various spiritual practices.

By 1992, I already had ten years as a practitioner of Therapeutic Touch. I had studied three times with Dolores Krieger, founder of TT, and twice with Dora Kunz, co-founder of TT. Through this study and practice, I was introduced to esoteric, ancient wisdom on healing and began studying various spiritual paths and religions with a focus on healing. Something deep within me knew that this contemporary version of the ancient "laying on of hands" was something that needed to be rejuvenated in our modern health care system. I was impressed with how Dolores Krieger, PhD, RN, made inroads with TT at New York University in the nursing department through a scientific study showing that TT recipients responded to treatments with elevated hemoglobin levels. Over the years, Dolores faced criticism, skeptics and resistance from mainstream health care. She endured despite great challenges and her community of holistic nurses grew. The same thing happened with some variations for Janet Mentgen. Pioneers face tremendous challenges when they introduce change in a cultural system. Let us be grateful for their courage to pursue their visions despite the many obstacles they confronted.

In 1992, my dear friend, Maureen McCracken, told me she thought I would enjoy taking a Healing Touch class which was being offered soon in the D.C. area. I had never heard of Healing Touch, as it was a fairly new energy medicine education program, but I was very interested and signed up. My first HT class with Sharon Scandrett-Hibdon, PhD, RN, HTCP/I, one of Janet's core team of "four" who helped her formulate the HT educational program in the late 1980s and early 1990s. Level 1 for me was *"love at first touch"* and seemed like another destiny moment. From there on in, I fully embraced Healing Touch as my full time vocational path.

**Early Days of the Healing Touch Education Program**

Back in the early days of HT, we were happy to receive "handouts in a folder" as the course materials along with demonstrations, guided practice and group sharing to learn the work. There were no websites or electronic newsletters, only hard copies of newsletters that Janet mailed out several times a year to students and practitioners. My first three levels of HT were taught in a retreat setting where we stayed overnight, and worked all evening as well. We were hungry to learn and relished in the long hours of being together doing healing work. We talked about how we could bring this new wave of hands-on healing to our various hospitals, health care facilities, and private practices in holistic health.

Three weeks after Level 1, I purchased my treatment table, and started seeing clients. My ten years with TT, and my background as a nurse psychotherapist and nursing educator enabled me to quickly and easily align with the teachings and philosophy of HT within a professional scope of practice and framework.

**Meeting Janet Mentgen**

I finally met Janet Mentgen in 1993, when she was my Level 4 instructor. I found her to be quiet and humble, not the kind of person who draws attention to herself. She dressed plainly, and spoke professionally with a sense of groundedness and *no nonsense*. She wore a watch and a cross pendant and no other jewelry. Janet didn't say more than was necessary in her teaching. One of her teaching styles was to ask the same question back to the student that was asked of her, and allow the student to come to her own realization that s/he knew more than s/he thought. I liked that about her... I told Janet at my Level 4 class that I would soon be moving to Boulder, Colorado just thirty minutes from her home. We agreed to reconnect at that time. We didn't really connect again until she was my instructor for Level 5, about a year later. While at Level 5, Janet encouraged me to take the HTP instructor training coming up in just three weeks!

In early June of 1994, three weeks after graduating from Level 5, I found myself here again at Shadowcliff Retreat Center, where Janet used to teach instructor training in the early years of Healing Touch. My life with HTP seemed to be on fast forward! On the last day of class, two giant double rainbows appeared over the lake outside our classroom. We all spontaneously deserted Dorothea Hover-Kramer in the middle of her presentation, in order to have a class photo taken outside with the rainbow. In the photo, the end of the rainbow touches my head, which over the years, has felt like an encouragement to align my vocational path with HTP.

In 1995, now feeling more like a colleague with Janet, I convinced her that in order to gain credibility in the world of mainstream health care, Healing Touch needed a department of research. I volunteered myself to create this role. After six months, the role of Director of Research became a paid position which I kept until 2000. My interest in HT then changed to a desire to teach the upper levels of Healing Touch so I resigned from this role to focus more on teaching and leadership.

The first years of the new millennium were busy with teaching Levels 1-5 for HTP which I found very fun and fulfilling. The momentum was wonderful and exciting and our HT community was filled with hope for positive change in the health care system of the United States, as well as for Canada, Australia, New Zealand, Germany, and Mexico, countries which had practitioners and instructors who wanted to integrate HT into their cultures in the early years.

**Transition Time for Healing Touch Program...**

The next time I found myself at Shadowcliff was in June of 2005, when Janet held a reunion of forty-four instructors at the retreat center for the last time. She was weakened from dealing with cancer for the last two years, and needed a walker as well as oxygen. The four days of meetings were video recorded, and included her presentation of the rightful roles of her privately owned Healing Touch (curriculum) Program, Healing Touch International (HTI, which was the second body to serve as administrators of the practitioner/instructor certification process after AHNA), and the Healing Touch Worldwide Foundation, the three organizations she created to serve different roles for the worldwide HT community. Those who had developed leadership roles with HTP, HTI and HTWF were all there. At her final Shadowcliff gathering, Janet surprised me with creating a sacred ritual and ceremony where she honored me as her successor in the role of program director. Her son Bill was there, as at the time, he was involved in running the business end of HTP for Janet.

Janet willed the business ownership of HTP to her family. Lisa Mentgen Gordon, her youngest daughter who had been involved with HTP from its early days, became the CEO, and maintains that role today. She has brought HTP into the twenty-first century by incorporating modern technology and communication within our organization so we could grow. Under her leadership, HTP became the only education and practitioner program to hold not only one, but two, national accreditations, one in health care (NCCA) and one in nursing (ANCC).

*DO YOU HAVE A FAVORITE JANET MENTGEN STORY?*

Yes. Three days after the September 2005 worldwide HT conference, Janet crossed the threshold to the other side. I was privileged to be with her during her last day of life and be touching her when she took her last breath. I felt deeply honored about that. It was a beautiful passing. I'll share a few highlights.

I had already been seeing her three times a week for the last two years. I would administrate Healing Touch to her each time I was with her, because she was dealing with cancer. That was always part of our day together. She had been gradually declining and getting weaker and more tired. But she remained very cognizant and involved. She never had dementia or "chemo-brain". She was sharp. She knew what was going on. She knew what she was doing.

I remember receiving a call the morning she died. She had had a severe coughing episode and was having trouble catching her breath. Hospice came and felt that might be the beginning of the death process. I arrived to her house within an hour. She lived with her son, Bill, and Tanya his wife. I went to be with her in her bedroom. She looked a little anxious, because of the dyspnea. I asked her "May I offer you the Chakra Spread today?" She nodded yes. So I did. It was something I shall never forget.

Carol Komitor (founder of Healing Touch for Animals) arrived later, as did Linda Smith (founder of Healing Touch Spiritual Ministries). Of course, Bill and Tanya were there too. We stayed with her throughout the day/evening. We were coaching her like midwives, reassuring her and offering comfort measures. I prayed with her quite a bit. We had some similar prayers in common. I prayed, she would listen, and we integrated prayers and loving conversation with Healing Touch.

At the end of the evening, Carol Komitor and I administered another Chakra Spread as a two-on-one treatment. Janet's breathing became a little more labored. At about 10:30 that night we were all with her. We could tell her breathing was changing. Finally, at the end she had these three sweet, gentle little puffs of breath... She left so easily. We were so grateful. We held quiet space for a while and just relaxed in the peace

After a period of time, Carol, Linda and I administered a ritual washing of Janet's body with lavender water. We brought in and lit candles. (Until then, we couldn't have candles, because she was oxygen.) We changed her clothes, dressing her in one of her favorite Healing Touch shirts, an image with open hands, a lotus flower and some sparkles. We prayed. We did a little singing. I sang four verses of "Amazing Grace" for her. We asked the family to delay calling the undertaker so we could have that special time with her. The men from the funeral home came after midnight and we watched them respectfully carry her body out the front door to the vehicle. It was so surreal!

Now the first major chapter of HT was ending….we prayed for guidance on how to gently help lead the unfolding of the next, unknown chapter….

## 2005 - Present

It is not uncommon that when a founder dies, that break off groups form, as that is part of the change or evolutionary process within organizations. Simply put, this happened with Healing Touch as well. While unfortunate and painful in many ways, wonderful fruits have also come from this unfolding. Long story short, we are thrilled that, with concerted efforts toward being the best we could possibly be, *Healing Touch Program became the only energy medicine education program to hold not only one, but two, national accreditations....National Commission for Credentialing Agencies (NCCA) and American Nurses Credentialing Center (ANCC).* These accreditations make Healing Touch Program a gold standard energy medicine program that we are very proud of.

The accreditations open the doors to many of our certified practitioners to create integrated care programs in health care facilities and to bring Healing Touch classes to these institutions. More and more practitioners are being hired as Healing Touch practitioners. Our Healing Touch Professional Association has grown, and provides services and educational opportunities for students, practitioners and instructors. At the time of this writing (2016), HTP has approximately one hundred sixty instructors around the world, with Japan being the fastest growing country outside the United States to embrace Healing Touch.

*DO YOU HAVE A FAVORITE STORY IN YOUR HEALING PRACTICE?*
Yes. I have two favorite stories.

**Story #1**
The first one took place in 1993. Mel was a man who asked me if I could help him quit smoking. He was the father of some boys I knew where my daughters attended Waldorf Education preschool. I replied, "I don't know. It can't hurt to try."

In the intake interview, I found out that he was happily married and a very dedicated father. He was a successful salesperson. He wanted to role model healthy behaviors for his children, which is why he wanted to quit smoking. He mentioned that he was an atheist. I remember thinking that's interesting, because most people who come for energy medicine have some form of belief in a Higher Power.

After the first session, he was not interested in talking with me in the post-processing part of the treatment. He just said, "I think I am going to go out and drive my car."

I was a little concerned that I did something wrong. He called a few days later and asked for another treatment. It proceeded just like the first one. After the treatment he really didn't want to talk. He said, "I think I'm going to go drive my car for a while before I go home."

This happened four weeks in a row. The fourth week, he asked, "How is it that you can mess with my brain chemicals and give me a spiritual experience, when I know there is no such thing as God?"

It was such a surprise. I left him, of course, free in his thinking and replied, "Well, it's a mystery. Shall we just keep going with it?"

He came back the next week. He told me two interesting things. One was, "You know, I called my father."

I said, "Oh really. What significance does that have to you?"

He said, "Well, I haven't talked to him in ten years. I felt like I wanted to call and start working on healing my relationship with him."

The second thing he said to me was, "And now I know I had a real experience....that there IS such a thing as Higher Power. The spiritual experience I had was real. I know that now."

I was very touched by that and felt much gratitude in my heart, as I have often wondered how people get through life without believing in a benevolent Higher Power.

A few weeks later, I referred him to another Healing Touch practitioner, because I was moving out of the state of Maryland to Boulder, Colorado. I saw him a year later, when I went back to visit friends. He insisted on coming to see me and say hello. We had a cup of tea together, and a conversation at a friend's house. We were just sharing the highlights of our lives. He was telling me that he was still receiving Healing Touch, that he was meditating, that things were going great with the kids, and with his wife and job. Then he looked at me and he said, "You know, by the way, I'm still smoking!"

We laughed about it, because clearly he didn't receive from our sessions what his stated intention was, but he opened himself to something much more. He established the relationship with his father, and he found his connection to God.

I joked back and said, "Well, now do you want your money back?" We laughed again.

It was a very special hour we spent together which I'll never forget. To me this was a powerful example of not being attached to any specific outcome for a treatment or a client because we never know where the energy will go and at what level of the human being healing will occur. We never know how we will touch another person's life and how they will touch us.

**Story #2**

The other story is about a young man named David, whom I had never met before. He had AIDS. He was my friend's brother. She was feeling distraught because he'd just slipped into dementia. She asked if I could go to the hospital and give him a treatment. She wasn't ready to let go of him, because they were the only living relatives of their family except for her young daughter.

I did go to the hospital and treat him. He greeted me. He didn't know who I was, but he knew I was his sister's friend and came to help him. I administered the Chakra Spread. He fell asleep, so I let him be. A few days later I spoke with his sister for follow up. She was so pleased to tell me that when she went back to visit him the next day (Mother's Day), that the dementia was not there at all. They were able to reminisce, talk about their childhood, talk about her daughter, and talk about his life, possessions, and his last wishes. They laughed and shared stories. They had a wonderful time together. By the next day the dementia started coming back.

A month later, David died. Then his sister told me that the significance for her of that treatment, and that day, was that they were able to complete their unfinished business. He wasn't yet ready to go. She wasn't yet ready to leave him. By having that one day together where they could talk about meaningful things in their lives, she was able to let him go, and he must have felt at peace enough to let go. She said having that one day of meaningful conversation that allowed them to come to closure was so healing for both of them.

## WHY I LOVE HEALING TOUCH...

Over the years, Healing Touch has become much more than biofield therapy and professional practice that I also teach and help administrate. It's more than an income, or an interesting way to work. It is my passion, my vocational life, and my life's calling to a major way that I serve humanity. I know that is true for many of you involved with HT. Healing Touch is in total alignment with my spirituality, faith and philosophy of life. I love that anyone from any culture or spiritual path who believes in a Higher Power that is benevolent, and who believes that human beings are empowered to support each other's healing process, can embrace and practice Healing Touch. That makes our work in the world very universal for all humanity.

I've been in classes and conferences with HT people from all walks of life and vocational work, and people affiliated with various religions and spiritual streams, and yet we all have a foundational set of beliefs and values that allow us to come together to support the healing of humanity. This is so beautiful and joyful! It gives me great hope for the world.

Janet laid down the foundation for the principles, guidelines and methods for Healing Touch in the 1980s and 1990s with the help of several close colleagues and friends, namely Dorothea Hover-Kramer, Sharon Scandrett-Hibdon, Myra Tovey and Mary Jo Bulbrook. Since her passing, the Healing Touch Program and curriculum have become more widespread, credible, scholarly, comprehensive, evidence-based, and theoretically based. The revised and updated curriculums pass the test of heart-centered professionalism. Our standardized curriculum has enough structure, theory and evidence-base to satisfy the academically and scientifically-oriented person. On the other hand, it receives enthusiastic support from individual practitioners who desire a spiritually-oriented practice where they can follow their intuition, be creative, and integrate with other holistic and/or mainstream therapies if they wish.

Healing Touch has gained steadily in credibility within health care, the field of holistic health and energy medicine, and has become a popular means for self-care among the lay population. Over the years, through anecdotal knowledge, research studies, and sharing of stories/experiences with thousands of students and practitioners, we know that HT is a great force in the world for alleviating suffering, and supporting healing of the body, mind and spirit. Its universal principles of energy healing allow people of all cultures, faiths and gender to be able to embrace it as an effective form of self-care, care for others, and a heart-centered philosophy of life. Not only is it gentle and effective, but it is non-invasive and affordable. No machines are needed. Ingestion of substances is not a part of it. All one needs is an open mind, compassionate heart and willing hands to learn the basics of this practice for self-care or care for others. That is why it has grown over the years and has been taught in over thirty-two countries! To me, Healing Touch is a form of care that is applicable to every person on the planet. It is a universal form of care of the body, mind and spirit that is based on caring science and heart-centeredness.

Those of us called to this practice and who receive it with the sense of awe, wonder and respect it deserves, are humbled to serve in this way. Many people have taken only the Level 1 course and have been able to apply it to their lives in very practical, effective and profound ways. Others have gone the route of the certification process (average of two years) which recognizes them as professional, accredited practitioners in the field of energy medicine with a specialty in Healing Touch. The beautiful thing to me is that both of these routes (or any of the levels along the continuum between beginner and certified practitioner) are powerful means to positively affect our lives and the lives of those who are part of our community. One does not have to be a certified practitioner to be effective. Healing occurs with HT not because of any credentials earned or because of any specific HT interventions, but because the person administering care is coming into the field of another with positive intention, a compassionate, loving heart and a willingness to give of her/his time and energy to serve another being. If you put those three things together, along with a recipient who is able to open her or himself to the healing process, both big and little miracles can and do happen.

I am especially encouraged to see more hospitals and health care facilities integrating Healing Touch into their clinical care. Nurses and other licensed health care professionals are aching for more meaningful clinical practices which minister not only to the body, but to the mind and spirit. When administrators and clinical leaders support their staff in learning and practicing Healing Touch, a whole new revolution in health care is possible... one of true, holistic healing where a person and family, as well as the staff, are seen for who they are, a being of spirit origin whose healing comes from heart-centered, "healing" touch and care. The world needs more Healing Touch!

I feel privileged to have been able to be a part of Healing Touch since 1992 and transition to a leadership role. It has given me an opportunity to see the world, understand various cultures and beliefs directly, and through ongoing administering and receiving of HT treatments, gradually understand more of the human body, mind and spirit, and the unfolding of the healing process in human beings. Teaching Healing Touch over the last 24 years has blessed me with meeting thousands of students and practitioners from different countries, spiritual paths, and communities and hearing their miraculous stories of personal/spiritual growth and development from "doing the work", as well as their amazing stories of witnessing healing in others. I am deeply blessed by meeting and knowing so many practitioners and recipients of HT who have touched my life in significant ways. YOU ARE AMAZING!!

*WHAT WOULD I SAY TO A PROSPECTIVE STUDENT CONSIDERING STUDYING HT?*

If you believe that we are placed on the Earth with a purpose of helping each other and to learn about love... If you feel a desire to alleviate suffering in others, to help them find meaning in their lives, and you find fulfillment in witnessing people's journeys and growth through life's challenges..... If you feel drawn to use light, gentle touch when you are aware of holding sacred space for another person.... If you feel open to the adventure of learning things that will blow your mind, open your heart, and stretch your way of being.... Then Healing Touch may be one of your paths in life!

If you feel you want to say YES to the inner calling to make a difference in the world, Healing Touch is a "learn as you go" path, because the spiritual world will always take you up on your willingness to serve humanity and Mother Earth with love, gentleness and evolving consciousness.

For me, Healing Touch has been a wild but rich and fulfilling ride.... many ups and downs, adventures, mysteries, fulfillments, accomplishments, heartaches, challenges and opportunities for growth! It has integrated easily into my personal and social life and my spiritual life.

Mostly, seeing how Healing Touch has been accepted and practiced has given me hope for the world. Knowing you are all out there, *"doing the work"* in your own individual and creative ways, in various communities, puts my heart at ease. Thank you to all of you who have said "YES!" to this practice and philosophy of life, who have taken the leap of faith despite discouragement from others, lack of self-confidence or what seemed like other barriers.

The WORLD NEEDS YOU and your Healing Touch. Your courage to take either small or big steps to being part of this community is what is going to, and what does impact the world and alleviate suffering, awaken administrators and leaders, give courage to those around you and deepen your own faith and knowledge of self. The world of energy healing is a mysterious and intriguing path that will lead you on a journey that is indescribable, fulfilling, growth-producing, adventurous and filled with awe, wonder, gratitude and hope. You will not regret it.

Thank you to Linnie Thomas for creating this opportunity for many of us to share highlights of our stories as a way to preserve the history and legacy of Healing Touch for future generations. I also want to thank Lisa Mentgen Gordon for having the courage to carry on Janet's legacy in a way that has taken us successfully into twenty-first century. Lisa and I have been through a lot together over the years. For those of you who don't know her, I want to share that she has a big, giant heart! It is my sincere hope that Janet's vision for seven generations will manifest *"that Healing Touch will become part of every home, every school, every hospital and every health care facility"*. May we all do our part to manifest this vision for humanity....

Love and gratitude to all,
*Cynthia Hutchison*
WWW.BoulderHealingTouch.com

You are invited to visit my website which is full of information, videos and resources and which has a store where I sell my CDs, body prayer DVD, and my daughter's energetic art posters. On this site, you can read about my other passion, Body Prayer, a practice that I've been teaching independent of Healing Touch since 2013.

NOTE: Background Information on the name Colorado Center for Healing Touch and Healing Touch Program

When Janet first developed Healing Touch as a curriculum program, she had to come up with a name for her business. At the time, someone encouraged her to include Colorado as part of the name, which she thought was too grand, as she was currently only teaching in the Denver area. She decided to "think big" and agreed to call her new business "Colorado Center for Healing Touch" (CCHT). Little did she know that it wouldn't be long before her curriculum would expand into Canada, Australia and New Zealand as well as through the majority of the United States. Before she died, she officially changed the name to Healing Touch Program, to remove the assumption that readers would think that her Healing Touch Program was only statewide. In fact it became international shortly after she created the CCHT.

Pioneers in Healing Touch

# Rita Kluny
## BSN, RN, BC-HN
### Elder

**Introduction**

Rita founded Healing Touch for Babies. She has been certified as a Healing Touch instructor and practitioner since 1994. She is certified in Holistic nursing, and was honored as the 1994 American Holistic Nurse of the year. She introduced Healing Touch into the Omega Institute for Holistic Studies Wellness Center, where she spent seven seasons giving private session to staff and workshop attendees.

She has over thirty-six years of nursing experience in neonatal intensive care. She created Healing Touch for Babies in January of 2000, to meet the needs of babies and their mothers at a deeper level. Her true passion is to give babies the best start in life. She envisions Healing Touch to be integrated into all areas of pre and peri-natal care.

**Interview**

*How did you get started in energy medicine? What attracted you to it in the first place?*

I got started in energy medicine long before I met up with Healing Touch. I was traveling and I had been in the Peace Corp. I was kind of a bundled, returned Peace Corp volunteer. One thing led to another and I wound up in England and Scotland.

I visited the Findhorn Foundation which, I don't know if you are familiar with, but they were one of the forerunners of alternative healing methods. While I was there I met some people who did rebirthing. I wound up in a training. I remembered some things around my birth. I immediately had a migraine headache afterwards, because a lot of what I was re-experiencing was traumatic.

I was sitting in the living room of a retreat house while everybody else was eating their dinner. I never get headaches, but it was a wallapalooza of one and even the smell of their food made me sick so I stayed out. One of the trainers, who wound up being one of my future teachers in healing, came up to where I was sitting and asked me if I was okay. I told him no, and I told him why.

He started to wave his hands around my head. In about five to ten minutes, later my headache was completely gone. I just turned around and said to him, "Number one, how did you that and number two, I want to learn." That was the beginning of a wonderful relationship.

Fast forward about five years later. I came back to the United States. (My dad had died.) I was in Europe the whole time after I met him. I helped him set up his workshops in exchange for him mentoring me.

Anyway when I came back to the United States, I did travel nursing. The thing that was interesting was I had met up with the American Holistic Nurses Association. That was through my relationship and membership with them, that I wound up studying with Janet. That was early on, because I had joined Holistic Nurses back in 1986. I was very much aware of who she was and what she was starting. I was lucky enough. I lived in New Orleans at the time. I was one of those people who traveled everywhere to go to the workshops. I got certified in 1994, both as an instructor and as a practitioner, because, number one, that's the way it started and, number two, we didn't have mentorship at the time. She told us to pick mentors. But I picked somebody in Holistic Nursing that didn't even have any Healing Touch skills, because it was Barbie Dossey, and I figured if she was leading a movement, it might be helpful to have support to know how to progress.

When I started working, nurses were getting fired for doing healing techniques at the bedside. This was before when I got certified, I was one of the few people – there was another girl, she was from the Seattle area, and I don't remember her name now. She has made her transition. She and I were the only people in the program, at the time, who worked with little people. You know, like babies and their moms. I seemed to be the go-to person when everybody was working with babies.

What I realized was a lot of people had a lot of fear around babies. I remember when Janet was teaching a class, she said that Dora Kunz, who worked with Deloris Krieger, said that you had to be really careful with babies. That equated to people being afraid to work on babies. I was never afraid to work on babies, even though they had said all that stuff, because I was so used to them and they were my element. I felt like just like they were little people with these little bodies.

I wound up participating in a miracle during my certification process. This baby wound up being my case study. She had developed a clot in an artery from cardiac catheterization. They were going to amputate her leg. Even though I was an OR nurse, people thought I was doing the work of the devil.

I worked on this baby for fifteen, twenty or thirty minutes at a time to bring circulation back to her leg. I didn't get immediate results, but she wound up being able to keep her leg. She did develop some gangrene. All she lost were some of her toe tips, but the good news was, they didn't have to amputate her leg. This was like a thirty-four or thirty-five weeker, that wound up needing to have cardiac surgery. We were looking at what we were going to do with this leg.

There wasn't any way I could say I did Healing Touch and it saved her leg. Again it was kind of like one of those life changing miracles that I got to witness.

The rest is history. I continued to work on babies. Fast forward to 2000, I was sitting next to Sharon Scandrett-Hibdon, and we were waiting for Janet to come to an instructor meeting. I kept getting this message that I was to start Healing Touch for Babies. I didn't know what to do. I didn't have any business leads, and I kept talking myself out of it. I turned to her and said to her, "Do you think this is a good idea?"

She almost fell out of her chair. She said, "I think that is a great idea."

So anyway, that's when I started. It's been a gestational journey, I guess you could call it. A lot of what I teach, along with Healing Touch, is not just one technique after another, but of giving babies, or giving people a sense of who babies are.

In my rebirthing training I remembered my construction and bits and pieces. I remembered my birth. I remembered the emotional circumstances around my mother's pregnancy. Luckily I did all that while my mom was still alive, so I could verify a lot of these circumstances. It wasn't stuff that I just made up.

In my awareness, I feel like I have this special connection, and also this special message to teach people, because I think, personally, Healing Touch for Babies is the ultimate medicine, because the other epiphany I had when Janet was teaching Level 5. She was doing the whole body technique or full body technique, I should say, on somebody, and while she was working on this guy, she asked him what his chief complaint was. He said that he had chronic neck pain.

She took him back in his life, because he said he couldn't remember the first time he had it. She took him back in his life, and every two years he had something happened to it, from falling off a bicycle, to playing touch football, to playing college football, to falling off a fence when he was a kid, to falling off his tricycle. The initial insult to his neck was being born with a cord around his neck.

I sat there, and I just realized that now, how different his life would have been if somebody had done Healing Touch on him shortly after birth. He would have had enough healing, that he wouldn't have had this indwelling weakness to neck injury that wouldn't have perpetrated itself throughout life. These are all the little ingredients that brought things together.

*Do you have a web site for Healing Touch for Babies?*

I do. It's www.healingtouchforbabies.com. The other thing I wanted to mention, was my workshop has definitely evolved through time. Initially it was pretty much just techniques and, like I said, I realized people really needed to know who babies were, in order to be able to feel safe with them. I also realized that most of the people that take my classes, it's like in any other class. Time and again I realized that everybody, when taking a class, it's personal to them before it's professional. It's pretty amazing how much healing happens during the weekend in reference to how even this person themselves was born. And their own ancestral history. Also, how their own children are born.

Somewhere along the way, I took this class in intergenerational healing. I have added elements of that to the class, because I think it's important for people to realize what patterns they were born into, that they've adapted to so early in life, that they don't realize it's not necessarily a part of everybody's reality. I have added that ingredient in teaching and model. All these things are coming up. They're also doing these techniques on themselves and on other people. It's really a very deeply healing weekend.

I think it's so amazing. I have one story after another where babies are exhibiting amazing distress, because these patterns aren't in them indwelling to the point of chronicity. They are so much easier to heal. The techniques themselves can have very dramatic results, because they're still in that acute episode. It's sort of like what you would see with somebody that you do Healing Touch and first aid. How things shift dramatically towards healing, because they aren't carrying this stuff with them and I mean even emotional stuff, because it gets healed.

One of the components of my workshop is I share research in my classes. These people are forerunners in their field in pre and perinatal psychology. A lot of psychologists wound up being together, because they realized that most psychological disorders have their origin during the perinatal period. That to me, is also exciting because I think, just like Healing Touch research has been done, and they find out that people who get Healing Touch, and have a history of depression, have significant relief of their symptoms.

These babies with neck injuries or whether they're suffering from unwanted pregnancies, or drug withdrawal, or need for surgery and quicker recovery from that, is pretty astounding. Some of the things I've seen, and again, yeah, all I can do is witness it all as a miracle. Some people aren't at the bedside and not always quite as convinced, but it just is so very rewarding.

Can I share a couple of healing stories?
*That's on my list.*

Aside from that one baby, there was another baby that I took care of. This is more in my beginning time where babies were put on ventilators for longer periods of time. They had more complications. They would extirpate and have them pre-intubated.

I worked in a teaching hospital. This one baby had a traumatic re-intubation. He had a lot of swelling around his vocal cords. They took him down to the OR, and they decided he was going to need a tracheotomy, because he had so much tissue damage from all the intubations that he had had.

Everybody always gave me the problem parents, because they thought I was good at helping them. In comes this mom that is livid, because she is totally convinced that we're the cause of the trach. Quite rightfully so. Anyway, after a barrage of anger, which I just kind of let her vent. After a while she fell silence. I think she was expecting me to defend myself. I just kind of went quiet. I said to her, "I can't imagine how hard this is for you. You're going to have to see your baby have surgery, and whatever, and I'm really sorry that this is happening to you."

I saw her put down her defenses. I said to her, "Do you believe in healing?"

She said, "Yes."

I said, "Well, I just want to let you know I've been doing healing on your baby and wanting to prepare him for surgery. I wondered if you wanted to do some healing with him. You can pray your prayers and I can do some healing. Two are greater than one, and so let's see what can happen before he goes to surgery."

I'll back up a little bit. When I was working on him, there was a lot of heat over that area of his vocal cords and over his chest. I had been doing Healing Touch on him, basically the basic Healing Touch sequence and some magnetic clearing. But throughout the morning about ten to fifteen minutes each time.

She came, and she started praying and I all of a sudden honestly felt like we were on this rocket ship. I was working on him, and I just felt an amazing amount of response. This whole area of heat that was over his vocal cords, totally lifted. What I realized, while I was working on him, was that this mom was totally scared to death.

I turned to her and I asked her, "I know you're really scared. May I work on you too?"

She said, "Yes."

I did the chakra spread in the chair on her. She really surrendered to me. It was really great. By the time I was done she was surrendered at that time.

The anesthesiologist came in just as I was done. It was perfect timing. She said, "I was down in the operating room with the baby, and I stayed upstairs. I thought I have lots of time so I'll take my time. I'm eating my lunch, when someone called up, and said the baby is coming back upstairs. I thought, "Oh my God! What kind of trach should I get for the bedside?"

They said they didn't have to do the surgery in the first place. Oh my God. We're home free. I go back into the room, and get ready for when the baby comes back upstairs. They said, "Yeah. When we got back down, they decided to just give him another shot of steroids, and that that would be enough. They have him back and he's incubated."

They were able to extirpate him a couple of days later. The interesting thing is the pulmonologist comes back in, and said, "I'm not going to go running around getting the bed space ready and what size trach tube did they put in?"

I said, "They didn't put a trach in, because they said it wasn't warranted."

He said, "Well, I was down there, and I saw it with my own eyes. This is ridiculous. He needs a trach."

I said, "Well, I did some Healing Touch on him."

He looked at me like I had spoken Japanese to him.

I shrugged my shoulder and said, "Well, you know, things change."

That was all I said, but it was really great, because when his mother had first come in before the surgery, she looked like she was fifty years old. She came back in, and she looked like her thirty year old self again.

She came up to me, and gave me this big old hug, and it was just like one of the greatest things that happened. That's the end of the story. He just progressed, and didn't need any further pulmonary intervention and hopefully lived happily ever after.

One of the things that I learned as a result of that, too, is how much babies entrain themselves to their moms. When the mom is in a sympathetic response, the babies act in kind. They can go into a state of agitation. At that point in time I realized how important it is for moms to receive Healing Touch, and sometimes I think that it is even more important for the mom, especially if she, like in lactation situations where the baby doesn't latch on immediately, that sometimes settling the mom down enables the baby to do what they know to what do. That's one example.

Another one of my favorite examples is to set up twins when they're born, and they're premature. Often they don't go home at the same time. They are often, also, at different states of recovery, because one has more delicate lungs than the other, and so this happens quite a bit. I also have to say, part of what I feel is that the Healing Touch treatment was talking to them as if they would be like talking to each other. This kind of gives them a bigger scoop of what is going on with them.

Their field of perception is acute, but it is also very limited as to the outside circumstances. You know, like telling that they were born too small and they have to be in the hospital until they get bigger and that kind of stuff. I always fill them in on the details. One of them goes home, and the other one is left to languish, because he is on oxygen, and instead of being able to leave, his needs are increasing. I started to do some Healing Touch on him and I realized that he was probably very much missing his mom and dad, because they had to be at home with his brother, and his brother was gone. He was all alone.

So while I did some Healing Touch on him, I talked to him about how his mother was probably thinking about him more than any other time, because she was missing him just as much as he was missing her.

It is kind of my mantra of treatment, telling them that their mothers, too, are just having a hard time not being there with them. It's not because they don't love them, and that they want to be with them, and they would be coming in.

It really helped him, because I could feel the change when I did Healing Touch on him every couple hours. His vital signs were gaining. By the time when my shift was over it made a twenty percent difference in his percentage of oxygen. He was back down into twenty-five percent instead of forty-five percent. He was less agitated. I guess it just felt like he was more at peace inside himself, because he got his questions answered.

It's interesting, because when I am holding them, it's the perfect time to do hands still. I feel like I am always in the mode of loving them, even when it's non-verbal. I teach parents hands still. I very simply say, "Your hands are an extension of your heart. When you put your hands on your baby, just send your love energy from your heart."

It makes such a difference. Babies really look up to their parents as a barometer for safety. I've lived in the South for such a long period of time. Here in California, it's like a breath of fresh air, where you can say more, and the parents are more, I'd like to say, less fearful of how you talk. But there I had to be really conservative in how I addressed things, and so I developed different techniques of how they could hold their baby in their heart. Put their heart around their baby. It would kind of like the Heart Math type of intervention without calling it energy. I have all these different little ways of helping moms to scan and envelop their babies with their hearts. Not to get too much in their heads by talking about energy, or anything like that. It's just very organic heart-felt energy therapies.

It's amazing to me how, sometimes it's really difficult to convey the depth of which people experience in my class. It's not just if you're a mom. I've had so many people saying, "Gosh, I wish I had known all of this when I was having kids."

Can you mention my book?

*Talk away girl.*

My book is called "The Easy Method of Parenting with a Deep Heart from the Start." Initially it was a project where I got my masters in spiritual healing. I morphed it into a "Reader's Digest" kind of written guide. It's very simply written, where anybody can understand it. It's not about Healing Touch techniques per se, but it's very much into helping moms realize their baby's an essential being. I teach them energetic ways to bond prenatally without mentioning the word energy. How sentient and perceptive babies are, and how important language is.

I teach something called remembrance in my class, which is very much how to live in your heart and to do healing, without a need for healing by using your hands. A lot of times we can't just whip out our techniques. The remembrance is kind of like a go to fail-safe technique that you can be in and living at all times in a therapeutic presence, using more holistic nursing terms. Actually, it augments everybody's Healing Touch practice quite a bit, including my own. It makes a point, that it augments everything they do from maternal instincts, plus with the power of intention. That's my book.

The things that I've written as far as scientifically oriented, and research-based, is in an article that I wrote – I can't exactly remember the name of it, but it's about the remembrance of pre-natal bonding and it's in the October 2014 issue of "Professional Peer Review Journal for International Childbirth Educational Association.". It's actually available on line. I need to send you a link for that. It's co-authored with somebody who has a research brain, which I don't have. But it was really nice, because I did the healing part of it. She did the research. It would show how healing can occur physiologically. It's a good article.

It stresses how babies imbed their stress patterns before birth. I refer to this woman, I would have to send you the name of her book. I think it's "Fetal Origins as a New Field of Science". They realize there's so much impact on a baby physiologically and emotionally before birth, They already determined that our health tablet is, not set in stone, but pretty set up by the time we're born, and how important that pregnancy aspect is.

I really want to branch out and help people realize how important Healing Touch is for the baby, while the mom's pregnant. She should have periods of time to download the endorphins and all the correct hormones to cover up the cortisol. It's relentless. Cortisol has already stress-patterned in the baby by the time they are born. That would need some work. It's important for the healthcare workers that are working with the mom before birth to be a part of their education.

*What do you see for the future of Healing Touch? Or what would you like to see?*

I would just love, honestly, I would love to see people be in their sense of presence, and have there be that inclusion of how powerful the mother is as an element of healing towards her baby, towards her children. It is so important. If you work on a baby, and not on the mother, it's kind of like filling the gas tank half empty. It would be like as incomplete a session as you working on somebody, who tells you their hands are shaking, without you finding out that they drink four cups of espresso every day. It's like that missing element of the whole picture of where you go to the root. Being your energy detective self, what is the missing piece that might also be creating something, a pattern or a stressor, that needs to be addressed so that the baby can be whole?

In this pre or perinatal psychology aspect, one of the foundational principles is, the baby will communicate the stress pattern. The baby will let us know. It's just that we don't carry our own capacity to see life from that baby's point of view. So that we can see what are they trying to tell us to bring coherence back into the situation. That baby is being entrained by the mom and the baby is trying to train the mom with coherence, using their own communication. That to me is just the most amazing thing. They are heralding a level of consciousness that we have fallen asleep to.

People want what babies have, but it's because they have forgotten their own beginnings. That's part of that whole magnetism of wanting to remember. That's why people buy books, and that's why that technique is called remembrance. It is all about coming back to Source and remembering.

*When were you certified? What year, do you remember?*
In 1994.

*Do you have any Janet Mentgen stories?*

One of them is, it was just so amazing, that living in the south, she would say at Level 1, "Let's start again."

It would be me and her in the room, because everyone else would show up late. I loved her. I never said anything, because I really coveted those times. I used to just sit with her. Sometimes we would just be in silence together. Sometimes I would ask a question.

One time I said to her, " Janet, you know, there is going to come a time where I'm going to be able to tell people, I had all of my levels with Janet Mentgen. And they're gonna say, 'Oh wow, you're so lucky'."

She looked embarrassed. You know how she was. She was kind of like that. She didn't like kudos so much. She didn't feel comfortable with kudos.

Another story, we had our first Level 6, maybe it was the second Level 6. She had some people around her that she had taught for years, that didn't take the classes, but wound up getting certified in teaching, because she was on her own way with her own thing, before the certification thing started. We wound up with going to Shadowcliff, and there was a lot of tension around. They were still trying to create curriculum. I was at Level 6, and I hadn't even done Level 5 yet. There was a lot of that chaos before order type of thing going on.

There were a group of ten of us from New Orleans. Janet really loved our group. I went up to her and, I know I'm bragging, but she really liked me.

I said to her, "Can we have about ten, fifteen minutes of time, sometime during the weekend, or whenever. I can't tell you what it is, but it's a surprise. Everybody's going to really like it."

She just looked at me with a kind of little smile and she said, "Okay. Yes you can have your time."

We had all brought Mardi Gras stuff. Beads and stuff. It was just so much fun. That ten minutes turned into more like half an hour, forty-five minutes. We had a Mardi Gras parade. I actually have a picture of her with Mardi Gras beads on with a plastic scarf. She was fun! In her own quiet way, she was like such a sweet angel.

When I was in Level 4, I had some very deep rooted incest stuff come up for me. Emotionally I was really pretty disheveled. Let me just say I was very emotional. I was crying a lot. We were in Delanica, Georgia, and I came up with shorts, tank tops, and bathing suits. It was forty-two degrees in Delanica in the middle of June. I was miserable.

We were sharing a house. What it was, was a bunch of houses on a retreat center. My roommates weren't very happy with me being emoting so much. One of them, who is no longer in the program, said, "You know what? You really need to deal with the issue and not be such a drama queen, because it gets old after a while."

I was like, okay. With that, it was two o'clock and I went into the room and saw Janet. I told Janet what was going on with me, and the conversation that had just transpired, about me being a drama queen. I just wanted to share, from the horse's mouth, since she had been witnessing my healing since Level 1. What was the deal? Was I over indulgent? Was I making a loud-mouth molehill?

She said to me, "Rita Kluny, of all the people that are in this program right now, I find you one of the most honest, and sincere, and hard-working people to do your own personal work. And I just want to tell you, not only how proud I am of you, but how much I respect you."

*That's Janet.*

I said, "Okay."

She supported me to the hilt. And we just sat there in silence. That's the way she treated me. That was Janet.

I had some consequent dreams about this very issue that came up in Level 4. I was lying in bed. She came to me and she said, she was really like right there, and she said, " Rita, just remember, if you can only see it, it's just change. To see it as change."

So that was good. I got to spend a lot of time with her in Australia, and the thing is, she's an introvert and so am I. We didn't have really great conversations. It was more like, I don't know, I just thought there was an opportunity to entrain myself with her.

I learned that from a previous healer in Nepal. I traveled to India, and then spent time with a holy woman. She could knock your socks off, but to me it was just like absorption. I had just started to learn Healing Touch through absorption.

My personal plans are, once I retire from nursing, which is imminent in the next couple of years, to start a radio show called "Birth Matters" and go public with everything that I know, without the constraints of being tied to my license. I'm looking for a sponsor. I don't have the wherewithal to create a dynasty. I want to get more political. Until I have that social security support, and clear up a few other issues, that's my plan.

I'm not interested in doing certifications and stuff like that, for nursing at least. You can put in that I'm ANCC (American Nurses Credentialing Center) approved. That was traumatic. Next time I would rather have my toenails pulled out instead. (Laughter.) That was crazy, but I'm glad it's done.

*Is there anything else you would like to add?*

I would love to find some instructors. They would have to have some kind of perinatal experience, and be a Healing Touch instructor. I don't think I can replicate myself, but I bet you, Janet felt the same way. I'll get over that, and let everybody's own natural talents shine through. Just to have, to be able to do that. I feel like it's a very juicy curriculum. Everybody can bring their own thing into it, but I also think they need to have some kind of exposure with babies, because they need to tell their own stories. It's just like your own life. So that they have a repertory, that's personal to them, and not be telling everybody else's stories.

Pioneers in Healing Touch

# Carol Komitor
CMT, HTCP/I, HTACP/I, ESMT
Elder

**Introduction**

When I first met Carol Komitor, it was love at first sight. This gentle, compassionate woman has, unknowingly, been a mentor for me for many years. Later, I took Healing Touch for Animals, Level 1. Carol referred to the energy we worked with as love, and I thought, "This is so true." I have thought of the energy in that light ever since. The following is a little about Carol from her web site: HealingTouchforAnimals.com and from my interview with her.

Carol Komitor is the founder of Healing Touch for animals and developer of the Komitor Healing Method, Inc. Based on years of experience working with world class trainers, veterinarians, animal shelters, private clients and through extensive studies (both animals and people), Carol Komitor formulated the curriculum for the multi-level, energy therapy program known as Healing Touch for Animals® (HTA). HTA techniques were created and cultivated by Carol through study, practice and experiential knowledge.

As a Healing Touch Certified Practitioner and Instructor, Certified Massage Therapist and Certified Hospital Based Massage Therapist, Carol witnessed the powerful, often dramatic, effects of energy therapy on humans. Her thirteen-year background as a veterinary technician combined with her studies and teaching experiences, inspired her to develop energy therapy techniques for animals. Carol's passion for animals and her knowledge of energy medicine brought about a hands-on, multi-leveled program offering a cooperative model that bridges holistic animal healthcare with traditional veterinary medicine.

Today Carol has an active HTA and HT practice for animals and their people in Colorado. Her continued close connection with the work has allowed Carol to keep expanding her knowledge and understanding of both the healing process and energy medicine. She is recognized as a leader for essential oils for animals and people and has developed specific applications to support the animal's energy system with the essential oils. Carol has also developed techniques within the HTA curriculum which incorporate sound therapy using tuning forks. Her practice also includes distance healing for those who are unable to visit her in person. Carol's private practice gives her the opportunity to develop new effective techniques to help animals with their healing.

**Interview**

*Way back in the beginning what got you started in energy healing?*

I attended a class where I was a support person for one of my girlfriends. The class instructor offered a different in-depth presentation weekly on health and self-care. The instructor presented Therapeutic Touch during the first class. This woman was talking about how, by balancing the energy system, and by providing health and well-being for someone else, you can help with their healing process.

The way it set with me was not good, and I started to confront her and politely argued with her in front of thirty people which is not my nature what so ever to have any sort of conflict. So to me it was like, wait a minute "What are you doing here? And I questioned myself; "What was it that set you off?"

After ten minutes of this obnoxious individual (me) drilling her with questions, she, in a very compassionate way, would answer my questions without any qualms. Finally, I decided, oh the heck with it, I am going to just endure this class and then Gloria and I can go out for coffee, and we can enjoy an adult conversation, because we both cared for our toddlers all day, every day.

When we started to do the actual exercises around Therapeutic Touch, I, to my amazement, could feel the energy. It was so dramatic that I did a three-sixty in my awareness, and in my understanding. Yet I didn't know what the heck I was doing, but I could feel something! The next day I went to the local bookstore, and they had a book called *Therapeutic Touch*. I bought the book and studied it.

As I shared my experience with another friend, she gave me a horse magazine that addressed the *same* topic, Therapeutic Touch. I wish I had the copy of it today, but I cannot find it. The magazine had an article on the front page about Therapeutic Touch with horses. I read the three page article, went to my friend's barn, and worked on her horse. The horse had a remarkable experience of relaxation and of calming. The horse was typically very high strung. The horse went into, what we see in our classes, a very deep relaxation state. His performance in his dressage activities was one hundred percent changed after the novice session I provided. He became connected to his rider, he was focused, and the horse did well during his competition. Each time I would come to the barn after that, the horse would meet me at the gate. The horse recognized what I did for him and we formed a bond for his healing.

In the meantime, I decided to go into massage therapy and the school I chose was because a class was offered named Therapeutic Touch. The person teaching the energy therapy class was Janet Mentgen. Janet Mentgen turned out to be the person who founded the energy therapy program called Healing Touch.

I didn't know who she was. I didn't know all that much about energy therapy. I went there, because she was teaching this class that I had been reading about and saw results of change during the short session with my friend's horse. I was eager to learn more about Janet and the work she taught during the weekly course that included Levels 1 and 2 of Healing Touch. Within the 8 weeks of training we had lots of time to practice between each technique that we learned, and I embraced the inner workings of the energy body. I was hooked in how I felt and how others reported the change that they made through HT.

I ended up working with Janet as her teaching assistant in her future classes, the whole time I was in massage school, and then took over her teaching position at the school after she decided to retire from her position there. So, that's how I got started with Healing Touch. Because of my massage training, and because of my understanding of the energy work, I had a lot of people to practice on. I did weekly sessions with friends, family and clients. Experiencing my own weekly Healing Touch sessions helped me get through massage school, and raising two little kids, and working through everything else that goes along with a new career.

I had my clients that I would integrate massage therapy with Healing Touch. It was an opportunity for me to accelerate in the Healing Touch work and be on the ground floor when Janet was developing Healing Touch Program.

By 1990 Janet had developed the whole program. I was able to experience first-hand the community she was building around the world. I coordinated a lot of her classes, got to hang out with her and as we sometimes traveled to teach classes in various parts of the country, I was able to be mentored by her on so many other levels.

*When did you become certified as a practitioner and/or instructor?*
I was not an instructor first. I completed my program for Healing Touch in six months as a Healing Touch Practitioner. I couldn't get my instructor requirements in at the same time but completed the criteria about six months later. At that time, I became a certified instructor and began teaching Healing Touch.

*You were teaching at the massage school before that?*
Yes, I was teaching at the massage school before the instructor certification was formulated, but I was pinned with the first group of Healing Touch Instructors in 1991.

*What do you like best about Healing Touch?*
How we can participate in someone else's healing process, as an observer, as someone who facilitates the work, and allows the empowerment of healing to happen for the individual.

*How did Healing Touch for Animals get started?*
Well, I have a thirteen year background as a veterinary technician, and was married to a veterinarian, at the time. When Janet found out about my experience with animals, she would send me all the animal questions that were coming into the Healing Touch office. I soon realized people didn't understand the differences of the energy system of the animals, compared to humans. In talking to Janet, or talking to my HT colleagues, I realized that I had skills that other people didn't have, or were not aware of yet.

I realized that I needed to share the information that I knew with my peers, and with people who desired to help their animals at a different level. I thought that I would develop a little class that I would teach in the Denver area a couple a times a year. And that would be the end of it. But what happened was a little horse came to me and changed the way I looked at the world through the animal's eyes.

The horse, a world champion horse, was injured so badly that the veterinarians wanted to put her down. Her owner/trainer called me, and I started working with this horse. This horse and the other horses in her herd that I worked with ended up being major teachers for me. She is a Texas horse that came to Colorado for training during that summer. Sharon Scandrett-Hibdon, another Healing Touch instructor, worked on this same horse down in Texas, before they traveled to Colorado for the summer.

The trainer got hold of me through the Healing Touch office, and I started working on this horse. She was a quarter horse and I worked on her two to three times a week during the summer. She brought techniques into my Healing Touch for Animals® program. She brought me better understanding on an energetic level than what I already knew. She gave me the curriculum and start-up for my program. Healing Touch for Animals® was born.

By the end of the summer, I had Level 2 in store, and shortly after that 3. I studied and worked with those horses in that barn for hours a day. There were a lot of horses with varied injuries, illnesses and behavioral issues within a training facility and breeding farm, so I had many opportunities to help the horses, but the horses were extremely helpful to understand what was happening to their energy system as I did my energy therapy.

I learned a lot from each of the horses I attended to, but worked mainly with this one horse. She was remarkable in her healing process. By the end of summer, she was doing well, and going into rehabilitation. Not only did she go into rehab but by the first part of the next year she was back into training and competition again.

It was remarkable to me the amount of energy awareness that came through by working with this horse, the other horses in the herd, and with working with the trainers. The trainers pooled their money together, and hired me to travel around the country with them to work on their horses for the competitions. I was working with high-end athletes, and world class athletes. I was working with some horses that exhibited behavioral issues. Some of them had physical problems and all of which I was seeing huge results. I was the one who was the most surprised at the results I was seeing. How could this be? But I was also enjoyed the process and basking in the realization that intention, and a big heart, and listening to the way the animal presented their energy was my gift, and that I could teach others the same process.

I was also listening to the trainers as to what they wanted for their performances and what they were desiring of their horses. I knew a little bit about horses, but not all that much, and I learned an amazing amount just hanging out with them for that quality period of time. That was in 1995.

In 1996 I offered the first Healing Touch for Animals, Level 1 course. It's coming up to twenty-five years and it has been a fun ride to see how the HTA program has developed. The techniques of the upper levels have also been proven to be amazing in helping the lives of our animals and their people.

*Have you explored other healing modalities?*

Yes. You mean other than Healing Touch or within the curriculum of HTP?

*Yes. Like Reiki or whatever?*

Yes. During my massage courses I took two levels of Reiki, and then I pursued, after I was certified as a Healing Touch instructor and was actively teaching HTA, I received my Reiki Master attunement. Then I studied Medicine Dharma Reiki which is a Buddhist aspect of Reiki as well. I studied Lightbody work at instructor level, but used the training for personal growth and development. I studied the use of tuning forks through Inner Sound® and incorporate the use of sound therapy with my HTA curriculum. And I continue to study, the use and effectiveness of essential oils to bring them into the curriculum, too. It is a joy to bring all that I have learned together to enhance the lives of others.

When I get a "download" for a new technique, I know it comes from the experience of whoever is in front of me, whether human or that it's an animal. I practice that technique until I understand it fully. I use it on animals. I use it on other people. I need to see how it works in my mind and I want to be confident in what the technique is doing, before I share it with someone else. I see the validity of keeping things clear, but I also see the validity of exploration. I do have a lot under my belt and love sharing the information.

*Why did you stay with Healing Touch?*

Because of the integrity of the program. Because of the integrity of Janet Mentgen and my colleagues. I love the professionalism. I love that we are based on a curriculum that has more than just "this is a technique thing that you do". The program has reasons for why we do what we do. It has understanding, and it gives us credibility. I feel, because of that integrity and the professional presence we hold, we are also able to explore our spirituality with ease. I love the spiritual part of us, too. I can get into the esoteric aspect of what we do just as much as anybody else, and yet, when it comes to the work I want to know the why's and how's before I hold healing presence for someone else. I want to understand the energy awareness under my hands and so that is why I have stayed with Healing Touch.

*Do you have a Facebook page?*
I do.

*Are you using other social media?*
My staff is using all of them: LinkedIn, Pinterest and several others that I don't even remember. I know that they keep track of it for me. I don't do all of my Facebook. I do my personal posting and I do some of the professional things on the Healing Touch for Animals® page. My staff is very good at helping me keep track of the technical stuff because I don't have time for to do it all myself.

*Does it help build classes and that kind of thing?*
Socially media helps to get the word out there! I have thousands of followers on my HTA website and on my Facebook pages. It's exciting to see how the word spreads, but also how people outside of my classrooms embrace Healing Touch for Animals®.

*Do you have any comments or advice for potential students?*
If they have the interest of energy therapies, I feel we're the top of the line through our Healing Touch Program curriculum. I feel each Level provides a superior approach through education and understanding of how an animal's energy system differs from the human. The understanding and the anchoring of what is needed and how to determine what techniques to use helps the students to

embrace the possibilities that can make a difference in another's life. It is the cream of the crop, as far as the energy work is concerned and the organization is dedicated to empowering others to support animals and their people with healing.

*Has Healing Touch changed your life and, if so, how?*

Yes! Absolutely! First, it gave me words for what I had already been doing my entire life, with the animals, with people. I was not a one who would say, "I'm going to put my hands on you, and heal." But I would be in a presence where healing would need to take place, whether someone was sick or whether they were troubled about something. Even as a child the adults would say, "I feel better when I am sitting next to you."

It also gives me structure to appease my logical mind, and as HT allows me to tap into my heart, too. I can understand the piece of unconditional love we must hold, and how that can help someone else in their healing process.

*Do you have a particular meaningful Healing Touch story?*

Like a human one? There's so many. Here goes: I have a PTSD Vietnam vet that I worked with years ago. This man was also a top executive with an international oil company. He oversaw hundreds of individuals and projects within his job.

He was coming to me for massage, but to make changes for his health. I shared with him about Healing Touch and how it helped to support the energy around his body and inside his body, so that he could let go of his pain. This man was injecting himself with prescription medication three times a day to alleviate headaches from shrapnel that was left at the base of his skull. He woke up with migraines almost daily. His self-induced medication he gave to himself was under the doctor's knowledge. He was not an addict, but he was in pain all the time. By working with him, and working around his head, with the intention to release his headaches he was engaged in our combined goals. I didn't always use the headache techniques, but when he came in with a migraine, I did. Within about a four-month period of time, where he came in for weekly visits, he not only got off his medication, but he was able to monitor his headaches with Tylenol. That probably was one of my favorite stories because of the dramatic results that we saw. It also proved to me the way energy therapies work to alleviate pain.

That honored veteran helped me with one of my fibro-myalgia patients, by helping me to really understand the energetics of pain and how pain works energetically in the body, and what pain does to the body. He helped me to understand that it isn't always a quick-fix, but that patience and perseverance gives us the ability to help others more profoundly. I feel he was a great teacher for me during the early days of my practice.

I teach the pain concept in my HTA, Level 3 and have the concepts online called the "Energetics of..." series. One of the segments addresses pain.

I've also seen cancer patients who have gone into remission and where working with others, I have had the privilege of seeing them through their death process. Cancer patients have been in my healing genre throughout my healing career. Many show up at my door, both people and animals. I honor my cancer patients as they are always great teachers and very receptive to the work provided.

*Do you have a particular animal one you would like to share?*

The horse I talked about early was just amazing. And she was the one who brought to me the Etheric Heartbeat™ technique to my program for the Level 1, HTA course. It is a remarkable technique.

Recently shared a case study about a dog who had a snake bite, a copperhead snake bite. The bite went undetected for about three days. The dog became lethargic, wasn't eating, and the veterinarian couldn't find anything wrong with blood work, other than a bit elevated white blood count. So there was some kind of infection going on, but nothing showed up until the swelling started in the neck, where the dog had been bitten. When they shaved the neck the tissue was actually dying around the bite mark.

I am going to back track a little bit. In my other modalities, I have pursued the tuning forks through Inner Sounds and Arden Wilkins' work. We offer two sets of tuning forks in Healing Touch for Animals® in the curriculum. I have also pursued and become a leader in the in the application and use of essential oils with the animals. The HTA program teaches people how to appropriately apply essential oils to our animals.

With this "snake bite" dog and the permission of the veterinarian, we applied Frankincense, Melrose™, and Helichrysum to this dog's wound, around his wound, and to his feet, to help support his health and well-being. The applications helped to release toxicity in the body caused by the snake bite. The woman who owned the dog was a Healing Touch for Animals Practitioner. She did a lot of magnetic clearing on the dog and used our HTA Bridging™ technique on him. (Janet Mentgen gave me permission to alter her technique of Magnetic Clearing to better work with our animals.)

The dog ended up having to have surgery to cut out the chronic and necrotic tissue. The veterinarians placed Penrose drains within the incision to release any accumulating fluid from the whole area. The entire side of the golden retriever's neck was shaved. The dead tissue was cut out, and then sutured back with these drains for a few days. Within a week's period of time, maybe a week and a half, the sutures were removed, and the dog started to grow his hair back.

He started eating. He was livelier, and with the support of HTA, I worked with him every two days, and with his HTA Practitioner/owner working with him a couple times a day this dog started to thrive again.

The veterinarians saw the results and how energy therapy really helped this dog, where he would perhaps not have survived otherwise and they were appreciative of the cooperative efforts that were provided for him. This experience was facilitated by distance work on my part, but his owner did her HTA techniques hands-on. She and the dog live in Kentucky and I was in Colorado.

*You knew Janet Mentgen personally, do you have any favorite stories about her?*

Yes I do. I have many, but I remember traveling with her to Payson, Arizona, where we had to fly into Phoenix. Our purpose was to go there to teach a Level 4 or a Level 5. I don't remember which. I went as the mentor for the advanced training. My job was to support the students and to help where I could during the class. We traveled together, as we had done several times with upper level classes, so I got to know Janet well. We had an hour and a half travel time by car from the airport in Phoenix to Payson. What I saw was Janet in her environment of the outdoors. She loved all things nature and she loved the desert. I remember one spring, maybe early March, as we made our way to Payson, the Arizona desert was blooming in all its glory. The saguaro cactuses were blooming, and all the other cactuses were blooming. We stopped along the road side and walked a short trail. Janet could tell me all the flora names and the Latin names of each cactus. It was amazing fun for me to experience the beauty of the sandy flora through Janet's eyes. It was also fun to share the energy exuding from those pregnant plants as they were blooming. They emitted such a strong energy presence as if they were proud of the beauty they showed.

That story wasn't even a class experience but an example of how we need to be energetically aware—where ever we are. I have many of those stories that showed who Janet was, and experiencing that part of her. It was showing me the essence of Janet's amazing brain. I couldn't even tell you some of the regular every day names of the cacti, but that short hike we shared was eye opening and fun for me. Janet came from a landscape and nursery background as Janet and her husband owned a nursery when she was married.

*What do you see for the future of Healing Touch?*

I see that, compared to the late '80's when I became involve with Healing Touch, to now, people are receptive to alternative energy therapies to help with their health and well-being. I like to call it the "cooperative" approach to healing. I love the word "cooperative" because it shows that we are cooperating with traditional medicine practice. We need that medical aspect in our lives, and yet we also need that energetic aspect.

I see that the cooperative measure is melding together. I see where medical doctors are seeking out other ways of presenting the health process, other than cutting someone open, or without killing their cells to get rid of disease, and I'm seeing it as a cooperative measure. Many times, traditional intervention is needed to help with the healing process, but more and more, we are seeing that traditional medicine is also seeking other means to help their patients to heal. I see Healing Touch is being recognized and at the forefront, as leaders in energy therapies. Because of Healing Touch Program and the organized leadership and the national accreditation, Healing Touch Program is leading the future's path for energy therapies. I am confident that the practitioners coming through their HT studies will have the extensive foundation of energy therapy training to provide assistance to others. Because the practitioner has been well trained, I can be assured that healing change can be offered. Healing Touch is a wonderful organization to embrace.

I see HT as better understood, more creative. I see where Healing Touch can be brought into a place where it is an everyday word. When I talk to people about what I do, "Oh I have heard about this." or "I have a friend who does this work." or "My Grandma used to do things like that." People are much more open, even though they don't exactly understand Healing Touch is or what it does.

*If you've got the time, you have answered most of my questions, would you like to tell the little horse story?*

Sure. It's in my Level 1 HTA workbook and I go into the big story during the class. I worked on a World Class competitor, quarter horse. She had a suspensory ligament injury that was so bad, that she not only tore the ligament, but tore bone away from bone with the ligament attached. The veterinarians thought she would not heal properly, and that she'd always be lame, therefore suggested that she be put down. Her owner/trainer contacted me. I started working with this horse two or three times a week. She changed a great deal within a short period of time: three to four weeks. Then she hit a "flat-line" where she stopped the acceleration of healing and became depressed. She was not eating as well. She was still stall bound. She wasn't getting out with the other horses and having interaction and she wasn't able to do her job as a competitor. With that, I saw this huge plateau. I had become so connected to this horse and so willing to help her to heal, that I made a commitment to help the owner/trainer find someone else to continue her therapies.

I went into my treatment room one day, before I started my travels to work on her, and did a meditation with the purpose of finding the person that could help this horse to heal her leg and provide a quality-of-life for the time she had left on this planet. I asked that she not have lameness. I did the meditation and felt good about the opportunities to find her the correct person to stabilized and promote her healing. During the hour and a half drive I kept diligent in validating the intent of the meditation and validating the purpose for her healing. When I arrived and began our HTA work, she was able to leave her stall and come into the alley way as I worked with her.

I started to do one technique, and it was as if someone grabbed my hands and brought both of them up to her heart. As I was monitoring the energy with my double hand boost over her heart chakra, I could feel the energy with an intensity that I had not experienced before. The energy from my hands was being drawn to the very fine point of the heart chakra and became vibrant and effervescent.

In my belief system, I feel like that the pinpoint of the heart chakra is the point where we hold our soul. It is where the heart chakra begins and where the soul seat resides that we teach in Healing Touch. What I experienced was that the heart chakra was not only taking in the energy, but it was creating a vibration and frequency that was higher in frequency than I had ever experienced before. I thought that was because of the large animal or because of the large energy that was needed to support this amazing horse. I soon found out that it was about a *new* technique.

As I facilitated the energy, and the energy was pouring into her heart in great volumes, it became effervescent and bubbly. It felt like my hand was over a glass of soda with the bubbles touching and tickling my hands. It was effervescent, vibrant and the energy became so full within her heart chakra that it actually pushed my hands away from her body. It drew my hands around her, not on her.

As I was standing there, my right hand went to one side of her and the left hand went to the other side. I was just holding the energy of that effervescence and energy flow that was going throughout her entire energy system, not only her physical body, but the energy field outside her. It was so strong that it supported my hands being held straight out from my body for almost forty minutes without effort. The energy experienced coming from her was so strong that it felt like someone was holding my arms up. I knew the technique was complete when the energy stopped moving through my hands. At that point my intention changed to a different purpose. I set an additional intent to have this vibrant energy re-circulate from her heart chakra through her entire body and to continue to work to maintain her health and well-being long after I stopped the session. I added to also help this amazing horse stabilize and strengthen her energy system. I ended the technique with that and I thought "Well that was pretty cool."

I saw a sparkle in her eye after that. I saw her head back up to normal position. I saw her engaging with the people that were taking care of her. I saw a difference, again, with how she connected to her owner/trainer.

It was at that point I realized that a *new* technique was born that day. And it will be called Etheric Heartbeat™. It was to become one of the highest frequency techniques I know to date. It's one of the most established techniques I know to help people and animals through a health crisis.

I ended up putting Etheric Heartbeat™ into the Healing Touch for Animals, Level 1 curriculum. I feel blessed every day that I was able to work on the sweet energy of that horse and listen to what the energy was telling me. To have that extraordinary experience of that horse showing me another way to support the healing process seemed like a guided blessing!

In my understanding of animals, they do not have the holding back that humans have unless they have been abused or neglected. There is no ego at work with the animals. They allow the energy to do their work for them.

It's like Janet Mentgen taught us from day one: "It is about the surrendering of the body that allows the healing to take place". It's about how the HTA Physiology Chart explains the body's physical response when relaxation takes place. It's about the relaxation which creates a physiological response as we work with the animals and the body surrenders to the natural healing responses provided through relaxation.

The people and the animals that we engage with during their healing process and the lovely training that we practice by maintaining our heart presence helps us to help others. As we hold the energy of an individual's desire, our intention of the highest and best is offered as a way of support and empowerment to the individual receiving our work. We are the observer and the instrument of energy flow and balance as we do our work—we get out of the way and offer a space for healing to take place. The energy does the work for us and healing happens.

# Nancy Lester
## HTCP/I, LMT, BSPA
### Elder

**Introduction**

Nancy is a nice mixture of professionalism and caring. She's loving, gentle and kind. At the same time she has worked with the ethics committee in various capacities for many years. That isn't always easy. She has a wise head on her shoulders which is useful for someone on an ethics committee.

She has some good ideas for helping you start a business, too.

**Interview**

*Do you have a web site?*
No.
*What position do you officially hold in Healing Touch?*
I have been a practitioner and instructor. I'm on the ethics committee, past chair, and I am currently Level 4 and 5 co-lead instructor with Janna Moll.

I just stepped down from chair of the ethics committee. I did vice-chair for two years and chair for two years, and then turned it over to Jerry Becker as chair. I am still on the committee.

*What is your job description as lead instructor for Level 4 and 5?*

That's a good question. We're writing one. Right now I have an email address. I don't have an official job description. It' taking care of any issues that come up in the classes, going through the evals quarterly, seeing if there are any issues we need to address. We just redid the books. That was the huge thing that they've been doing. Now that that's done we can focus on some of the other things.

*What does being on the committee entail?*

Whatever ethical issues come up. It takes a lot of investigating and trying to work out the best solution to whatever the issues are. They can be pretty broad. It depends. A couple of times we had to come up with a corrective plan of action with people.

*What attracted you to energy medicine in the first place?*

A dream.

*About what?*

I was doing a lot of dream work, just in my own health journey. I was doing lots of workshops, but that was one of them that really spoke to me. I had a couple of friends and we started a dream group. We would go to workshops, and then we would get together monthly and work on our dreams. I was used to getting a lot of my insights and my guidance through my dreams. I woke up one morning and I had this vision of energy moving through me, kind of like light. I didn't know it was energy. It moved through me and out my hands. It was like this powerful vision.

I shared it with my dream group and one of the women there said "I think you need to learn energy work." I said, "What's that?" That's how I got started exploring. Really my personal journey led me to all these holistic workshops around my area in Annapolis. This is in the mid '80's.

I heard about the Holistic Nurses Association. I thought, well gosh, I love this stuff so much, maybe I could weave it into my nursing. I was doing critical care at that time. I spent the first fifteen years of nursing in trauma and critical care. I joined the American Holistic Nurses Association. The first flyer that I got, well they used to send out newsletters, and the first one I opened to a page advertising Healing Touch. I lived in Annapolis, Maryland, but I went to Charlottesville, Virginia for my first class. That was the closest one.

*When did you take your first class?*
I think it was '93.

*When did you become certified as a practitioner and then again as an instructor?*
'95 I became certified as a practitioner, and in '98 I became certified as an instructor.

*What made you decide to certify in both of those?*
I loved the work. I used to go, and help at all of our local workshops. They came to Baltimore right after that. A friend of mine, who I got know, Dimitri, was coordinating them and I would go and help her. As one of the helpers, I just kept going to the classes. I got hooked on the work. I just loved it, and knew it was something that I needed to pursue.

At the same time I was doing the Holistic Nurses Association certification. That was through Season Bridges, way back then. They didn't even have a core curriculum yet. I became certified in both holistic nursing and Healing Touch at about the same time.

*How has Healing Touch changed your life?*

It's my whole career now, pretty much. I am just so grateful. I was ready to leave the hospital nursing. My last seven years I was a hospital administrator. I knew that this was the work I was meant to do, but I couldn't figure out how to get there. I was sole support of me, and two children. I just kept asking for guidance.

How I ended up in private practice in 1995, I was a senior administrator of a major hospital of interdisciplinary services. We merged with another hospital. In the beginning, my CEO was named the CEO of the new facility. I was so disappointed, because I thought that this was how I would move into private practice. Within three months it was reversed. My CEO just had an emergency meeting, and she resigned. The other CEO took over in the merger.

That allowed me to have a little bit of a severance package, and I was, just like I said, finishing up everything. I had my certification. I went to basic massage school. It started with a Healing Touch practice. I went to people's homes with my table. When I got certified and licensed in massage therapy – at the time we didn't have licensure in this state. It was just becoming a massage therapist. I opened a practice. I got an office. It was the right thing because the connections just happened so easily. I had a full practice going within months.

*Do you have a particularly meaningful story with your Healing Touch practice?*

Oh, many. My case study was a young woman with a melanoma. When I met her she had already had surgery. She had already had radiation, and she was about to start chemo. A friend that I had treated, a nurse practitioner, suggested Healing Touch. So anyway, I started working with her. One of the things that we did, one of our goals, was to protect her ovaries. They had already told her, and she was young, that with all this treatment and all, she may not be able to conceive as an outcome of all this treatment, the chemo. We did that. It was really fabulous that my work with her counts as a session. I didn't know how often to see her. We were kind of playing it along. She called me one day and she said, "My white count's really dropped."

She is a child psychotherapist. She was working around the children and they wouldn't let her work when she was too low. She said, "I really want to stay with working part time. Do you think that if we add an extra treatment, that would help?"

I said, "Well, we can try. We can see what happens. "·

Anyway, she bounced up incredibly. She had never missed a day's work. We then adjusted according to her chemo. I saw her about three times a week then. She did beautifully. She continued to see me, like monthly, for two years. When two years was up, they okayed her to try to get pregnant. They wanted her to wait two years. She got pregnant immediately. She's had two children. I still see her.

We lost touch with each other when she got busy with both kids. She lived pretty far away from me. All of a sudden one day, it had been about four years that we kind of lost touch, we ran into each other in a grocery store. I've been seeing her ever since. She comes to see me for maintenance, just for health. Staying healthy. I look back at a time when I was seeing her son. I did a home visit, and we ended up with a baby on the table with her, when she first had him. It was wonderful. He's now in high school. He's looking at getting his driver's license. It's really fun. She reminds me of the anniversaries and stuff of our work. It's really just special.

*Do you use Facebook or other social media to promote your business?*

I don't. I do have somebody in the community who puts my classes on Facebook.

*Do you think that helps build classes?*

I don't think a whole lot. I ask people where they heard about the Level 1's, where they heard about us. Very few people said Facebook.

*Have you explored other healing modalities?*

I teach Anatomy for Healers. I forgot that. Level 1 of that. I guess that's the work that I embrace. I've studied other classes like craniosacral I took with Ledger and what not. But I wasn't drawn to them enough to go on to certification or anything additionally. I use them a little bit. Absolutely, in an integrated way. Like still point, I use that a lot. I mean, it just goes naturally with mind clearing, but I don't do their thirteen step process. Or whatever it was. It was a long time ago since I took that.

When I started doing the Anatomy for Healers, I do integrate a lot of that work with my Healing Touch now.

*Do you have any comments or advice for potential or new students?*

I think, to me, it goes back to Brugh Joy. Make no comparisons. I see a lot of students get into kind of comparing where they are, and what their able to feel, and do, and what not. I think it's so important to make it a very unique journey. And to be open to who they are meant to work with. Because I think that was the thing that helped me the most. I think I was really in a place, when I went into private practice, to just be open.

I took a massage class for pregnancy, a very spiritually based class. I could see how well the energy worked to integrate with it. I thought my practice was going to be a lot of working with pregnant women. But it turned out that didn't happen. I worked with some, but I see more of a variety now than I thought, I guess, I would.

*What do you see for the future for Healing Touch?*

I see it continuing to grow, and to be more integrated with healthcare.

*Do you have a Janet Mentgen story you would like to share?*

Yeah. Actually that's what I thought this call was all about. More so than me. I just feel so grateful and honored to have known Janet Mentgen, and it took me a long while after she died, to realize that none of these people would ever know her. She was so involved with all the communities. I've been to every conference from when we started in Lakewood at that little – I've forgotten where we were, a Hyatt or Hilton or something, in Lakewood, Colorado.

I guess I was so impressed that Janet was just so down to earth about everything. I am a very practical person, myself. We kind of hit it off that way. I think the funniest story that I had, was in the very beginning when I was helping out with a class. We used to have a Level 1, and then a Level 2 or a Level 3. So we had two concurrent classes going on at Shepherd Pratt in Baltimore. Janet came in and the people she was teaching, a 2 or a 3, I don't remember. Then the Level 1 instructor, was the one who had taught there before. So the students coming in knew the Level 1 instructor, and, of course, everybody has warm feelings towards their Level 1 instructor. They're all coming up and hugging this person and what not. Nobody really knew who Janet was at that point. It was really on.

I was standing there beside Janet. She had come in, and she said, "This is the way it always goes."

I'm standing by the program director, but everybody was so excited to see their Level 1 instructor. She was laughing about it. Of course, then we got to know Janet, and things changed. In the very beginning it was like nobody knew who she was until they got know her and meet her in real life.

*Is there anything you would like to add?*

I would like to talk more about building community, because that has been such a big part of my heart's work. It's not just about seeing my clients and my private practice and the teaching, but building community. I think it's so important for people to have that support, because a lot of people coming into this work, their spouses, and sometimes even their closest friends and all, just don't understand the ah hah moments that we have in this work. I think it's really important. I started a practice group early on, when I first started teaching and that is on-going. It's been, I don't know, I started teaching in '98, probably we had that going by '99.

I did turn it over to two certified people eventually, and they ran it for years and years. One of them still is. I started a mentoring group when we started getting people up to those levels, and it still continues. I have groups into my house once a month, and it's for anybody who is certified, whether they have a mentee or not, if they just want to give back and help mentor apprentices, it's a way.

I encourage – well, now that things are changing – I used to encourage people who wanted to mentor. People would ask me. I would say that I would love it if you would come to a mentoring group and see if there was anybody that you resonate with that I could be, you know, help. But they would choose another mentee and I would be part of the team. Then it became qualified mentor for mentors. Anybody in their apprentice year can come. Anybody from Level 4 on can come for help through certification, and then they can come back once they're certified to help mentor the others. I think that is supportive of the whole community. That's been ongoing for years here.

The whole community gets involved. We share, like we put on a health fair. We get people to volunteer to work with that. It's just been wonderful. We do focus on the work that needs to be reviewed, either for certification or for Level 5. People have great input, and they do it in a very kind way. We have a lot of fun. People share stories. It's just great. It's really worked well here. Like I say, it's ongoing. We're getting a snow storm, so I have to cancel tomorrow's meeting. We're going to get six to ten inches.

The other thing with community is having people come back and be helpers. I always encourage that, especially in Level 4. When they are in their apprentice years to come back and be a helper in classes. I think that is very beneficial, because so much is covered in each level that everybody who has come back as a helper has always given great feedback about how much they got out of it.

When I started, I wanted to be a helper all the time. It helps you to solidify the information. There is always something new to take away. Just being in the energy the whole time. I think it's nice for the students. I usually have three helpers in every class. Occasionally I'll let one or two more come in. We have a bigger area now. Our conference center at the hospital that I use, they built a new conference center, so we have more space. It's really nice.

Another thing, in the beginning I spent a lot of time learning about starting a new business. I went to the small business administration, and had classes in the area. I went to the classes and all. Sharon Robbins and I actually started what is called the business council. I don't remember what year. I think we presented in '93. That was an interest of mine was to help people start their businesses. We did two years back then, up in a break-out session at conference. The first one, I know, was called "Profit from Your Passion." It was all kind of nitty-gritty. Anne Cathcart did self-care. We had various people speaking about the different parts of it. That was something I was always interested in. It's nice to see the way that's developed through HTPA and the support that's there now. We only did it annually at conference.

Janet came up to me, it's another Janet story too, after that presentation, the first one, and said "I love your handouts."

Which basically is just nitty-gritty stuff. It's in Level 4. It's been revised and edited a little bit over the years. She said, "May I put this in our 4/5 notebook?"

I was really pleased. That's the only thing I have ever had published.

# Renata Maniaci
## MPH, HTCP/I

### Introduction

I met Renata at an instructor gathering. Her enthusiasm for Healing Touch is infectious. Her stories come from the heart. I just knew I had to add her to our list of pioneers in Healing Touch. She lives in Washington DC. That's not an easy city in which to start an integrative medicine practice. She has managed to build a practice and is teaching Healing Touch classes there.

Renata is younger than most of the Healing Touch instructors. I think that is one of the things that make her special. She also reaches out to heal a part of our population that has endured a lot of pain and suffering due to prejudice and misunderstanding of what it is like to be a member of the LGBTQ (lesbian, gay, bi-sexual, transvestite, questioning) community. She has great courage and I honor her for her work.

### Interview

*What got you started? Why did you take a Healing Touch class/*

The year was 2013 and I was getting a lot of information from my guidance that I needed to look more in depth into energy medicine. I don't know how else to explain it other than that. Of course, Reiki being the most recognizable name at the moment, I found and enrolled in a Reiki Level 1 course which I took near the end of 2013.

It was good. It allowed me to feel things, see things, but that particular instructor couldn't answer some of my more scientific based questions. I was coming from a strong academic background. I had graduated from Columbia University in public health, with my master's in public health earlier that year. I had been involved in research for the previous decade. I was really left brained.

I wanted to understand how energy was working. I thought I wasn't going to continue with Reiki, but I was really interested in this energy medicine thing.

I had experienced Healing Touch before. I am from Wisconsin originally. The first time I ever experienced Healing Touch was with Jerry Becker, who's in Milwaukee. I remember having a really positive experience during that. So I looked up Healing Touch.

I went to Nancy Lester's Level 1. Immediately, that weekend changed my whole life. It was January of 2014. During that weekend I was like, "This is what I need to do." I remember I called my mom after the class and I said, "I think need to quit my job and go into Healing Touch."

*What was it in this class that really hooked you?*

Everything. There was no part of that class in the philosophy behind Healing Touch that I didn't innately agree with. It's the principles of energy medicine.

Every single one of those, it was like, "Yes!" All of those made sense. Everything else in the class was also amazing and I could just see it. I could see in front of me, "This is how I want to live my life." Not only that, but it felt like I was remembering how to do it, not learning how to do it. I had never experienced that before. I am avid learner. I like being in school and academia. This was like, "Wow. I know how to do this. I am remembering how to do this." That was a really profound feeling for me.

I did Level 1 in January, Level 2 in February, Level 3 in March, and Level 4 in May. The reason I could do that is because I literally quit my job and I devoted all of my time to working on friends and family, whoever would let me put my hands on them.

I did feel ready to go to Level 2, even with just a month, because I put hands on more people than probably a lot of other students may have done, even though they may have had a year in between both levels. I just kept going from there. It felt right.

*How are you using it in a practice now?*

It's my primary modality. I have a holistic wellness practice right here in Washington DC. It's called Hana Healing Arts. Hana is my middle name. Eighty per cent of my clients come in either for Healing Touch or another thing that I do called Spiritual Response Therapy (SRT). Often I mix them because they're very complimentary. SRT is not hands on body work. It works with consciousness and you're more talking and clearing things using charts, and then I go to the table and use Healing Touch. When clients are on the table I am only using Healing Touch. It's not a mixture of on the table modalities. All my clients today were Healing Touch this morning. And I think all my clients tomorrow are Healing Touch.

I am also a Level 1 instructor, a new Level 1 instructor. I had my solo last year, about this time. I won't lie. I've been having trouble filling my classes. I had to cancel the last couple. I think the new price range has something to do with it, because that was in April and

January. I also teach Intro for two hours. I love it. I love teaching the Intro class and I joke that the Level 1 class is like year one at Hogwarts, if you're a Harry Potter fan. It's mind blowing. I really enjoy teaching both of those classes, Intro for two hours and Level 1.

I hold a practice group once a month for my students. That's been really great. I am on the board of the Healing Touch Worldwide Foundation. This must be about a year and a half into my three year term. I have been on the ethics committee for the last two years.

*How did you go about building a practice?*

It came gradually. Honestly, as soon as I made the decision of I'm leaving the nine to five public health world, and checking into holistic health and energy medicine, it was like the whole universe conspired to support and help me do that. It was a gradual move.

I was going through the first part of the program, where I was an apprentice for that year. The latter part of that year I also applied to going to massage school, which was a part time, eighteen month program. I was learning how to do massage and I was giving energy medicine. I was seeing as many friends and friends of friends as I could during that whole year.

Sometime around the beginning of 2015 I was seeing people out of my small studio apartment. They were all people that I knew, you know, friends and friends of friends. From the early part of 2015 I was getting really good at Healing Touch, because I had been doing it solid for a year. I had seen a lot of people in that time. Plus I was in my apprenticeship, so I needed to get my hands on as many people as I could.

Around the midway point of 2015, I decided I had seen enough people and it was time to find an office space. I was able to find an office space right down the street from me. I was sharing an office space, so it was only a couple of hours a week. It was a really gradual thing while I was doing my apprenticeship. I was still in massage school. I would see clients and charge a little, not a lot, like whatever apprentices charge.

I went to Level 5 in May of that year. It was just all very gradual. I kept adding on hours at this office because there was time and space there. It was very natural.

I was also, at the time, seeing clients at a holistic health center across town called Freed Bodyworks. I still work there once a week when I am not in my office. It works for me because I love the community. It's an amazing place to see clients. It serves a lot of the LGBTQ community in the city.

I was working at another place just doing massage while I was graduating from massage school later. So I had my hands in different places in the city, just building up my skills and my practices. But now being 2018, I have had my office for three years. I am in my office down this street most of the time, Wednesday, Thursday, Friday, Sunday. I see remote clients on Mondays and other times if I need to.

*Do you have a favorite healing story?*

I have lots of them. The first one that came to mind, and this might be interesting because I am kind of like on the next generation side. When I was at Level 4, which I also took with Nancy, it was a really profound experience. In Level 4 we get our partners for all four days that we're there. You're just working with them. This came to mind because it was the first really super profound experience and I have had many since then. Since it is the first, it is the one that came to mind.

I think it's interesting, because I do believe that when there's multiple people in the room doing healing work, the vibration is raised. You have a higher vibration than you normally could do, or at least a student could, alone in their own space working by themselves with just one other person. The energy was so high, at one point where I was working on my partner - I'm a feeler. I am what they would call clairsentient (ability to sense emotions and feelings) and claircognizant (inner knowing about the present or future). I feel things and I know things. I am not usually a seer, I don't usually hear things, or taste things, or smell things.

For this particular thing I was working, or the intention was to clear some fearsome childhood stuff from my partner who is probably around your age. She'd been holding on to a lot of stuff for many, many years: dynamics with parents and the ways she had been raised and such. The energy was really, really high and I was doing chelation or I was doing etheric template clearing. I could see. I started to see wisps of white energy just leaving her. That was just ready to leave her. I was just in it. I could see it. It was so high vibration.

I think what made it more interesting and memorable is that two things happened. She reacted in two different ways that I've seen very little since then. You know how people release in many different ways? You know how people twitch? Some people burp, some people yawn, some people cry. There's a million different ways to release.

She started laughing out loud. She could not stop laughing. It was a little inappropriate because, remember, there were like ten other people in the room, also doing work. We were kind of getting glares and stuff. But she was releasing. That was her way to release because, and we talked about this afterward, she wasn't allowed to laugh as a kid. That was fascinating.

This had to do with her mother and the tension growing up with that. At one point during the session, she smelled her favorite meal that her mother used to make her. It was a very distinctive smell and she smelled it perfectly while we were working. This was while I am seeing all this stuff, you know, come off her. It was really profound with the laughter and the smells. I mean because, those were things I don't see that often, or my clients don't experience, or they at least don't share that experience with me that often. Smells and tastes are always rather interesting.

We're still close. We've stayed in each other's lives since then which was May of 2014. She lives in another state. She describes it as one of the most profound healing sessions that she's ever had. That obviously stuck with me. From there, there's been so many.

*What do you see for yourself in the future with Healing Touch? Where would you like to go from here?*

It's an interesting question, Linnie. I'll be honest. You can choose what you want to put in the book, obviously. It's changed the last few years. As much as a year and a half ago, I could see myself doing something like Cynthia does or did. Her role is changing a lot right now.

Cause I love Healing Touch. I believe in it. I think it is so important. I do. I think it is so important for the country, for the world. I think if everyone took Level 1 the whole world would be different. I really believe in it and I love it enough to volunteer for things like the foundation and the ethics committee.

There's this big thing that I am trying to understand about myself. I am trying to bring in what's my guidance for me not being able to fill my classes this past half a year. Where's my guidance there? Where am I supposed to be heading? The last week or so I have been thinking about, I love teaching don't get me wrong there, but am I supposed to be teaching the full Healing Touch Level 1's, or am I supposed to be that spark that gets people interested in Healing Touch in general?

I am still pondering that question and I am kind of realizing that I might be really interested in pursuing a class about self care for people who weren't necessarily ready to go into becoming a practitioner and working on other people. What they would really need first is to get themselves in line before they can even look externally. We have so many good tools in Healing Touch to do that.

Some people are getting stopped at the price tag of a full Level 1 course which focuses on other people. It's self care too, but you're learning how to do it on other people. This is something really recent, Linnie. This isn't something that I have been focusing on for the last three years. This is coming in now.

Maybe expanding the already rich resources we have around self care in the healing Touch community for people who need to do that first before they can even think about doing it with other people. Something around that. I love the community.

*I like what you're saying very much. I have a mother who has dementia and I belong to a support group. It suddenly dawned on me, a class like what you're talking about in self care is so needed for the care givers. The need is huge.*

And so many other care givers too. I mean, dementia of course, but there's people who take care of somebody who has cancer in their family or some other illness. You know what? There is a curriculum or there was a curriculum. I've been talking to Sue Walker recently about revamping a self care, shorter Healing Touch for self care, class that is more cost effective for a lot of folks. It's only a one day class. It's only five or six hours. Something like that would probably be super useful.

That's one thing I have been thinking about and making moves towards. The other part of it, and you might have gotten a little of it out of the instructor gathering, I don't remember everything that I said there, but making this program more appealing to a wider range of people.

*I heard you. You really opened my eyes on that idea. I sing in a church choir that's one third gay community. I've just finished another book and I have dedicated it to two gay men. There's something very special about the gay community that I just love.*

I, obviously, am a member of the LGBT community and I love that community. It's as simple as we receive the people of who we are. If we are mostly white women, that's who we're going to attract. That's just what makes sense. That's the vibration thing. That's the energy we're putting out and that's the energy we're going to get. This is so much bigger than that demographic of people. I want us to shift our vibration so that other people feel welcome. So other people are excited and can see themselves, because I - I could talk about this for a long time and I don't want to say anything that is - It's just that there's more room. There's more room for more people.

Sometimes when we've been in a way and we're super comfortable with the way that things are, we assume that that will be comfortable for everybody else, too. But it's not like that all the time. If I were a person of color looking in on the Healing Touch instructor meeting, there is hardly anybody else that would look like me, if anybody. We can't imagine what that's like. We can try to imagine what that's like, but we don't actually know what that feels like. We just don't.

It's nothing that Healing Touch is doing wrong. It's just there's more room for growth. There's more room for accessibility. There's more room for people who are on the outside to look and see themselves reflected, so that they are like, "Oh, I could be comfortable here. I think I'll meet people who might share some of my experiences."

I think what we're missing right now with our advertising and our marketing is we're missing the story of people who aren't that one vibration that we all seem to cover a lot of. I think that the people of color, the more men, and the more young, and the otherly-abled people. And non-American people that you can get in the book the better.

There's going to be more, but we have to do the work. We have to do the work to shift into a higher level of vibration that is more open and accessible to other people. We have to make ourselves a little bit more uncomfortable, so that new people can be a little bit more comfortable to commit. That's growth. That's what happens. That's the biggest growth that any of us will ever experience and certainly the fastest. I speak for myself. It's when you feel uncomfortable, you grow and you shift quickly, because "Oh man, I'm uncomfortable. I'm learning a lot right now."

I think that it's natural to avoid change if it might be a little uncomfortable or maybe we don't know how to do it correctly. But the truth is, there is no way to do anything perfectly. I think Healing Touch Program could grow astronomically in different realms and different communities if we took a little bit harder look at how and where and who we're advertising and marketing to, and all of those things. I think it could shift and I think it could grow and hit more people. Which I think is what Janet Mentgen always wanted. She wanted this in every home and every school. I want that, too.

You mentioned a desire to teach Healing Touch to a gang. I think it would do great things. The first thing I would think about is that most gangs are men of color and you're a white woman. How do we train a man of color to become the instructor so that that person could go into that community and teach the class? He'd be a person that these people would automatically feel more comfortable to be around, and they would be more willing to listen because he is of their race and of their gender.

A white woman going in to teach gangs is one thing. A black man or a man of color going in, it's a different vibration. They're probably going to be more open to it. That's why we've got to get more people in. We've got to get and train them. We've got to encourage diversity. We've got to train instructors. We've got to encourage students of color. We need to encourage any of our Healing Touch Certified Practitioners or Healing Touch Practitioners who are of color, who are of the younger generation, and who are men.

We need to encourage those people to become instructors, not just practitioners. Those people need to be tapped on the shoulder and say, "Hey. I think you'd make a really good instructor." We need to do that more often.

*I get it. I need to find a man of color and have him do it. I have no trouble attracting men in my classes. I have an engineering background. I am used to that kind of language. But I am also aware that I speak 1960's English. My publishers have made me very aware of it. Language that is normal for me, is not necessarily of your generation.*

That could be too.

*I mean the expressions I use. For example, I am fond of saying 'Oh good grief." Well that's not really your generation language.*

You have a different experience. You grew up in an entirely different time than I did, you know. That's also a thing. It's a shared experience. You lived at the same time that this thing happened. You've gone through experiences I'll never understand, that I wasn't alive for. I can't possibly understand what it was like during that time.

That's where it comes in. The more diversity we can have in our instructors, I feel, the more diversity we can have in the people that are attracted to and come to Healing Touch.

*Right on girl. I'm right behind you. Is there anything else you would like to talk about? What would you say to a student who is reading this or a prospective student might be better?*

I guess I would say it' one of the most profound healing and spiritual journeys that you can go on. It's worth every penny. Every minute in class is worth way more than what you are actually paying for it.

Even if your journey might take you all the way through all the levels or it might just take you through Level 1. Level 1 was the most profound experiences I ever had. But if I didn't continue going through the program, my life would have profoundly changed just by taking Level. No student will be making a mistake. You'll not regret taking this program. If you can be open enough in your heart to learn and to pick up whatever you can, it has the potential to be a life changing experience.

I also just want to throw out there that I have been so well supported by elders in this community and folks who have been in the program for decades longer than I have. I want to make it known just how much I appreciate everyone who came before me. It makes me tear up. There's a lot of really good stuff in this program. And people.

I wouldn't be who I am today without Cynthia, and without Nancy Lester and Jerry Becker who were both my dual mentors. I asked for both of them to be my mentors during my apprenticeship. And for other people who have stepped in along the way and given me amazing guidance. Sue Hovland and the list goes on. Everybody at the foundation and everybody at the ethics committee.

I had a really beautifully profound experience at the instructor gathering and felt very welcomed in a place where I kind of felt I would be out of place. It was a really lovely experience. All of it.

# Tim McConville
## HTCP/I

**Introduction**

Tim's devotion to Healing Touch Program shows in his work. He teaches Levels 1 through 4. He is a Qualified Mentor and co-teaches the mentor training classes. He has been on the Healing Touch Certification board for a long time, just recently resigning. He has a thriving practice working both in hospitals and long term care facilities. He is a joy to talk to. I love his enthusiasm.

**Interview**

*What I would like to know from you is how you came to take a Healing Touch class and, once you were in the class, what hooked you to continue taking the classes?*

At that time I was doing environmental engineering. I had an engineering career for many years. I was a closet mystic. I had read literally every book in the library on healing back in the '80s. I did some things with healing work in some meditation groups I attended. But, you know, in the engineering community there's not a lot of people like me. There's probably more than we know, but they're all hiding like I was.

In the '90s I took some Reiki. The path was kind of convoluted. I look back and just sort of laugh. I was doing some volunteer work in a child nursery. I found that fulfilling and was interested in doing more volunteer stuff.

A local hospital, Abbott Hospital in Minneapolis, started an integrated medicine program. I heard about it and for some reason, I wanted to volunteer there. When I look back, I go, "Really? How did that happen?" I called them up and I asked what it would take if I could volunteer with that new program that had sort of piqued my interest.

They said, "Well, you could take Healing Touch and do Healing Touch as a volunteer."

I said, "That sounds like fun."

I signed up for a Healing Touch class. I fell in love immediately. It was just like I felt like I was at home - that same phrase you hear again and again. It felt much more like home, much more so than Reiki did. I kind of dabbled in Reiki, but Healing Touch I just fell in love with and jumped in with both feet. I started doing HT every chance I got.

I called them up and said, "I've taken my class and I would like to volunteer." And they said, "Well, you have to be Level 4."

I said, "Okay. I'll see you in a year."

In the next year, I took levels 1 through 4. I did start volunteering at that hospital right after Level 4. I volunteered there for probably three or four years working primarily in the long-term rehab floor, but also all over the hospital. I continued my floor volunteer work until I started instructing. I started teaching Level 1's in the hospital. The way they were paying me as an instructor, they weren't taking anything. I didn't think that was fair. I wanted to give them back something. I said, "I'll volunteer a hundred hours for their research department for integrated medicine". They had a research department with a dozen people just for integrated medicine. I volunteered my hundred hours. At the end of that they said, "No. We want to keep you." I ended up working there in a paid research position for about three years as well. That gave me some good experience with research. That hospital went with the other program, so I stopped teaching there

That's what got me interested. In some ways I think it was this odd desire to volunteer that hooked me into Healing Touch. Obviously, it was what I was supposed to be doing. That volunteer stint at the hospital gave me a lot of healthcare experience both on the floor and in the lab.

Once I was in Healing Touch, I immersed myself in it. In my year of mentorship, the work just came easily. Even though I was working a full-time plus job as an engineering manager I found time to do the homework and had double the number of client sessions needed for Level 5. It took me just over two years to get certified after my Level 1 class. After certification people kept telling me, "You should teach." And I said, "That'll never happen." And then I started to hear these voices in my head saying, "You need to teach."

Eventually I listened to the voices and signed up for instructor's training. I love instructing!

*That's quite a story. What do you do in Healing Touch besides instructing? You're in the mentor training program aren't you?*

I have a client practice and I do a lot of mentoring. Right now my wife Pam and I have a mentor group of more than a dozen students. I teach levels 1 through 4 now. I teach the Mentor Training. We have been talking about teaching Level 6. I have helped with it before and would enjoy teaching with the new instructors. I've also been on the certification board, for I don't know, a long time. I really enjoy reviewing the work for certification and renewals. I think it makes me a better mentor. I'm just resigning from the certification board. A lot of family things happened this year and I've got so much going on that I need to shift priorities and let someone else take that over.

*Tell me more about the mentorship program.*

The mentorship program, Janna really got that going. I think all the kudos need to go to Janna for that work. I probably took the first one or the second mentor training class with Janna. I started helping her with it almost immediately. Co-taught with Janna for a few years. Later Franny and Dawn also joined as Janna has stepped away. I think she had too much on her plate. It's the three of us now who are teaching the mentor training course. I think it's a wonderful thing.

The course has really paid off in consistency and overall quality of the mentoring that students get. I wear a lot of hats. In my certification hat, I could see the shift in quality of what's coming into the certification process. Case studies were better and there were less problems with the certification packets. Once we started doing the mentor training, you could see it shift the quality of work products coming in Level 5. As a reader in those classes I could see who got good mentoring and who did not.

It was always amazing. You'd get people in Level 5 saying, "My mentor said this." And another would say, "My mentor said that." There was this huge spread of what mentors were teaching their mentees. It caused lots of anguish, I think, in Level 5. It's not completely gone away, but it's considerably better than it was in the old days, I think.

The overall quality of the program has gone up because we have a much more commonality with what mentors are being trained with. Overall for the whole process, it's been a huge improvement.

## Tim McConville

*I think it's terrific. I'm all for it. I became a qualified mentor long before I took the mentor class, which I just audited, because as a qualified mentor I didn't think I needed to take the class. I still wanted to know what was going on in the mentoring class and I am glad I did. I usually pop in and check on it at least once a year.*

That's a good thing to do. I grandfathered in to it as a qualified mentor right away too. But I really think I had just gotten enough students through the process to qualify. It was nice that I could be grandfathered in. I didn't have to pay for the class. I was able to audit. But then I just thought it was a really great thing. I was working with Janna on certification at that time, so. she invited me to come join and teach with her.

*Do you have a favorite healing story?*

There are so many. I think one of my favorite ones, and I couldn't tell it for a number of years without tearing up. My wife Pam had a good friend whose father died but been revived. He had choked on a steak and suffocated. By time the paramedics came in and revived him, he had been dead for a while, so it would have been better if they let him go. He ended up transported to the hospital, "alive" but, essentially brain dead.

I was in a meditation group that night. I intuitively sensed her call for help while I was in the midst of my meditation. During my meditation, I imagined going to the hospital and did a chakra spread and worked with him. The next day, her friend actually called and invited me to come out to the hospital. I didn't say, "Well, I was there last night." I went to the hospital and at that point he was intubated and on all this life support stuff to keep him going. In Minnesota, if you revive somebody, you have to keep them on life support for at least seventy-two hours.

The families are in this watch period, for seventy-two hours, which is just a huge stress for the family. Things were going badly. His IV lines were all backing up and going septic. They were going to have to do some more aggressive things just to keep that body going.

My wife's friend, who was a nurse, was afraid to touch him. I talked her in to going in with me and we did a chakra connection, the two-on-one. That allowed her to feel like she could actually touch her father. It bridged that gap just by inviting her to touch. That alone made a big impact on her.

When I walked in that room, I sensed his spirit was not in his body. He was off somewhere. I couldn't even sense him whatsoever. The body seemed kind of lifeless. After the two on one Chakra Connection, I followed with the chakra spread while she watched. At the end of the session his spirit was back in the body. His body started functioning better, the IV lines cleared, and everything was fine. He did not return to consciousness

Just as we were finishing, the nurse walked into the room. She looked at him and said, "I don't know what just happened, I've never seen this before."

His spirit stayed with the body keeping things going until they pulled the plug. Then he left. He died as soon as they took him off life support. But it changed the dynamics of the whole family in a pretty unique way. The impact through that family system was amazing. Obviously, the patient died. But it was beautiful the way it came back in such a healing way for the whole family. At the funeral they were immensely grateful.

*What would you like to see for the future of Healing Touch?*

I think Healing Touch is a marvelous foundational program. I would like to see, just like Janet's dream, Healing Touch taught in every school. Everyone ought to know this stuff. They should have taught us what we're doing, all in kindergarten. It's part of who we are as a human being. I would like energy awareness knowledge spread everywhere and be a part of health care systems.

Part of what I am curious about, is how do we add to the system? I see healing Touch as a wonderful foundation, but it's not the end all. There's more things to learn that go on top of the Healing Touch foundation. Those foundations were installed in the 1980s and clarified a bit since, but not radically changed. The world has energetically changed, so more gets added on top of what Janet was originally teaching as the certification program? I think there is a lot more and the world's evolving. We're evolving too.

Energies are different now, than they were when she was teaching back in the beginning. People's core stars aren't where they were in the pictures any more. We need to be doing this higher frequency work. It would be neat if it could be part of that, or some adjunct. I am not sure how it all works out. We need to keep moving as the world evolves. It would be good to have a greater expansion of the work as it's not stagnant.

If you look, everybody's doing more than what was taught in Healing Touch.

*For an introductory program, it's the best I have found anywhere.*

I think so, too. As an instructor I get people who are from all sorts of different modalities. When I first started teaching, and I used to be a little bit nervous, because I would get people in my classes who come in with five or six different modalities, masters of this or that and the other thing. And I'm thinking, "What am I going to teach them?" It turns out those people often got the most out of the classes.

The other things I was finding as a generalization, some of the other modalities are good, but in general I don't think they teach the fundamentals as well as we do. I don't think they are grounded properly. I don't think they know how to manage their energies very well, as a generalization. Obviously it varies with individuals. I think Healing Touch has the best basic foundational program of energetics out there.

*I agree totally. Anything else you would like to say about your work or Healing Touch?*
I think it' been amazing. The world keeps unfolding in absolute brilliance. I love teaching, of watching people open and expand and grow. Part of my job is to wake everybody up. I'm an alarm clock for the universe.

*What would you say to a prospective student? Somebody who is on the fence.*
I would say that in many ways this is the most valuable thing you can actually do for yourself. Its value is far beyond the money you're paying for it. Our spiritual wellbeing should be the most important value in our life, yet we seldom spend time on it. Compared to other things in life, the few thousands we would spend to learn Healing Touch is hardly anything. What else can you do for that kind of money that could profoundly change your life? Where else can you do that kind of value?

*Even with just the Level 1 class you can do that.*
Yeah. For five hundred bucks.

*Which is cheaper than a lot of insurance payments.*
Absolutely. or if you look at how much people pay for therapies. The list goes on and on. And the things people buy to supposedly better their life. People keep pouring money into things

that don't help them. I don't think there's a better value on the planet. I think everybody can benefit from it. With all the people I have interfaced with, hundreds of them, I see so many beautiful stories on just how people shift at their core and end up with a better quality of life. Happier and more joyful. It's so beautiful. It's very fulfilling work.

Pioneers in Healing Touch

# Janna Moll
## HTCP/I. MSN, LMT

### Introduction

Janna was my mentor, so naturally I have great affection for her. She is a fabulous mentor and has done considerable work in writing and offering the Mentor Training classes and in helping to write the Qualified Mentor guidelines, as well as HTP's transfer policy – among other things. Uniformity among the mentors has been needed for a very long time and this course has successfully increased our mentors' skills.

Janna was instrumental in bringing about the National Commission for Certifying Agencies (NCCA) accreditation. She jumped through a lot of hoops, just learning about accreditation. It is her persistence that has brought us to where we are today. We owe her a debt of gratitude.

Janna is also the developer, founder, and owner of Energy Medicine Specialists. She teaches advanced classes in energy medicine. Two of my favorites are "Advanced Chakra Diagnosis and Treatment" and "Advanced Hara Diagnosis and Treatment". Janna is always very up-to-date on the latest scientific research and approaches to energy work.

If you ever have an opportunity to attend one of her Level 1 (or other) classes, go. It is well worth spending the time to take or retake the class. (Or be a helper.)

**Interview**

*What was your role in getting us started to become accredited?*
When was it that Janet died? 2006? *(September 15, 2005.)*
A lot of things changed for HTP in April 2006 and later that summer, in August or September, Dale and I made a presentation to Bill Mentgen. Cynthia was there as well, and possibly Lynn Mentgen or Lisa.

We made a presentation on why the NCCA accreditation was important to HTP. We showed a power point on the benefits, the trends in oversight – especially in healthcare. We presented this highest stakes credential, because it was the upcoming, accepted standard in health care in testing.

They appeared very interested. But it took another, I'm thinking, two years - two and a half years, before they actually signed with us as consultants. They didn't go for some of the things that we recommended, like using exterior testing through Pearson testing. Eventually we were contracted to begin the process with them as consultants.

For the first year or so after Janet's passing, Energy Medicine Credentialing was established. We planned to be the credentialing agency for the field of Energy Medicine. As we got more deeply into this process we realized that we couldn't do this, because we already owned course work. You can't be a credentialing agency if you own course work! We couldn't credential somebody else's course work (program) under that situation, so we decided to become consultants after spending a year learning credentialing.

What we presented to Healing Touch Program, was how important it was to be self-policing with the trend toward legality of touch laws coming in at the state level, which started to peak right about then. With industries that are self-policing, the government leaves them to oversight within their industry. That's why psychotherapy and massage therapy are so regulated, because they aren't self-policing. They do not have national organizations that provide oversight – or they didn't at the time when serious issues came to light around ethics, appropriateness of touch, etc. We learned that being credentialed under the highest level of scrutiny in healthcare provided the self-policing process we desired. We also felt that achieving this oversight would ultimately provide recognition as a full occupation for our practitioners aligned with healthcare.

It took HTP a while to be able to move forward with the project. Energy Medicine Specialists consulted to them for about a year and half. Eventually we parted ways and Chris Gordon took it over himself. Up until that point we had done a validation study, looked at our domains of knowledge, identified subject matter experts, and oversaw the writing of the initial test questions. That's what happened under our watch. Finally in December of 2013 they got that accreditation for the credential HTCP.

Before 2006, Janet was at the helm. If she didn't like it, it hit the highway. Ultimately, people who were invested in having Healing Touch as a hobby or an occupation, were to come round into Janet's way of thinking. She made some mistakes along the way. I think she was a reluctant business owner. I think she just wanted to do the work and that's why she said, "Do the work."

I think, HTP has been charmed, nobody could question it. It has survived through this intensely challenging time-in spite of certain actions. One person owns a company, and you don't like the decisions they're making, but it's their company and I think that's why we're in a lawsuit currently. It was, literally, Janet Mentgen's business. She was the head of Healing Touch International. She was the head of the Colorado Center for Healing Touch. Then the business name change to Healing Touch Program came just before her death. Literally, she called the shots. She could have sold the business and she decided instead to leave it to her children. It's been fairly charmed against all odds. Before her death, I think there was a tighter scrutiny and a tighter holding of the reins.

*Who was the one who came up with the idea of accreditation in the first place?*

Dale Ferg. Dale and I. We had to build a board of directors and everything. We had everybody, basically, who was anybody in the field of energy medicine on our board of directors. We were very excited, but in the end, we couldn't do it. We disbanded and went to the consulting side. I was talking with several disciplines about accreditation and when HTP was interested, we thought, "Here's an easy one. I know the program really well, inside and out. I know everybody who's anybody in Healing Touch. This'll be our first step out into consulting". Truly, it couldn't have been harder. If we had started with a different discipline, we might still be consultants.

*What got you personally started in energy medicine? And why did you pick Healing Touch?*

I started by training with an individual instructor. I was taking some local classes in meditation and self-development in Nashville, Tennessee, when I lived there. My girlfriend dragged me to everything. One night she dragged me to this evening where this guy who had just moved from California was going to 'channel'. John

LeMay, had been actually searched out in the US by an African Sangoma for training in healing. He had training in fifty different energy disciplines. He was a very powerful healer. This evening when I went for the channeling, I was across the room from him. He channeled Archangel Michael. I didn't really want to be there, but the love in that room! It was so thick, you could cut it with a knife.

I said to myself, "I want more of what he has." I studied with him for a number of months maybe nine months. We met weekly at his house and he channeled for a group of about eight or ten of us. After about nine months, he kept three of us on to teach us hands-on healing.

When he was done with the two hour training he said," Go out and do it. You know everything you need to know."

I said to myself, "I don't think so."

It was at that point that my friend, who dragged me to see him in the first place said, "You know, I see a Healing Touch practitioner regularly and you might want to go see her and receive treatment yourself."

So I did. It turned out she was one of the local Healing Touch Level 1 instructors in Nashville. This was in 1995. After a few months of receiving HT (with some very profound results) she suggested I might be interested in taking a class.

I thought, "Well, sure. I know I don't know enough." I was in school full time, so I got Healing Touch for a hundred bucks a weekend. I thought, "Well, yeah. Why not?"

I went to the Level 1 class. Back then Level 1 was a Friday night, Saturday and Sunday. This Level 1 was a large class with some thirty people in the class. Friday night we would go around the circle and hand scan heads. I remember I put my hands in someone's energy and I pulled them out right away.

I said to the woman, "Have you had a recent death in the family?"

She said, "Why yes, I have."

The instructor said, "Now, rotate to the next person."

I thought, "Okay. That was weird."

I put my hands in the next person's energy and again, I pulled them out right away. I said to the person, "Does the word 'acidic' mean anything to you?"

He said, "Yes, it does. I'm a nutritionist." And he ran out and got some carrot juice to drink.

I thought, "These people are weird, but I 'm probably just as weird."

That was about all I got out of the Level 1 class, other than learning the techniques, of course. And getting on the table and receiving.

I continued receiving Healing Touch sessions after the class. About six months later, my practitioner said, "I know you didn't get anything out of Level 1, but you might be interested in taking a Level 2 class."

I thought, "I don't know how she knows I didn't get anything out of Level 1. I never told her that. Okay, I'll go to Level 2."

I felt like I was starting to learning more in Level 2. I never had an intention of being a practitioner of HT. My goal for taking HT classes was simply my own healing. I took levels 1-3 in Nashville.

I graduated with my undergrad degree in December of '95. As a family, we were transferred to Australia for my husband's work. One of the benefits of taking HT classes for me was in starting to build a community of like-minded people. In order to have a community like I was building in Nashville, I decided to hook up with some Healing Touch people in Australia. I signed up for Level 4 and then went on a month long tour with Mary Jo Bulbrook. Janet

Mentgen was on the tour as well. I also attended the Holistic Nursing Conference, took AP1 (*Advanced Practice 1*), and then traveled and studied with the Aborigines and Maori (the traditional indigenous peoples of Australia and New Zealand).

We traveled for a month. We did interactive studies with the Aborigines. At Thanksgiving, we went over to New Zealand to study with the Maori. That trip was pretty overwhelming and definitely life changing.

In January of 1996, I was told by my mentor, who was the only certified person in my town that I was on a path towards certification. I thought Level 4 was just another weekend of getting together and giving/receiving treatments, albeit a long one! It wasn't my intent to get certified. She hauled me to community fairs to start doing my community service work. I begged, borrowed and stole anyone I could get on my table.

In three months I completed all the Level 5 homework and also my certification application. I flew over to the U.S. to do Level 5 in Denver and a week later, I attended teacher's training (Level 6) with my mentor. I got approval to do that so quickly, because they had so few instructors in Australia and had great need.

At the time, there was this ugly corporate takeover happening. Mary Jo had taken Healing Touch to Australia and New Zealand. She had the business set up to keep most of the funds in the country. Her executive director for Australia was Rosalee Van Aken. Rosalee changed the names on the bank accounts and took over Healing Touch Australia. She set up a new ownership and membership organization. All of this was done without Mary Jo's knowledge. (This is my understanding of what happened, of course.) There was a real showdown happening in Australia.

When my mentor and I came to the US, me for Level 5, and both of us taking teacher's training, we had a meeting with Janet. We said, "Look. You've got to back Mary Jo. We've been told we won't get our classes. This was Mary Jo's business and there's been this ugly corporate takeover." Janet backed Rosalee. Australia fell apart, big time.

In Australia, I had to travel the country from coast to coast to coast to get my classes. I could only get them when Mary Jo and Donna Duff were in Australia offering classes, because Rosalee wouldn't let us in.

We were told, by Rosalee, that we weren't going to get any of the teaching opportunities that we needed for teacher's training because we had sided with Mary Jo. It became really ugly. I did certify as a practitioner while in Australia, but I finally certified as an instructor once I was back in the U.S.

While I was in Level 5 Healing Touch, I was presenting my case study. Classes were here in Colorado. What was common was, Janet would come and other instructors would come by (as HTP was headquartered here), and sit in on the Level 5 class. They'd listen to case studies, critique them, and connect with the students, creating community.

I was literally, presenting my case study, when Janet walked in and sat down, and listened to my case study presentation. Once I finished, she got up and went over to the table, and twelve people worked on her. She'd been hit by lightning on the way to class. I think there was this trauma logged in Janet with regard to me, hearing the sound of my voice, having this connection through Mary Jo, etc. I believe there were all these things that happened over the years that aligned us with that trauma.

There were some really interesting occurrences that happened around that time. It's only in hindsight that I realized that on the tour, Mary Jo and Janet were not getting along very well. When it came time to back somebody in Australia, Janet backed Rosalee. From that point, until the end of Janet's life, Mary Jo and Janet were struggling to get along. I think I got in the middle of it, because of the relationship of teaching for Mary Jo, telling Janet what she should do, being outspoken, etc.. All those things that an older, more wiser, more mature person would know better than to do. (HAHA)

I certified as an instructor in '99. I taught ten Level 1 classes and had a big student network, and I also taught for Mary Jo Bulbrook. I was senior faculty for her for five years and held her certification as well. I then trained to teach Level 2 Healing Touch in Wisconsin. I proceeded to teach ten Level 2's and I started asking to teach Level 3.

Janet was pretty picky about who she let teach above Level 1 and 2. She kept telling me, "no. no. no" .Once I quit teaching for Mary Jo, Janet said, "Now you can teach Level 3."

I trained to teach Level 3 under Steve Anderson. Janet was undergoing chemo at the time. She would come by the class during parts of the weekend. She cornered me in the hallway and said, "Now. You aren't going to be teaching for Mary Jo any more, are you?"

I said, "No." She said, "Okay. You can teach for me."

Janet died in 2005 and Lisa Mentgen Gordon took the helm. I became very active in HTP, serving as the first Ethics Chairperson, writing policy and procedures, serving as a certification reviewer and working with Cynthia Hutchison, the program director. I finally got approval to train to teach Level 4. Cynthia was given an opportunity to camp and raft down the Grand Canyon on a lottery system. She called me up and said, "Can you take my Level 5 in Chicago?" This was a scheduled combined offering of Level 4 and 5.

I said, "Well, I will do it if I get to teach the Level 5 class."

She said, "It's okay with me. Okay it with Lisa."

I talked to Lisa and she said, "No. You're not trained to teach Level 5."

I said, "Lisa, I won't go if I can't teach Level 5. "

She said, "You've got to go through the training."

I said, "Lisa, look. I'm the ethics chairperson and a certification reviewer. I'm a consultant on accreditation. I've trained to teach Level 4. I know every level of this program. I'm trained to teach Level 5". Basically, I just talked my way in.

Mary Ann Geoffrey was going to teach Level 4 and had an instructor-in-training scheduled. Lisa kept saying, "You take the Level 4 and Mary Ann can teach the Level 5 and the instructor will be with you."

I said, "I haven't taught Level 4 yet! You can't have me train an instructor. You can't expect the instructor to come that weekend, pay to be there and not be trained to teach Level 4. You've got to have Mary Ann teach the instructor who's coming and give me the Level 5."

I think I finally wore her down. I taught the Level 5 in Chicago. I think about three weeks later, I taught my first Level 4, which had been scheduled.

That's how I got to teach Level 6 as well. I kept paying my own way to go to Boulder. I would help Cynthia teach the Level 6. I would teach parts of it as we went through the four days. That's how I needled my way into teaching all parts of the program. I call it being fatally available.

Janet really was on to me. I think she was cautious of me. I was scheduled to teach a Level 1 class in St. John's Hospital in Jackson, Wyoming. I announced it at one of the local instructor meetings that we used to have at the office quarterly. I said, "I've got a class in the hospital in Jackson!"

Janet looked at me and said, "You're not a nurse. You had better take a nurse with you into the hospital. You can't teach in the hospital. You're not a nurse."

I said, "Janet, Watch me."

My HT classes went on to be the first in the country that offered CMEs to physicians because of my work presenting and promoting to the holistic physicians organizations as well.

I learned fairly early on, to fight for everything I wanted. I made myself 'fatally available' to HTP after Janet's death.

*What's your favorite healing story?*

As a practitioner I have a very telling story, but I'm not very proud of it. In classes I will sometimes tell a story from the early days in Australia, when I was trying to build a practice. The other practitioner in town, who was working toward certification as well, was going on vacation. In Australia when they go on vacation, they go for three weeks or more. She asked me if I would take one of her regular clients that she saw weekly.

I said, "Sure."

She dropped off her client's file. This woman scheduled to come to see me. The woman was heavy set, and depressed, and just whined for an hour. She bitched and moaned about her ex-husband who was abusing her. Her kids abused her. Her employer abused her. She had been off on disability and she was scheduled to go back to work. She didn't think she would be able to handle it. Whine, whine, whine. She wore me down.

She left. The next week she was scheduled to return and was late. I didn't want to see her. I really didn't want to see her. I noticed that my son had forgotten his lunch, so I took off. I left. The client was about ten minutes late. I left to deliver my son's lunch.

When I got back, the client had called and apologized. She said, "I know I was here the week before. I don't know how I got lost. I'm driving around the neighborhood. If you can see me, give me a call, and I'll come see you while I'm still in town."

I didn't call her. I sat in my office feeling really horrible about myself and I said to myself, "What's wrong with you? You call yourself a healer? Why are you in this line of work?"

I've really got to give you the back story. This woman drove four hours from the outback to see me. This woman got up at o'dark hundred to be at my house by nine AM. I'm sitting here, as a practitioner in energy work, supposed to hold this heart-centered space for this woman's healing, and I literally took my first opportunity to avoid her. I said to myself, "There's something seriously wrong with you, that you would do this. You need to consider, what is your roll? What is your job here?"

I decided what I needed to do was stand as the Divine would, and look at her as though she were Christ incarnate, that angel in disguise. Just love her, if she would ever come back.

The following week, which was the third week my practitioner friend was going to be gone, the client came back again. I was prepared. I showered more love on that woman. That's all I did. I just loved her. She whined and I loved her. She was a victim to her family and I loved her. Her employer was out to get her....and I loved her. She got on the table. I worked on her. She went home.

About a week and a half later, my practitioner friend called me and said, "What the Hell did you do to my client?"

I thought, "Oh no. She's found out. I'm no good in this field. I'm a disaster. I'm a failure."

I took a breath.

She said, "That woman has made more shifts in three weeks than she has in three years. I just wanted to thank you and share her gratitude."

I thought. "Oh my God. Thank You! This is what our work is all about!"

It's one of my favorite stories, even though it's not very flattering of me. I think it illustrates what it is we're really doing. It's not about technique. It's not really about sitting with someone, though presence is important. I think our work is really about engaging that Divine love energy, which I believe is the healer. It is about holding/offering Divine love and allowing the client to come into that space as much as they can come. I truly believe that when I stand in that place of embracing Divine love for someone, I'm the best person I'm ever going to be in this life!

*What do you see for the future of Healing Touch or what would you like to see for the future of Healing Touch?*

I know that I'm supposed to be really pro Healing Touch, and have a vision for them and all that kind of stuff, but it's getting really hard. It's been a really hard process for me. I'd never been much more than an independent instructor and practitioner when Janet was living. When HTI blew up (was fired), I immediately took the side of Healing Touch Program, because I worked for Healing Touch Program. I didn't work for HTI. I was a member of their membership organization, but even at the time of Janet's death, they were changing their charter without letting the membership know. They did things without a vote of the membership and then said, "Now you have to vote for this", but they'd already made the decisions and changes! Therefore, I didn't have much of a loyalty to HTI, but I knew whom it was I taught for.

When Janet died, I became very, very involved with the organization. I probably have PTSD because of it. (She laughs.) As I said, I made myself fatally available to HTP. When EMS stopped being their consultants, I burned out. I didn't want to do anything anymore. I quit Ethics, Certification and turned over mentor training. At that point I was very hurt and angry. I felt unappreciated and unheard. I had been pushing the proverbial boulder uphill and it rolled over me on the way back down.

It's been a process for me to step back and not be so affected by HTP decisions and actions. My passion is for holding the highest standards. This has not always put friends in my court. At this point I'm tired of fighting toward that end. Fighting those who say, "It is good enough' when it falls below the standard. I've invested a tremendous amount to that standard within HTP. Cynthia holds quality control over the curriculum, agrees with having a high and improving standard, has great passion and holds Janet's vision. As I healed enough to step back into a roll of any kind, I chose to serve on the Curriculum Committee as a Lead 4/5 Instructor. I think the reason is that I'm pretty sheltered here from the business practices.

In the last year or so I have pulled away even further. I have my own business and write my own course work. Right now, my course work is based on a platform of Healing Touch and everything EMS offers is for the EM practitioner, and is directly applicable to a person's private practice.

I have no idea what's going to happen to HTP. It really doesn't matter what I see for the organization. What matters is what Lisa and Chris see for the organization. Great strides have been made since they took over HTP and far more are still needed. A lot of personal 'sweat equity' has been put into the organization to keep it going since 2006 as well. And that has cost us some great people over the last decade.

. I truly know that we have some amazing people in our organization – ones who regularly work energetically to keep it ethical, strong, viable, on mission and moving forward. We have the tightest curriculum in the field and I'm very proud of contributing to that.

*Do you have a favorite Janet Mentgen story?*

I do. When I was first mentoring, Cynthia was my supervising mentor. It was quite a long time ago. I had only been in Denver a couple of years. I've been here eighteen, now. Maybe it was back in 2000, 2001, or 2002. I was mentoring a guy who was inappropriate with his touch. He was combining massage with Healing Touch. He was not draping appropriately and things like that. We were hearing all kinds of stories about him. It went on and on for months. Cynthia and I met with him. I told him he had to cease and desist in combining Healing Touch with massage. We also found out that he didn't have any formal massage training, which was required in his county.

I suspended our mentorship for a period of three months, I think. I required that he undergo weekly counseling. He had to change all his materials separating massage from Healing Touch. There were about four things I required of him. He signed the agreement, Cynthia did, and so did I. We each had a signed copy.

I said, "Now, if there's another complaint that comes up in these three months, you're done."

What happened was, another complaint came to light, although it wasn't a new concern. It was very difficult to get anyone to officially write a complaint and my frustration level was high. Here was a person practicing unethically. I called Janet.

I said, "Janet. Here's the background. Here's what's going on."

She said, "You are to cease and desist from having any contact with him. No phone calls, no meetings, no explanations. Nothing. You're done with him."

I said, "Thank you."

She said, "It is now in the hands of our attorney. He will be asked not to associate in any way with Healing Touch. He won't be allowed to attend conferences or further his education with us. Nothing."

I said, "Okay."

She said, "You need to know, I will take the word of a mentor over a mentee and that of an instructor over a student any day."

I felt really good with that. I felt like, what's the word, like I am at a very high level. I felt seen and valued. I really felt appreciated with that.

*I hope that somewhat filters down.*

Me, too.


*Is there anything else you would like to talk about?*

Healing Touch isn't where I'm most involved any longer. I'm teaching EMS courses around the country. I have an active private practice. I have a National Coordinator and a volunteer program. I love teaching HT at the upper levels, but am having a harder time keeping to beginner levels of information anymore. I look forward to my coordinator taking over the teaching some of the HT classes. I will still stick to the curriculum aspects and continue to be of service I think, but otherwise, I'm excited to get to do my own thing.

Another story. I knew few people when I moved here. I had levels 2 and 3 with Janet and traveled with her on that journey in Australia. I knew Judy Turner because she housed me when I traveled to the US for coursework (Level 5 and Level 6). I knew Cynthia and Carol Komitor, because when I travelled to the US I co-taught with each of them as part of my instructor training. We used to get together at the HT headquarters about quarterly to discuss class schedules, what was new in the field, research, development issues, etc. At one of my early meetings I was seated next to Carol Komitor. She lived near me and we would ride together to meetings at the

CCHT office. We'd have these local instructor meetings at the office, usually with a catered lunch.

We would go around the long table giving highlights of what was going on with the teaching in our communities. At this particular meeting everybody around the table was saying, "I can't fill my classes. I can't get students. I'm having trouble." One right after the other said the same thing.

From Fort Collins down to Highlands Ranch, Boulder to Colorado Springs they were having trouble getting classes going. When it is my turn to share I said, "Well, I've been here, like a year and a half. I talk to people all the time. It is strange, but not one person that I've talked to has heard of Healing Touch. I have to ask why is this? Denver is the foundation of Healing Touch. This is where it started."

I turned to Janet and I said, "Janet, you need to be on the radio. You need to be on TV. You need to be interviewed. You need to be talking about Healing Touch publicly."

You could have heard a pin drop in that room. Everybody's mouth was gaping. Carol was slowly sliding down, getting lower and lower in her chair.

I said, "You know, you asked me what we can do about this. So I'm telling you what we can do about this. "

Basically Janet changed the subject and the meeting ended shortly thereafter.

When we get in the car to go home, Carol starts laughing hysterically. She says, "I can't believe you did that."

I said, "Did what?"

She said, "I mean you told Janet how to run her business."

I said, "Did I say anything that wasn't true?"

She says, "Oh no. Of course not."

I think I sort of got started on the wrong foot with Janet. But then, no one has to guess at what I think or where they stand with me. Although I think Janet had my number, she was supportive if you deserved it. I felt she always supported me.

Question about social media? I use social media a lot. I have a periodic blog that goes out to my database from Constant Contact about the energetic trends I'm seeing with clients in my practice, along with notices of my classes. I use Facebook (FB)-both for my business as well as personally. I post pictures on Instagram. I think using social media and having a website and FB presence are essential these days. I know personally I prefer to put a little time in on the computer rather than put time in on the phone. I can answer emails and post on FB at night when my client practice is finished for the day. If you are building a practice and want to appeal to the younger crowd – you have to have a web presence.

# Kathy Moreland
## RN, MScN, HTCP/I
### Elder

### Introduction

Kathy Moreland is one of my favorite friends in Healing Touch. She is a fabulous story teller and sneaks in humor when you least expect it. No matter what is going on for me, I always feel better when I am in her presence.

She is the expert when it comes to research and also Canadian laws concerning energy medicine practitioners. Until recently, she was the chair for the Healing Touch Program Research and Science Advisory Council.

Right now she is taking time to be with her family.

### Interview

*What brought you into energy work in the first place, and specifically Healing Touch?*

It was 1994. I was a newly divorced, very stressed out, nurse manager at a large teaching hospital in downtown Toronto. I had a colleague who kept saying to me, "I'm really worried about you. I want you to go see my friend, Susan."

I said, "Why? What does Susan do?"

She said, "She does a combination of Therapeutic Touch and Healing Touch."

I said, "Do you mean that stuff where people wave their hands over you to make you feel better?"

She said, "Yes."

I said, "I'd rather have a martini."

She persisted over the next few weeks, because she could tell I was extremely stressed. She finally said to me, "What are you doing next Thursday?

I said, "Why?"

She said, "Because I've booked an appointment for you, and paid for it."

I said, "You're not going to let up until I go, are you?"

She said, "Nope."

So I went. I happened to meet Susan Mayer Morales (Kosinec), who is one of the founding elders of Healing Touch, with Janet, who brought Healing Touch to Canada. I actually was extremely skeptical going in for my first treatment. I lay on the table with my eyes wide open.

I said, "Go ahead. Get it over with. "

I found the treatment to be so profoundly, deeply relaxing, and cathartic for me, because I completely lost track of time. I felt my body relax fully. I had never felt it relax. I know I cried.

It was almost like a coming home sort of healing. I came home to myself in that moment.

When we sat and talked, we realized we had very similar backgrounds in nursing and palliative care.

She said, "I would really be honored if you would join us in our class. I don't say this to just everybody, but I really believe this will help you."

I realized she was right. I was in the second Level 1 class in Canada. I did not look back after that. It became a huge part of my personal healing. Then it became a part of my professional practice.

It took me approximately four years from the time I had my first class to certification. Which wasn't overly fast, but I was working on my master's degree at the same time. I left Toronto, having lost the job that I was so stressed at, which was sort of a Godsend. I ended up returning home, and doing my master's degree. I did my master's thesis on the experience of receiving Healing Touch for women with breast cancer. That got me really interested in Healing Touch research.

*Do you have a favorite story where you have used Healing Touch on a client?*

My most profound recollection involves my skepticism. I've always had a healthy skepticism about energy work, because there is a big part of me that is left brain dominant. I still consider it to be rather strange to do the therapy, but I've learned to trust it.

Even after doing Level I, and knowing my own personal experience, I really still didn't have a sense of whether it made any difference to anybody else. Was it just my caring presence that made the difference?

Soon after my Level 1 experience, I was teaching nursing students. We had a patient who had had a below knee amputation of his leg. He had profound phantom pain. He said it was profoundly painful, and no amount of narcotic or medication was helping. He was just really suffering. He was a fairly young guy.

I said, "Well, I've just learned this new therapy that, I'm not sure that it will help or not, but we can see what happens."

He was open to trying anything. I have never had any difficulties doing the work I do in hospitals. There was no concern about doing this therapy, except I mentioned to the students that this might look rather strange. I told them to trust the process, and hold their intention as this would help.

While treating him, I had this very strong sense that what had happened during the surgery was that his leg was bent backwards under his body. He was actually lying on his phantom limb, as if it was right behind him. I could actually sense the immense amount of pain. I thought that if his leg was under him, maybe if I straightened out his energetic leg, it would help to relieve it. He had his eyes closed during the therapy. I just set my intention that I was going to help bring this leg, this energetic leg, out from under his body and straighten and smooth it out so that he was laying with his leg in repose, as opposed to laying on it. I thought that would be really uncomfortable. It was as if he had been kneeling and then fell back onto his leg.

As I did this maneuver, I literally felt it energetically shift. His eyebrows went down like this was really strange. I finished, and he let out this big sigh.

He said with his eyes closed, "I don't know what you just did, but it feels like you just straightened out my leg."

Just like that.

At that moment I thought, "Okay." I had no idea of what just happened, but that is what happened. At that moment, I thought this is more of a faith than belief now. There is just faith that there are things beyond my understanding, because I had followed my gut and didn't fight it.

After that he said, "I actually feel like I can feel my feet, and my right leg. I feel like I can wiggle my toes and relax that leg finally, even though it's not there."

He didn't require narcotics after that.

For me, that is one of the most profound recollections of the work I have done. I have a gazillion stories that I still cannot explain, but that created relief for people where nothing else had been able to do that.

I became a nurse practitioner and counselor. I use Healing Touch often in my practice. One of my other favorite stories is one where I was working in the States at a large NCI (National Cancer Institute) affiliated cancer center. I used to do two to four bone marrow biopsies a day. I was working in the leukemia service. I did Healing Touch all the time to help people relax before their treatment, and afterwards. After seeing the benefits of HT for patients and themselves, all the nurses in the outpatient area ended up taking a Level 1 class. It really shifted things in the whole department.

Getting back to the story, JCAHCO (Joint Commission on Accreditation of Healthcare Organizations) had set down really strict guidelines around conscious sedation at that time, so that would have been in the late 90's. You had to have an anesthetist, or a nurse anesthetist, with you if you were going to use short acting barbiturates to sedate the patient.

We had been using these medications to sedate patients for bone marrow biopsies. So we had to stop doing that, and we ended up using morphine and things like that which were very sedating, but not anesthesia per se.

For my patients, I used to treat them with Healing Touch beforehand, rather than using narcotics. Narcotics didn't make all that much difference. I got called up to my director's office one day. She said, "I got a call from the call center that people are willing to wait up to two weeks for you to be their bone marrow biopsy nurse. Are you using conscious sedation? You'd better not be using conscious sedation because we can't do that anymore."

I said, "No, I'm not using conscious sedation."

She said, "Well, what are you doing that is so different that people are willing to wait two weeks for you to do their bone marrow biopsy?"

I said, "Healing Touch."

She said, "Do you mean that woo-woo stuff you do?"

I said, "Yup."

She said with an exasperated grin, "Get out of my office."

The next day her secretary called me again. I said, What for?"

She said, "She wants you to come up here. She has a severe migraine and she has to do a presentation tonight and nothing has helped. She wants you to come up and see if you can do anything."

I came upstairs. She was literally sitting in a dark room. She couldn't function, because she had such a severe migraine. She said, "Can you try that stuff on me. I am willing to try anything at this point."

I treated her headache. After I left, about an hour later, she called me and said, "I don't know what the heck that is that you're doing, but I want every nurse in the cancer center to learn how to do it. My headache's gone. I still feel a bit woozy, but I can do my presentation today."

That is how every nurse in the cancer center got Level 1. We used it with all our patients to start IV's and other invasive procedures and for anxiety management. She still calls it that woo-woo stuff.

*What is the story about "healing presence"?*

As soon as you go into a caring intention, your energy field changes. When I describe energy work to people, I say to them when they act skeptical, "Have you ever walked in a room and you can feel the tension" because that's usually a pretty powerful energy. Can you feel the tension like when you say that you feel the tension so thickly that you can cut it with a knife."

They go, "Oh yeah."

So I say, "Have you ever felt like levity where you think about huge world events, when something wonderful happened, and you could feel the levity? Or when tragic things happen?"

Often times they'll share world events like when 9/11 happened, and they could feel that connectedness between people, and that sense of tragedy. Other celebratory events, like if Canada won the world championship in hockey or something like that; things that unite us. You can feel that levity and people go, "Yeah."

For me, caring presence is once you set that intention, it's almost like turning on the spotlight right from your soul and from your heart. You create a beam of energy around yourself that envelops the people around you.

When I am helping to design research, I talk about how we tend to control the presence by having someone else in the room. I always worry. How can you be around suffering people and not send out or emit some of that consciousness, some of that light and create some of that energy that helps you to be around someone without creating that energy? That's what I always worry about when setting controlled presence. I believe that all of us have the ability to heal through that kind of presence. Healing Touch takes it to another level, where you're actually, intentionally trying to shift the energy. That's what I worry about. You walk into a room where someone has got cancer, and you care. You care about them. I think that creates energy.

When you ask people, can you tell if someone cares about you or not? Caring is a feeling, not any actions necessarily. When I talk to my students about creating caring moments between themselves and patients, it can be as simple as coming from your heart and touching someone, to me, can be an energy treatment in itself.

There are very skilled technicians out there, who are at the bedside, who shut their hearts off, because they believe they are going to give away too much. They would be very skilled, but people can tell that they don't care about them necessarily. That probably opens up some debate, but I also believe that showing caring is a practice, is an excellent practice. My heart goes into that.

I tell my students that if you just wanted to be a caring individual, you probably should have gone into volunteerism. To be an excellent nurse, caring has to be transmitted through all of your processes and interventions as well. Caring means that you set your intention to do the best you can for that person in all ways. Within your own professional body, that means you excel and work towards excellence in all that you do. Your heart is always at the center of it. That's the reason why you become the best that you do, is that you care, not because of what it necessarily brings you. It is not about technique.

That's the same in Healing Touch practices.

*What advice do you have for new students?*

Keep it simple.

Recognize that true caring involves receiving, not just giving. It's a reciprocal process.

Keep your eye on the prize, if your goal is to become a practitioner.

There is learning in all things. Everyone's journey is different.

Don't compare yourself to other people.

Realize that the greatest healing that has to occur in your journey is with yourself.

The last piece would be, don't take yourself too seriously.

As an instructor I would say, remember that the hand movement – remember the words of our founder, Janet – no matter what, the energy goes where it is supposed to. Remember that sometimes the techniques are meant to keep you focused, and that energy will go where it is supposed to.

*What do you see for the future of Healing Touch and/or what would you like to see in the future for Healing Touch?*

I am already seeing one of the things that I wanted to see, which is a much more open dialogue and acceptance of energy practices. I anticipate that, as research support and the understanding of energy, and subtle energy healing, becomes more available, and becomes more accepted in the allopathic world, it will become a part of what occurs in healthcare. It will be part of the prevention and treatment. It will be a tool. I hope that will occur in my life time. I figure I've got another thirty or forty years here. I think that will occur as a process like this.

I think what I don't necessarily want to see happen, is that it becomes a product. I think that the practices can't become a product; but that the programs can become a product.

*What do you mean by a product in this case?*

I am often asked whether I think Healing Touch is better than Reiki or is it better than Therapeutic Touch? I always say that if you truly believe in energy, it's that the vibrations between you and another entity and environment that you're in, because you have to remember that it's not just an exchange between two people, but we're within the context of an energy as it is. We're within another energy which is that of everything going on around us.

There is this tendency within Western medicine to try to package products, because of the consumer aspect of it. The thing that I would say, is that it doesn't matter to me whether Healing Touch or Reiki or Qi Gong or whatever else is out there is better. It's like asking me to tell you which music is better. I think what we have to recognize is that, although they are all under the umbrella of energy medicine, that the vibration that occurs between you and another person and the environment you're in, can be very much subjective.

If I tell you I like jazz, but that I don't like fusion jazz, for someone else it may be that fusion jazz really rocks their world. It's not up to me to say what's better. Now having said that, the next question might be, why do I like Healing Touch? The answer to that would be I believe that the development of me as a healer was an integral part of the program. The requirement for me to look within was an important part of the program. I wasn't just taught techniques.

I loved the fact that it was inclusive; that I was encouraged to look at other practices to help others. There wasn't an ethno-centered component to it, for lack of a better word. There was work required to get there. There was an ethical component to it, and standards involved.

I think the fact that there was a community that had a similar experience anywhere in the world I went. It's not just like other programs. I don't know that if I was to take a Reiki master course in Toronto, if it would be the same as a Reiki master course in New York or Florida. It's just probably that there's some sense of organization, and that appealed to the left side of my brain.

The other piece of that is, there is skepticism out there, I don't mean there aren't healers out there who are profoundly talented in their own right. Absolutely not. But in the world that I walk in professionally, I can show credentialing. I can show the process that I went through to become certified. I think that creates a vibration of acceptance in the allopathic world.

For me, it was not so much that I didn't believe that there may be someone else as good. You get people who say they were taught by a native elder. Do I believe that they are not a powerful healer? That they can do wonderful things? Absolutely. I believe that that is true. But in terms of being able to walk into an allopathic setting and say, "Here I am. This is part of my tool box. This is the process I went through to get here." has created much greater acceptance. Now having said that, I think that if I was a flake professionally, if I wasn't exemplary in my allopathic skills, nothing I could have done, would create acceptance of my Healing Touch practice.

The only way I can give my advice to practitioners is to go back to that place. Do not proselytize your practice. Be the change you wish to see in the world. I did not proselytize my Healing Touch practice at the cancer center where I worked. I just was who I am. I treated when I could. It was walking the walk and talking the talk. I was held in high esteem for my allopathic practice, so that when I spoke about energy work, people wanted some of that.

I would hear things like "What is it that makes you happy when you work? What is it that makes that connection so strong between you and your patient? Why are the patients saying that they want you, and not someone else?" It was about *being* energy work, not *doing* energy work. So my advice is again, be healing. Don't do healing.

*To change the subject a little bit, do you have a favorite Janet Mentgen story?*

I was fortunate to do an Advanced Practice with Janet, back in '97. I think my favorite part of the story with her is that I had heard how direct she was and unassuming. My recollection is that I was surprised that the woman I had heard about for so many years, was how unassuming she really was. How soft spoken she was, and yet direct at the same time.

She was very unassuming, and you gotta remember I was educated in Healing Touch at a time of big hair, big earrings, and shoulder pads. People who were leaders in healthcare and especially in nursing, were pretty corporate looking. Janet arrived at class in her sweat pants and her sweat shirt and no make-up on. Yet she held the room the whole weekend.

I don't have anything that she actually did with me. I was just so honored to finally meet her. I know of her stories up in Canada. She had her favorite beer, and she had her favorite chicken wings, and stuff like that up here. They had to bring her those things every time she came. So she had her favorite foods.

The other story I heard of her was how important she was in bringing Healing Touch to Canada. Whatever the founders needed, she made sure it happened. That's how Healing Touch Canada got started.

*Let's get into some things I know are near and dear to your heart. What would you like to talk about concerning studies? I know lots of people who would like to get involved, but they have no idea how to get started, what to do, or even if they are credentialed enough .I mean there's a thousand questions around it.*

I'll start by saying the conduct of research, in any form, is not for the faint of heart. I would strongly suggest that anyone interested in doing research in Healing Touch, affiliate themselves with someone who has the credentials to do research, and the opportunity to create partnerships that get funding.

The problems in Healing Touch research are similar to those of any complementary or alternative range of therapy. To get really solid evidence of the work doing anything in any area of practice, in any type of illness or practice requires large clinical trials. That costs lots of money and takes lots of time.

When people talk to me about where are the best studies, I would say there are only a few that I can count on one hand of that kind of study that have been done in Healing Touch. That's meaning that there's large enough sample sizes, that there were controls and variables, that there was randomization of subjects, that there was excellent statistical methods used, etc. That's why, not only clinical significance but physical significance that meant something, that there was a confidence in that work in that it was the Healing Touch that made the difference.

Those are the studies like Dr. Shamini Jain's team did that involve PTSD with veterans; the studies that Dr. Barb MacIntyre looked at for the reduction in anxiety, and length of stay for patients with coronary bypass surgery and Dr Susan Lutgendorf and her team did with natural kill cell preservation during cancer treatment. Lutgendorf's study was an NIH (National Institute of Health) funded study exploring Healing Touch and its impact on killer T-cell function in women who were receiving chemo therapy and radiation for gynecological cancers. The group that received Healing Touch, had the best preservation of killer T-cell function, which is the lymphocytes, that actually attack cancer cells and viruses in the body. Good NKC (natural killer cell) function is an indicator of your ability to prevent relapse. That's one of the best studies to date.

The best way for Healing Touch practitioners to be involved in research, is to provide practice free of charge to researchers. They should find someone who is looking to recruit people for research and who might want to do studies. Usually, most of the HT studies that are published are those that are pilot studies, which means there are less than thirty subjects in each group. Many are done for a master's thesis or a PhD dissertation. The best studies are the ones that are getting funded and reviewed.

If someone is really interested in being involved in research, they should approach either a nursing department, or a psychology department at an affiliated university close by to determine if there is anyone with research background who wishes to conduct a study. Healing Touch practitioners could act as a consultant in the development of the research. I would also encourage people to replicate studies that have shown some promise. People are choosing research topics with no clear plan. I would also encourage you to do research in areas where the funding is.

In the United States, right now, there are funding opportunities in veterans' recovery from PTSD and things like that. Also, in cancer and recovery for the secondary effects in chemo therapy and radiation treatments, like fatigue, and anxiety, and things like that. There are papers out there and people you can talk to with that information. I would encourage people to do that.

Now, having said that, I won't discourage people from exploring potential outcomes or areas, because what hasn't been done yet is a systematic review of any one particular impact area in Healing Touch treatments. When a lot of small studies are done and are well conducted a research might be able to systematically analyze those findings.

*I think a lot of people who would like to get involved or see studies going, just to validate what they are doing.*

I would never discourage that desire, but the reality is, you have to find someone to affiliate with. We're not that organized yet. Researching Healing Touch is still very much in its infancy, even though people might not think that. You have to remember that the practice really only started in the eighties. Research methods have become much more scrutinized. What saddens me, when we go back to that thing about the caring presence, is that when you have small numbers in your study, and you get significance, you probably will get published. There's a publication bias, which is studies that have significant results tend to get published. But, someone scrutinizing that would look at it and say, "Well, you might have just been lucky enough to have picked the part population under your curve that would have gotten positive results regardless. If you had had larger numbers, you may not have had significance." Or, what I like to point out is that, depending upon what control review you used, how do you know that you would have gotten significant results if you hadn't had people in the control group with great intention in creating that same energy field.

If you are trying to control the treatment and treat it like a drug it won't work. I don't know any practitioner who's on the same "dose" (frequency) of treatment every day. If I'm giving a Healing Touch treatment in fifteen minutes, and the next day I give the same treatment in fifteen minutes with a different person, I don't know if I'm delivering the same energy "dose" or not. It's an interactive process. We don't have those measurements yet to know that we can deliver.

There are some scientists out there, who are actually measuring the energy of practitioners and things like that, and recognizing that they deliver with consistent frequency. But how do I know that I don't have some young Level 1 person who delivers treatment with far greater intensity, than a qualified practitioner who has honed their craft, but may not be delivering the same frequency.

There's this disconnect with the idea that being able to give a treatment is like a dose of drug. I don't know from one day to the next if my intensity is greater or lesser. I like to believe I do. It goes back to that simple philosophy that energy is what it is. Energy is going to go where it's supposed to go.

Practitioners will tell you that they have come across people who have walked through Hell and back, and finally come to seek treatment because they don't even know what else to do. These individuals seem to pull energy from you. You can feel energy going through you like a torrential river in the spring. They need that energy. Am I delivering a bigger dose, or is that something coming through me? I don't know the answer to that. Energy goes where it's supposed to. If your philosophical idea is that you are a conduit, not a deliverer, and as long as I'm open, they'll get what they need, that's where the whole irony of research comes into play in the first place. It's a belief that I am delivering a specific dose, because you're using a certified practitioner and in the best, perfect world it's the same practitioner.

How do I know that that practitioner isn't extremely gifted? Or are not gifted at all? Or we're just having a bad week that week? There's so many factors.

*It's actually the client who makes the decision in the first place, and there's no way you can measure that.*

No. I've talked about mythological issues in research many times. We've talked about the fact that we're trying put a square peg into a round hole, because we're trying to use methods of research that are used for things that are controllable, like drugs or frequencies. Energy is a consciousness thing that can't be necessarily prescribed in doses. That is some of the problem beneath the surface of these studies.

You say to yourself, "Well, how many studies that would have had significant impact, they need to publish because they didn't happen to pick people under the curve who didn't have significant results. If you understand statistics, then you understand that there's a certain number of people who have to be under that curve in order for you to say there's enough positives, that what you saw was a direct result of the treatment you prescribed and that the results weren't just a result of chance. If you don't have enough people, you might have been just really lucky enough, that people rate in the middle of the curve versus the people at the end of the curve.

I'm trying to speak as pragmatically and practically as possible. That's the statement. My advice to people about research is, go back to the Healing Touch research page, or go back to the Level 1 notebook, the current Level 1 notebook, and look at what makes a good research study good.

Don't go in there proselytizing that you've got a list full of research studies, because a lot of them are not well conducted. It doesn't mean that the work wasn't worthwhile. It does suggest that there is something to this work, but isn't by chance alone. There's not a lot that's really solid. That's why, like the Lutgendorf and her study, the Shamani Jane study on PTSD and that group and the study by a number of other people. Like I said, there's about four or five that I usually say are good studies.

Other people will either say, "Is there one on arthritis pain? and I say no, or "Is there one on blood sugars?" "No, nobody has explored that yet."

There's so many practice areas that people wish there was research in, at least quantitative research, like what we call the gold standard, randomized clinical trials. There aren't, because they cost so much.

The other piece is, that because energy work is not a product, you don't get the funding like you get for drugs.

*It comes back to money.*

Yup.

Keep creating the vibration and keep looking for opportunities that other people have solved. People say to me, "How do you design or control a study involving Healing Touch?" When, in fact, you don't know what treatment you are going to provide until you have assessed at the energy field. The pragmatics of it are, you can't tell me to walk in and do the chakra connection, when, in fact, it may not be the chakra connection that's needed. Because in the process am I going to change my energy field?

When I talked to Shamani, Jane who is developing and designing research, I suggested that she use the Healing Touch sequence as the "treatment". That makes a pragmatic approach to it, so that the practitioner can decide what needs to be done and for how long. That's the way it's really done. If you really want to know what a Healing Touch treatment really is, use the Healing Touch sequence as your treatment. What we decide within that, is how we take where we need it.

If I meet someone, and I decide all they need is spiral meditation, then that's what I would do. Or if I see what they really need a chakra connection or that they need magnetic clearing or whatever. Or a combination.

I think that's where research is going to shift. It can become much more pragmatic in that perspective. At least, that's my hope. Then the energy is authentic. You aren't walking in saying, "I have to do chakra connection. No matter what I feel, I have to do chakra connection." Then the left side of your brain's in there way too much.

People are basically practicing, according to this is where the square peg goes into a round hole thing comes in. Instead of the round hole telling the square peg how it has to be, the square peg is dictating where the round hole has to be. We're trying to make those shifts.

That was my big drive in becoming the Chair of the Research and Science advisory council. For me, the big job in Healing Touch Program at the time, was not about the research, because we knew there were new studies that were coming out. It was about people understanding what was good research. There are people who were so passionate about the practice and wanting to bring it in to allopathic care. People were running into administrator's offices with these studies in their hand, and having the door slammed in their face, because the research wasn't good quality.

For me, the big drive in becoming advisory council chair was about educating people about being good research consumers.

*Is there anything else you would like to add about anything having to do with Healing Touch.? You are open-ended for the moment.*

Here's my closing thought. Given the drive of healers to help shift our ailing planet, I would always ask people to remember the difference between the business of energy work and the practice of energy work, and to continue to stay centered in the faith that things always work out the way they're supposed to. There is definitely success to be had in becoming energy workers, but that people have to clearly go into themselves to determine what success really means. I think, when you are in the corporate west, that needs to always be in your consciousness.

There is no "better than". There just "is". But there are differences between the practicing business of energy work and the practice of energy work.

# Bonnie Morrow
## BNH, ND, HTCP/I
### Elder

**Introduction**

The following information comes from excerpts found on the Healing Touch Program and Healing Touch Worldwide Foundation (HTWF) web sites. I have not met Bonnie, until I did this interview. She was delightful and so full of enthusiasm.

Bonnie hails as a true "Healing Touch Elder" and an amazing woman. She holds the honor of being personally asked to serve on the Healing Touch Worldwide Foundation Board by Janet Mentgen. Healing Touch Worldwide Foundation sponsors Healing Touch research and service projects. She served as a board member prior to becoming the foundation president at a time when the foundation consisted of only three members. She provided leadership that ushered in expansion of the HTWF Board for greater participation and ultimately grew the HTWF bank account by nearly three times during her tenure. She continues to serve the board in an advisory role, lending her historical knowledge and passion for spreading Healing Touch worldwide. She also is a member of the nominating committee.

Bonnie has visions of greater financial success for HTWF. Carrying Janet's vision of having Healing Touch in every home,

Bonnie has a special interest in supporting Aparna Bhatta's journey as a certified instructor, establishing Healing Touch in Nepal.

Bonnie is also Healing Touch Certified Practitioner and Certified Instructor of Levels 1, 2 and 3, and in training for Level 4. She is a charter member of Healing Touch Professional Association. Bonnie is currently completing her Doctorate in natural medicine. After retiring from Exxon Chemical Company, she established her private Healing Touch practice. Bonnic is the CEO of Healing Touch Texas, a corporation that provides training throughout southeast Texas. Her vision is to have Healing Touch readily available throughout Texas. Bonnie often states, "Healing Touch changed my life.... Healing is my passion." That passion is demonstrated in her teaching technique where she brings enthusiasm, creativity and a sense of humor to her classes. Bonnie continues, "I am privileged to teach Levels 1, 2, and 3 of the Healing Touch Program and I love to see the light come on in the students eyes. I have taught throughout the US, in Romania and Nepal. I have my books packed and will travel. I love my students and it is mutual. Healing Touch changed my life and I'm ready to support you to have to the same experience. Bonnie is available to present Healing Touch introductory workshops and presentations. Either one-hour or three-hours and there are CE credit available for those who might want it. Compensation for classes and introductory workshops is negotiable, depending on your number of students.

**Interview**

*What positions have you held in Healing Touch?*
I was president of the foundation. I was on the board for three years and then Janet said, "Will you be the president?"

I said, "Yes."

I was president for six years, nine years total on the board. I have been with it ever since.

*Were you the first president?*

I think I was. I don't think she took that title for herself. I was right after she decided to turn loose the reins for the foundation.

*How did the foundation come about?*

As my understanding, some lady was helped, I don't think healed, but helped by Healing Touch. She left money in a will for us. I think it was $32,000 that she left us.

*What got you started in energy healing?*

I was sitting at my desk at Exxon, one day. I said, "God, isn't there something more you want me to do with my life than this?

The next day there was a Healing Touch flyer on my desk.

"It's like, okay, okay, I got it God."

I went to the class. When I got to the class, I knew I was home. I have been a healer for many, many lifetimes. I didn't know that at the time. I don't know how that came about. Somewhere.

*What did you do for Exxon?*

I was an artist, which is really a round peg in a square hole.

I retired from Exxon when I was eligible to do that, to do my Healing Touch business. That was way back there, sometime. I have been doing Healing Touch ever since.

*How has it changed your life?*

Oh my gosh! Well, it put me on a spiritual path. It completely changed my life. I almost don't know how to answer that one.

I went from a regular person to a completely spiritual one. I have studied and I have gone to seminars. It changed the kind of person I was.

Getting to know the Healing Touch community, getting to know Janet, that was a big deal for me. She was very spiritual, very accepting, non-judgmental. I think I learned those things from her.

I was coordinating classes and she was the easiest instructor to keep. The rest of them were not demanding, but wanting this or that or something else. Not her. She was so easy. She would announce that she wanted to go to bed, and she would do that. She didn't have to be entertained, I guess is the thing. She just was there.

How did it change my life? I just was walking a different path. I was walking a path toward God and away from the world. I guess that's it.

You start meditating and you start journaling. Both were things I never did. Now we teach them in Level 1 to do that. Maybe that was it. Of course, I didn't set out to do teaching. I did a lot of helper work with the classes.

*Do you have a particularly outstanding healing story?*

I have done so many. The one that comes to mind was a lady who came to me, who had been going through chemo for cancer. It was when she went back to the doctor and he said, "There's a spot on your liver."

I said to her as I was working on her, "Let's just ask God to take that thing away."

We did that. She came back the next time and said, "It's gone."

That was like, oh wow. I says, "Well, you know I didn't do it. God did it."

She just laughed and said, "Yeah. I know."

That happened fairly recently. It's a neighbor and she was across the street from me.

You know, yourself, when you've been doing a lot of Healing Touch, you're seeing a lot of clients.

I lived on Whidbey Island for a year. My husband was in the navy and I didn't get connected with any of those people that are there and very spiritual. That's what it was. My life became very spiritual, when I started Healing Touch.

*Have you explored other modalities besides Healing Touch?*

I fiddled around with a little Reiki. But to answer your question, specifically, no. I did oils, that sort of thing. I never really pursued them. I just kind of dabbled in them.

*Do you have any comments or advice for new or potential students?*

Just let yourself be led. Don't force it. Follow the directions that you're given. And, of course, that comment, from me, means from God. To listen when you're meditating and when you're praying. Go where you're led and keep on keeping on.

*What do you see for the future of Healing Touch?*

My vision, and consequently the vision for Healing Touch, was Janet's vision, too. To have Level 1 in every home in the world. Every household needs Level 1. I really, firmly believe that. So what am I doing to get it there? I have taught in Nepal. I've taught in Romania. That's about it. I haven't stretched farther than that.

*Do you have some stories from those times?*

Well, out in Nepal, the gal is still out there. The foundation has decided to take her in under their wing and do some promotion for Parna. She lives in the mountains, and does work with women. She is a, oh my God, she is a fireball. If you have a chance to interview her, do it.

Nepal is a communist country. They only have there, electricity two hours a day. It's at odd hours. She is hard to get. She is worth the price of admission. I want to make sure she is up and running. I want to make sure she has enough money to finish out her clinic. A lovely, lovely lady.

*Do you have a Janet Mentgen story?*
Just that she was easy to keep as an instructor when she came to our house. She was such a delight and such wonderful energy. That's my fondest memory of her.

*Is there anything else you would like to add?*
Right now, I am doing a thirteen week of Voice America. She is interviewing people and giving the Healing Touch story out there. I am about that. I am coming to the end of my thirteen weeks. I don't know if I will be invited to do more or not. You can hear us on Voice America on the wellness channel.

*What all are you telling people?*
I am interviewing people. I have had Cynthia on. This week, I believe is Linda Smith. I do people that I think the listeners would enjoy what they have to say.
It's interesting. These people who have been around a long time say, "Ah, I can't do that." It's like, bologna, you can do it.
I had somebody talk on mediation. I had somebody talk on a business plan. It's been different things and different areas of Healing Touch. Cynthia spoke about the energy fields and the chakras.
It's fun.
When is your book coming out?
*I don't know. It's when I get it done.*
That's what I'm talking about. When Spirit says you're done, you're done. When spirit says, "Well, I think you've got a little bit more work to do here." You've got more work to do.
That's what I was talking about when I said, "Follow where you're led."

# Monica Nebauer
### RN. PhD, CHTP/I

## Introduction

Cynthia suggested I interview Monica. She teaches Levels 1 through 3 in Australia. What a delight she turned out to be. She is amazing. She has taught nursing classes at the university level for many years and Healing Touch for over ten years. It wasn't easy to get started as a practitioner in Healing Touch as her stories will confirm.
 There is a little more interaction between the two of us. It was my first experience using Skype. I was thrilled to be talking to someone in Australia and to be able to see her as well.

## Interview

I have been in academics at university for a number of years. I was also involved with Therapeutic Touch since 1990.

*What got you interested in Therapeutic Touch?*
 I took the Therapeutic Touch class. Janet Quinn came to Australia and I took another class with her. In the early nineties Mary Jo Bulbrook brought Healing Touch to Perth in western Australia., Then she came to the eastern part of the country where I am. I took Level 1 and 2A, back to back. Then I went to Perth two weeks later to

do the third level. At that time we had Levels 2A and 2B and levels 3A and 3B. I missed out on 2B, which is now Level 3. I took that some time later. I did a repeat of that with Janet Mentgen when she was over here in 1996.

I've been a certified practitioner since 1997 and I've been a certified instructor since 2008.

*What happened in Level 1 that hooked you on Healing Touch?*

My answer to your question is that I realized that Healing Touch would give me more tools in my nursing toolkit with which to help my patients. I was excited by that possibility because I was concerned that the biomedical model within which I practiced nursing provided very limited opportunities for nurses to practice autonomously and holistically. And here was this wonderful, holistic modality that offered so much potential for healing, not only for my patients, but also for myself! I was ecstatic and also intrigued to learn more as the possibilities in learning more about and using HT appeared endless, very deep, and very exciting at that stage.

*What's your favorite healing story?*

I always tell this story when I'm teaching Level 1 students. It's not actually a story that I was involved in. I think it is a really lovely example of the focus of intentionality and the importance of hands on healing.

Out here in Australia we have a particular hospital, that's a specialist hospital, a very large one. People go there from all over Australia if they have cardiac or respiratory problems. The staff in the hospital who work in infection control were looking at their statistics, and noticed that for a particular doctor, had a very low, almost non-existent post-operative infection rate. He was a respiratory surgeon. His patients had a much shorter stay in the hospital than the other respiratory surgeons. They thought this was very interesting and wanted to find out what was happening here.

They looked at all the procedures that each doctor went through. The only thing that turned out to be different was that this particular doctor set his intention for the patient at the beginning of the surgery in the operating theater and nobody was allowed to talk about anything like golf or what went on during the weekend. Nobody was allowed to play heavy metal music or whatever was the current practice in the operating theater. Some surgeons played some pretty raucous music while operating. There was just quiet and focus on the patient.

At the end of the surgery most surgeons will just simply do the closing up internally and then leave the external closure to their assistant doctor, usually an internal something. This particular doctor would insist on staying right to the end and then he would place his hands on the patient's chest and pray for their healing. The result was astonishing, which the hospital realized could be proven statistically in their figures.

I love telling that story to my students, because it explains clearly the importance of intention, being centered and grounded, and focused on what you're doing and focused on the person you are working with to have these amazing outcomes. In that case, it had been measured. Even though I wasn't involved in it personally, it is still my favorite story.

*I'd like to tell that one in my classes. Do you have a personal one that you like?*

There are so many it is hard to pick one out. I'll pass on that one.

*That's okay. The first one was good. Do you have a Janet Mentgen story?*

Yes. I met Janet here several times. I absolutely loved her as everybody did. I remember going up to her at the end of a repeat Level 3 that I did with her. I asked her a question. I can't remember what the question was now, but it was something to do with the layers of the energy field. This is about twenty years ago.

She just looked at me and she said, "Monica, all is one." She stood there and kept smiling at me. I got it. She explained it so simply. There were other students who weren't getting it, until she said that. I learned so much from those three words that she said. I'll always remember that story and the look on her face when she gave me the answer. She could have gone into a very long and complicated response to my question, but she answered it in three words, which meant a lot to me.

*That's Janet's way.*

"Do the work," was one of her other three word sentences that everybody used to love as well. "Get on the table," was another one.

*What advice would you give new students just coming into the program?*

I guess it would be more along the lines of telling them the importance of self-development. This is a program of not just learning techniques, but it's a journey into the self. It's a journey into understanding the importance of self-care, self-development. Unless you're working on that and working on increasing your own vibration, you're not going to be as effective as a Healing Touch practitioner. It's an ongoing work. It's a journey into the self. It's a journey into self-awareness and self-understanding.

*That was well said.*

Thank you.

*What do you see for the future of Healing Touch?*

I think we've been going through a scientific paradigm for about two hundred and fifty years. According to Thomas Kuhn, paradigms last for about two hundred and thirty years. I think we're witnessing moving into a much more holistic paradigm. People who are starting to learn Healing Touch now are really conditioning themselves very well for the future and for what consumers are wanting in their health care. They're wanting to be treated holistically. They're not wanting to be just a body with a disease, where the practitioner has about ten minutes to see them. They want to have a say in their treatment and they want to be treated as an equal with the practitioner. I see that as a big part of Healing Touch. Where we're working with the person, we're working to help the person to self-care, and we're not creating a dependency. We're helping them to be their own individual spirituality and I see that as part of the holistic paradigm that we're moving into.

As with any changing paradigm, there is a lot of trial, chaos, uncertainty. There is a lot of fear. We just have to go out and be centered and grounded as a strong basis for what we're doing. Having an understanding of what's happening is the background with this huge social and spiritual movement that's occurring in the world, and know that it's meant to happen and trusting that everything is going well for us. It will take time.

*How is Healing Touch doing in Australia?*

It's a real challenge. I don't know if you'll be talking in your book about the split.

*We can't avoid it.*

The same happened here. In 2008, when the split happened over there, we had quite a large national foundation. It was called the Australian Foundation for Healing Touch. We all belonged to it.

Unfortunately, the organization went to HTI. It meant that there were only a handful of us left with HTP. I was a brand new instructor. Since then, two of the other HTP instructors have retired. So I'm on the east coast as an instructor, and I have a mentor on the west coast who is an instructor. Between the two of us, we're the only ones in Australia who are teaching Healing Touch for the program. There are teachers for HTI or HBB, Healing Beyond Borders, but only two of us for Healing Touch Program.

We've more or less had to start from the beginning and rebuild out of the air, trying to build up a community. I am still trying to get someone through to instructor level to take over for me when I want to retire. It's quite a challenge. But I love it.

It's a challenge in that the size of our country, twenty-two million, might be about the size of one of your largest cities, like what New York would be. Do you know how many you have there?

*Last I heard eight to ten million in New York. It's probably grown since then.*

Last time I was in Shanghai, China, they had a population of twenty-two million in that city. When I was there I was thinking, "Oh my gosh. This city is the same population as my entire country."

Our population is very spread out. We're mostly along the coastlines. Travel is very expensive. To travel within Australia, it's more expensive than going to Japan or someplace like that. There are really challenges to spreading Healing Touch in Australia, and getting the classes happening what with our population.

*I had no idea.*

We're hoping that we will eventually come back together with the other Healing Touch people here. We're about to set up an Australian Healing Touch Program Association, which will be an umbrella organization for HTPA chapters. I had a Skype conversation with Chris Gordon a few mornings ago. They had to look at our constitution, which is dispatched regarding registration.

We are hoping that by establishing this association in Australia as an umbrella for HTPA, we will bring more people into HTP, and it will also mean we'll get our wits together. We have not had this quality with HTI, while loving HTP. That's some of the stuff that I've been doing here. I've been trying to get HTP more visible here. It is a lot of challenge, but it is done joyfully.

*Good for you. We are blessed in the Pacific Northwest. Both Washington and Oregon instructors have all gone with HTP. We haven't seen the struggles with Healing Beyond Borders.*

The foundations that we still have here, and that I was a charter member of, and helped write the constitution, the decision was made by one person who sat on the certification board in the US, but lived here. That person made the sole decision that we would go with HTI. Most people didn't even know what was going on. It was just business as usual for them.

For others who had some idea of what was happening, right from the start, we stayed with HTP. I am hoping with the association, and with all this legal stuff finished, that we can get back together.

*Anything else you would like to add about you, your classes or Australia that might be of interest?*

Talking to Chris the other day, I am also on the ethics committee, with Cynthia and a number of other people in the US and Canada, all of the classes have waned, which is our biggest challenge, because we can't see ourselves as some sales people or marketing. I just want to do the work and I want to teach the work. I am no good at marketing. Getting classes has been my biggest challenge. And as I said, traveling to teach classes here is very expensive. That has to be done. Otherwise you can't grow and you can't just keep trying to attract people in the same city of maybe a million people. You've got to move outside to continue to grow. That is probably our biggest challenge here.

*It's a challenge here too. It's everywhere. I think sometimes we rely too much on social media. They are really working on this issue at the home office.*

They're doing a good job, too.

*They are so good to us. I feel their support so much.*

Just spending an hour with Chris Gordon talking about the association and what we're planning to do, I felt very supported by him. He was very nice. Lisa came on and said hello and introduced two of their three kids. It was lovely.

It's really nice that Skype can allow for that kind of thing.

*It's a big thrill to be talking to you. And to get Skype going. That's a big accomplishment for me. I have one more question. What did you do before you got into Healing Touch?*

I am a nurse. I had been teaching nursing. Actually I had been working in intensive care. I was becoming concerned, because I could see, obviously, the focus on high tech and the medical model of care. I found the longer I was there, the more focused I was becoming on the patient and what was happening to them when in and out of a conscious state.

I was more focused on their families. I was helping their families adjust to what was happening to their loved ones, and helping to prepare the family if I was bringing them in to see their loved one in an induced coma or whatever it might be.

I could see that other people were much more focused on the technology. I thought there had to be more that we could offer a patient to this situation, other than suctioning their airways and taking their observations, and giving them all these drugs. There must be something we as nurses can offer them.

That's when I took Therapeutic Touch. I was really excited. It opened up this whole different world to me. I did that for a number of years before Healing Touch came to Australia. I was so excited by Healing Touch, because I could see it was such a structured program. There were techniques for particular conditions. It had this worldwide community that was developing. I wanted to be part of it. It connected deeply with me and where I was at and where I was going. I could see there were opportunities for village work about things and to learn about many of the spiritual things and see folks help others with spiritual things living in this world.

I have had lots of thanksgiving. It's made such a difference to my life. It's made a difference to my teaching of nursing. It's made a difference to my family. I can't begin to tell you what a change it's been to my entire life. It's been such a blessing to me. I just love it.

It's such a promise there. I just live and breathe and dream about it.

Pioneers in Healing Touch

# Reverend Rudy Noel
## In Memorial

### Introduction

Rudy Noel brought us several healing techniques that we use in Healing Touch including mind clearing and the Hopi techniques. To talk with him was such a joy. I learned much from him in a very short period of time. I think that is true for most people who knew him.

Rather than go into a lot of detail, I thought the two following articles about Rudy made better reading. I added one of his favorite stories to give a taste of what he was like.

### From Franny Harcey

In addition to being close friends, Rudy Noel and Janet Mentgen studied together when he moved to Denver in the 1980's. Rudy also studied and was on staff with Rosalyn Bruyere at the Healing Light Center in California in the late 1970's and early 1980's. He brought teachings from Rosalyn to Healing Touch, adapting her Mind Clearing, as well as, the Hopi Technique, which are part of the Healing Touch Program curriculum.

We all know how teachers come into our lives as we need them to appear. Four years ago I met Rudy Noel when I worked for Healing Touch Program. I had an instant connection with this master healer and he became my next teacher! (I would be inclined to say that I was presented as his teacher as well). We spent many hours together - learning and sharing. I bathed in the plethora of information he shared with me about his years of studying with Rosalyn Bruyere.

As our friendship grew, we delved deeper into the mysteries of healing and of what life presented each of us in every moment. His bountiful wisdom always flowed from both his mouth and his hands as we shared healing sessions. Rudy was the most inquisitive man I know. He never settled for an answer, but always wanted to understand the deeper meaning. He truly reminded me of my son, who at age three, had the ever present "why?" flowing from his mouth! It makes me smile to think what I learned from Rudy when he asked "why?" It will be a delight to read the book Rudy completed just a few months ago. His casual, conversational style as he shares his philosophy, some of his teachings and techniques, as well as how Rosalyn Bruyere influenced him will be as if Rudy is sitting next to you as you read his story.

Rudy's message about having an open heart chakra was one of the first things he shared with all those to whom I introduced him - my mentees, meditation friends and other healers who wanted to experience and gain his wisdom. He was a gift to so many on this planet. I am honored and blessed to have had this dear man as my friend. God bless you dear Rudy -- send me a message every once in a while! –Franny

The Huggin' Healer may be purchased through the Healing Touch Bookstore.

**From Heidi Van Vleet**

It was 2008 at the national conference when I first met Rudy. I had made a Native American talking stick that my husband and I presented to Lisa Gordon that represented the changes that the organization was going through. It had wood burned petroglyph symbols on it and glass and stone beads hanging down on it. That evening Rudy was studying the talking stick that I had made. He seemed really interested in how it was made. He asked me how I made it and after I had explained it to him, he told me that when I hold the stick to ask it what symbols I should put on it. Even today that is part of my creative process when I make a talking stick. I knew within about ten seconds that this man was someone I really needed to listen to very carefully.

    Then he started talking to me about Love. He wanted me to tell him where I feel it in my body. He kept prodding me until he could tell that I was feeling it. I felt like I was in an intense therapy session with all his questions and the deep way in which he was asking.

    Finally when I felt it, he had me give him a symbol. I gave him two thumbs up because he had given me two thumbs up a few minutes earlier. When I told him that was why I picked it, he said that he had given me two thumbs up because I wanted him to. He had me do the two thumbs up to anchor that feeling in my body. He told me to do that action, two thumbs up, before I started Healing Touch on someone, and that my unconditional love would mix with the client's unconditional love.

    Then he was starting to talk to me about where do I feel God in my body. Just as we were getting started Cynthia Hutchinson brought Jerry Becker over and he started with him and where he feels love in his body. Jerry came up with his own anchoring symbol. It was such an amazing moment for both of us. As Jerry and I were walking down the hallway and talking about our experience, I said to him that we had been "Rudy-ized".

    Throughout the rest of the conference when Jerry and I would meet eyes, we would each do our anchoring symbol to each other. Even now when I do that symbol I get that same feeling of the unconditional love that Rudy taught me to feel.  Rudy and I became good friends after that and he would always go out of his way to see me when we were at a conference.  I gave him a talking stick the next time I saw him and he gave me something that he had carried for years.  I feel so grateful for my relationship with him and still think of him often.


**One of Rudy's favorite stories**

*A Man, a Boy & a Donkey* ~ shared by Rudy Noel

An old man, a boy & a donkey were going to town.
The boy rode on the donkey & the old man walked.
As they went along they passed some people
who remarked it was a shame the old man
was walking and the boy was riding.

The man and boy thought maybe the critics were right,
so they changed positions.
Then, later, they passed some people who remarked,
"What a shame, he makes that little boy walk."
So they then decided they'd both walk!

Soon they passed some more people who thought
they were stupid to walk when they had a decent donkey to ride.
So, they both rode the donkey.
Now they passed some people
who shamed them by saying how awful to
put such a load on a poor donkey.
The boy and man figured they were probably right,
so they decided to carry the donkey.

As they crossed the bridge,
they lost their grip on the animal
and he fell into the river and drowned.

Rudy Noel

The moral of the story?
If you try to please everyone,
you might as well...
Kiss your ass goodbye!

Have A Nice Day And Be Careful With Your Donkey

# Sally Nyholt
## RN, LMBT, HTCP
### Elder

**Introduction**

I have yet to have the pleasure of meeting Sally face to face. I found her interview to be very human and heartwarming. She has some great stories and insights into the very early years. So many challenges face us as we begin the Healing Touch journey. Listening to Sally talk reminded me of some of my own struggles. For those of you who are new to Healing Touch, take heart. Sally made it and so will you. I especially liked her stories about distant work.

You'll find out more about Sally when you read Amelia Vogler's chapter.

**Interview**

*Have you ever held any positions in Healing Touch?*
Not within the organization, no. Other than being certified and an instructor.

*What Levels have you taught?*
1 and 2. Or what used to be 2A.

*What attracted you to energy medicine in the first place? How did you get started?*

I live in North Carolina now, but I lived in Illinois prior to that, while both my husband and I were going to school. My husband has wonderful sisters who are interested in all types of esoteric things. One of them introduced me to tarot when we were visiting with them in Wisconsin. I went back home to Champaign, Illinois. I didn't know anyone who was interested in tarot. I had bought a deck in Wisconsin and I started doing my own tarot study.

Then suddenly, there was a whole page with a huge article in the life style section of the Sunday paper featuring a photo of a woman who had all these tarot cards spread out in front of her. I was like, wow! There is somebody else here that is interested in tarot. I contacted her and became part of a weekly tarot study group that morphed into other things. One of them was studying energy therapy.

There's a fellow, I googled him not too long ago, so he's still around, named Alan Mesher. We got him to come into the area. One of the other gals in the group was familiar with him. He did a weekend workshop. It was my introduction to energy. He led us through a meditation which I know now is a grounding and centering exercise. One person lay on the table. Six people surrounded the person and placed their hands on different parts of the person's body and just relaxed. Alan guided us into communicating energy through our hands. It was remarkable. All kinds of things happened. With that many people communicating energy to one person, you know, people were having past life recall and all kinds of healing work happened. We were blown away by it.

Alan left. He lived in Texas and we were in Illinois. We started, in addition to the weekly tarot group, a weekly energy group in which we would do what Alan taught us.

That kind of steered me into Healing Touch. I had a very good friend who was actually the nurse director of the local hospice. We met and had champagne in her hot tub like a week before I was supposed to move to North Carolina. I hadn't seen her in a very long time. She told me that she had been diagnosed with multiple sclerosis. I told her all about the energy work we were starting to do. She was intrigued. I met with her and a really good friend of hers, literally a week before I moved, and taught them all I learned from Alan Mesher. They were very excited, and we worked together again one more time before I headed to North Carolina.

After I moved, they went through massage school and started studying all kinds of complimentary healing modalities, reading everything they could get their hands on. They both experienced a great deal of healing, and became active in the Healing Touch Program.

Two years later, I got a phone call from one of them. She was incredibly excited. She said, "We just attended this workshop. It was fantastic. It was Healing Touch with Janet Mentgen, and it was life changing. I just got a little money from an inheritance and I'm sending you and my daughter also."

Her daughter came down from the DC area and picked me up. We drove down to Gainesville, Florida. The class that we attended, I believe, was one of the very first Level 1 classes that was offered outside of Colorado.

The class was in late October or early November of 1989. Of course, we were absolutely taken with it. That was kind of it for me. Janet taught it and fellow students in the class were Dorothea Hover-Kramer, Sharon Scandrett-Hibdon, MyraTill-Tovey, and Judy Chiappone who wrote "The Light Touch". It was just fantastic. It was a star studded class. That was it. I mean I took Level 2A shortly after and then Level 2B. I went into Level 4 and then into instructor training. A lot of us from that class were in the first group of instructors that Janet taught.

It was whirl wind, once I had experienced that first Level 1. Like so many of us, that was it. That was going to be my thing. It was really remarkable.

*What happened in Level 1 that hooked you on Healing Touch?*

I think that my response to Level 1 was immediate, visceral and intuitive. Certainly, Janet was a very dynamic, wonderful teacher. But I felt so immediately connected to the work. It felt like a coming home, a discovery of a piece that I was missing, an awakening to remembering something vital. I didn't feel like I was learning something new, as much as that I was remembering something important that had slipped just outside of my consciousness. I was so grateful. And that was it. There was a deep certainty that my world had changed forever.

*How did it change your life?*

Well, I attended that first Level 1, like two or three months after I had opened up my massage practice. I had been an oncology nurse. I had gone to massage school and graduated in July. I opened up my office in September, and had that Level 1 class at the end of October, beginning of November. I immediately began incorporating it into my work. I combined massage and Healing Touch for a while. Eventually I had clients that just wanted Healing Touch.

Of course, it enters every phase of your life. The word "energy" became pretty prevalent in my life. I would talk about things in terms of energy, and describe things in terms of their energy. It just felt like, instead of learning something new, I was remembering something that I already knew that was deep inside of me. It was like a homecoming. I am certain a lot of other people will describe it in the same way, but that is what it has been like for me is the remembering.

My experience of life is very much through the focus of energy. It has changed everything: the way that I live, the way that I relate to other people, and certainly my practice. I was really grateful that I already had a practice. Then I could just integrate Healing Touch into it.

I did massage for between ten and thirteen years. I started to phase the massage out after about ten years, because my hands gave out. They couldn't handle it. I gradually transitioned my practice into just energy work. I do some foot reflexology, cranio-sacral therapy, some crystal and gemstone therapy, but the bedrock of it is Healing Touch. It's just become so prevalent in my life.

*Do you have a favorite story that you like to tell of a healing experience?*

Wow. Interesting to try to pull just one out. One of the top two dearest people in the world to me lives in another part of the country. That's hard for us. We talk every week, and we're very close. Twenty-four years ago, she began her journey of recovery from alcohol abuse. We're accustomed to meeting at the Carolina coast. There is an island with a beach that we would go to once a year in the fall.

The year that she began her sobriety was with one of those visits. I had brought my table to the beach. She missed her flight and had to take a later one, because she had had a black out the night before. She barely scraped it together to get on another flight. When I met her at the airport, she looked horrible. She felt horrible. She felt like her head was any second going to fall off of her body and roll across the room.

I'll back up just a little bit. In the airport where she lives, she had run into an old friend while she was waiting for that second plane, who had begun his journey in sobriety. He happened to have a copy of the "Big Book". He gave it to her. They had a short conversation. She got on the plane. When I met her at the airport in North Carolina, I gave her a big hug. She started to cry.

She said, "Sally, I think I'm an alcoholic."

I said. "You can't imagine how happy I am to hear you say that." I'm tearing up as I'm talking about it.

She was taken aback by my response. I was really hoping that at some point she would be able to confront this. We went to the island. I had my table set up. I got her on the table. This was near the beginning of my Healing Touch journey, and I had only the basic skills. I worked on her for about forty-five minutes to an hour. I did the chakra connection, grounded her really good, and I also did the magnetic unruffling *(magnetic clearing),* I think that's what it's called now, to clear the alcohol out of her system. I was really committed to that technique, which you need to do to get down through all the layers, until it feels like glass as Janet used to say.

She got up off the table feeling perfectly fine. Felt great. She felt clear and calm. She took a long walk on the beach, and committed to her sobriety. I would say that is a really important story for me, and it was a big validation for me about the work. In forty-five minutes to an hour it was such a turnaround for her physically. Also spiritually. It helped to bring some momentum into what had already started for her. She was amazed.

Human beings, we can't help it. We're stubborn. I think we really appreciate validation, and validation helps us to believe even stronger. It would be nice if we didn't need it, and we could just believe, but I think that validation is important for us. That was a big validation for me. It was a very special and very treasured experience with the work. That is the first thing that popped into my head, of course. In twenty-six years I've had a few. But this one was especially special.

I started doing distance work and have been doing distance work for a long time for my family, and friends, and clients. The other story that popped into my head, I had a call from someone whose mother lived in Fiji. She had just been diagnosed with Dengue fever. She was in her late 80's, and very frail to begin with. She was just not well. They were very concerned about her. I said, "Okay, what the heck", and did a distance session with her. I visualized myself doing Healing Touch techniques with her. She had been bedridden completely and they were really worried that she was going to leave her body soon. I was told that after I finished, within an hour she got up, got dressed, and wanted something to eat. All these years later, validation is always a welcome thing. With that, it was remarkable. I was like, whoa. Thank you to all of my helpers and everyone that went down there to help communicate the energy.

I remember back in the old days, gosh, when was it? I have a picture of the person in my head. She was a student in one of Janet's classes, and worked in home health care in hospice. She was active in the program for a long time. We were talking about how there were times when she wanted to work on some of her patients in the hospital, but she didn't feel comfortable. She felt like it would call attention to her in a way that would be difficult for her to explain, etc. She told Janet that what she would do is just get quiet and imagine herself, hold pictures of herself doing the work, doing the techniques on the person.

Janet was like, "Yes! Absolutely. It will work when you do it that way."

Of course, that impressed all of us. That was the basis for doing the distance work.

I do a lot of it now. I have one client, who works in New York and in Florida. She wants to have work done weekly. So when she's out of town we arrange a time. If she's able to, she will sit or lie quietly during our time. I do work on her over distance, and she says she really feels very nice changes. I also work on animals over distance. I've been doing it for a long time, and both people and animals seem to benefit from it.

I taught for a while at a local community college. So here's another tangent. There's a local community college that's in Raleigh. They were starting up their Curriculum Therapeutic Massage Program. I ended up coming in, and helping design the curriculum program. I built into the curriculum an energy therapy module that I taught for a few years. I turned it over to another Healing Touch person.

I would talk to the students about distance work. I would say, "Can you agree that I'm affecting the energy field when I'm doing the unruffling (now called hands in motion) 6 inches away?"

And the students would say, "Yeah. You're definitely having an impact on the energy field."

"Let me back up a little bit and do you think I'm affecting the energy flow from here?"

"Yeah. We can see that."

Then I go to the other side of the room and I'm like "Well, what about from here?"

And they're like, "Yeah."

Because it's intention. The intention is to focus energy. Then I go out into the hall and say, "What about from here?"

Most of them were like, "Well, yeah. Yeah, I can see that."

I'm like, "So what about from the other side of the city?"

It's easing them into the idea, that with intention and focus you can affect an energy field from quite a distance. That's how I would explain it to students. I encourage them to try it also.

It's fun. You listen to the little whispers in your ear when you're teaching. Go with what comes to you as it's happening.

*Do you have any comments or advice for new or potential students coming into Healing Touch?*

I'll go with the first thing that came into my mind.

*It's usually the best.*

I'm a person that, over the years, has long ago taken the training to heart and have been listening to guidance as far as doing the work. The techniques that I use look very similar to, or often the same as the Healing Touch techniques that I learned. Eventually you do take off the training wheels and listen to the energy. Let the energy guide you. Someone who's starting, I think, a bit of advice that I would give is, in the beginning, learn the techniques as they are taught, and practice them as they are taught for a while, before you start experimenting. I think that early on, at least for me, and I would encourage this in my students, having that basic structure to be able to take off and fly from, it's really important. Do what your instructor tells you to do. Let them guide you and practice it the way you learned it for a while.

I guess what's popping into my head is that I love figure skating. In figure skating as they're practicing a routine, it becomes muscle memory. Let the techniques become like muscle memory to you. Then you'll have more experience working with energy, with assessing, with engaging the energy and with correcting the energy. Then take off and do what the energy tells you. I think it's really important to have that structure, to have basis in the beginning, because even twenty-six years later, you rely on it. At least I do. I do rely on it. Doing what I just said, learning and practicing those techniques really benefited me.

*What do you see for the future of Healing Touch?*

Hopefully continued growth. I think, like a lot of people, the separation between Program and International was heartbreaking for me. I don't think that it's possible at this point for there to be any kind of combination of those two again. I think that ship has sailed, at least from what I've heard. I feel like Program is where I personally have aligned for a number of reasons. But everyone, all the old timers, the elders, went through their own process about deciding where to align. I know some people have still aligned with both. But I chose to align with Program.

I guess I would really like to hope that each of them can find their own feet really firmly again. I'm not articulating it very well. I apologize, but I guess I long for the old days, to be honest with you, when there was one organization with HTI being in charge of certification and when things felt more complete and more grounded to me. I'm feeling like things are coming together again for Program. They seem to be coming together for HTI, I guess it's a different name now, even. I hope there won't be any repeat of that schism that happened in either organization, that each of them can become whole and complete and continue to spread the word and continue to get more people interested in energy, and more people practicing. I did not articulate that well, probably partly because it still exists on a level of emotion for me. It's a very painful subject. How many years has it been? It's really a shame. It really was heartbreaking for me. I didn't understand it, and I still really don't understand it, especially on an emotional level.

The program was and is still home for me. It's like a divorce, a really painful divorce. Children in a divorce, it's like where is my home now? I'm just realizing it as I'm talking to you about it. That is kind of what I went through: where is my home now? I have been settling in with Program. I have decided this is my home. I'm hoping that things will become, will feel more safe to me.

There were things that happened early on. There was a period of time when there was almost sort of a little mini coo staged in which Dorothea Hover was wanting to take over the program. She wanted to declare Janet unfit to continue as the program director. I heard this from Janet and Mary Jo Bulbrook. This isn't hearsay. I don't know if you were familiar with it. That shook me. It was the beginning of me starting to pull away a little bit. I couldn't believe that it was happening. Of course, it blew over. Janet handled it.

Dorothea pulled away and started her own little organization, and then she eventually came back to the program when that sort of fizzled. There were a lot of rocky periods in the beginning. It wasn't okay, but it was growing pains. I think that the program grew so quickly, that Janet was chasing after it trying to catch it at different points. It was certainly a challenge. That was nothing compared to the schism that developed.

I just really hope for healing. I hope for healing for all of us who were impacted by it for HTI and for Program. Just so everything will settle back down again and stay settled. The word can get out and more people can learn, and practice, and take it out into the world. 'Cause God knows, we need it.

*Do you have a favorite Janet Mentgen story?*

Oh gosh. Two of them pop into my head. I was invited to write a little article for the newsletter. I think I was identified as an elder, and they reached out to me, and asked if I would be willing to write an article. I talked about one of the things that was very special to me about Janet, was her humanity. Incredibly gifted healer, visionary. I mean there is no question about that. But it really helped me that she was so human, because it helped model for me that I could be, I could go to the office and do healing work and have amazing experiences working with the energy, and working with spirit, and then come home and watch Grey's Anatomy. I could be a human being doing this work. That was one of the things that Janet modeled for me personally.

One of the things that I thought was so adorable was that she had this little stuffed weasel that she carried with her when she traveled. It wasn't very big. It was like her constant companion. I think its name was "Weazel" and she loved it. It was just part of her entourage. I thought that was so sweet and so dear. It was like this incredible person, that everyone kind of deified, loved her little stuffed weasel.

There were other things. She would have a beer when we went to dinner on Friday night or Saturday night, when she was teaching in our area. She liked to have a beer every once in a while. There were so many people who were into the really healthy diets. She ate very well also, but she listened to her body. When her body told her that she needed beef, she would eat beef, because she told me that beef is very grounding. Sometimes, when your body needs grounding, it will tell you.

This is segueing into my second story, when she was here in the area. Janet was the instructor, and both of us who were assisting her, went to a restaurant for dinner after class. Janet started it. She got out her pendulum first. We all got out our pendulums and we were penduling the menu to see what we were supposed to have for supper. It was lighthearted. We're kind of giggling about it, but we were also taking it fairly seriously.

The server came over and said, "Would you like to hear about the specials?"

We all stopped and looked at each other for like a couple of heart beats. Then somebody jumped up, and held the pendulum over his head and said, "Okay. Go." We all totally cracked up.

I love to remember the lighthearted moments about her, and also how she did take care of herself. She was shy and more introverted than I think most people knew. I saw that side of her, too. When she taught big groups, it was a lot of energy for her in the room. As someone who was assisting her, I remember that her health was starting to get a little iffy at one point. As soon as she called for a break, the assistants with her would flank her and escort her out of the room. People would want to come up to her at the breaks, and want to hug her, and ask her questions. Sometimes she wasn't up for that. It was a little too much. She needed to go and be quiet. I really respected that. That she took care of herself. If that's what she needed, then she listened to that. She was a role model for me in many things, but definitely in those things.

Like I said, I really appreciated and learned from her about being a human being doing this work. That was important for me personally. It made me feel more comfortable with myself as a healer.

*Is there anything else you would like to add or say?*

A good question. One more thing that popped into my mind, right away, is that when I heard that Janet had left her physical body, the first thought that popped into my head is "Oh, how wonderful. She is going to be free of the limitations of that physical body and now she can be wherever we are, watching us and helping us do our work."

It freed her to step into the next phase of her beingness or her existence as a healer. It would allow her to be a guide and a helper to us anytime, anywhere. So I was very joyful for her, and also for us. It was like, "Oh, how lovely. Now she can step into this next adventure, and this next phase of assisting us with Healing Touch."

I have felt her energy, not every time, not all the time, but there have definitely been times when I have felt her, her energy in the room when I've been working. And it's been, oh, I can't even describe how wonderful.

Like I said earlier, I do have so much hope for the future, for the program, for the work. I'm so grateful that, over all these years, energy and energy therapy have gradually, gradually, gradually, but definitely become more accepted and more real as a part of health and healing, as a recognized part of health and healing. It's so nice that all types of people have more of an openness to it. That wasn't always the case. I think that, way back when, we were real pioneers as far as the work was concerned.

I'll never forget the time that my youngest brother called me and said, "Sally. I just saw something on the news about Healing Touch. It was on national news, just a little blurb about Healing Touch and Therapeutic Touch energy work. That's what you do isn't it?"

I said, "Yeah."

He said, "Wow. It was on the nightly news."

It was so cute, because it was obvious he didn't take me seriously until that moment. And again, it's validation. He got validation that what I was doing might actually be something real.

That is happening more and more. I am really grateful for that. I would just love to see that continued.

What a group of people in Healing Touch. It's so varied. So special. Each and all.

# Sharon Robbins
## RN, HTCP

### In Memorial

I first met Sharon when she invited me to a meeting about Healing Touch Professional Association (HTPA). I don't think we even had a name for it then. My first impression of her was that of a shy woman with a big dream. Her enthusiasm was infectious and I found myself jumping right in. A couple of meetings later, I found other obligations took me away from continuing my share of the work on the founding of HTPA. I really didn't want to stop, but life has its way and I don't regret it. I know I missed out on a lot of the fun.

Sharon took off in a big way. We all thought it was very much needed. Sharon accomplished things. She didn't just sit around and talk about what was needed. She got it done. As Executive Director for HTPA, and due to her determination, we now have liability insurance for students, practitioners, and instructors, not only of Healing Touch, but other energy medicine modalities as well.

She helped create the Community Connections Volunteer Bank, monthly business support calls, Healing Touch service for the military, and started the formation of HTPA chapters. The Practitioner Support Column in Energy Medicine began with Sharon. She wrote many articles for the column.

I was with Sharon and Lisa when speakers came to an ISSSEEM (International Society for the Study of Subtle Energies and

Energy Medicine) conference introduced us to the Voice for HOPE (Healers of Planet Earth).

It was Sharon, with some encouragement from Lisa, who became a member of Voice for HOPE and later became a representative. She actually went to Capitol Hill for one of their HOPE on the Hill events in Washington DC. She met with Congressman Dennis Kucinich for over half an hour. You can see her on YouTube where she tells about her experience.

Sharon had vision. She believed in herself and her dreams. She had the strength to stand up for what she thought was right, often in the face of some pretty critical people. She never gave up.

She is very much missed.

# Sharon Scandrett-Hibdon
## PhD, ARNP-BC, HTCP/I
### Elder

### Introduction

My experiences with Sharon are all over the map. I first perceived her as a very strict, follow-the-rules type person and she is to a point. My later experiences opened up a whole different side of her and I have come to like her very much. She can be warm and caring, and has an unexpected sense of humor that shows itself from time to time.

She did our interview while driving a truck, which showed me another side to her life.

Sharon was very instrumental in the forming of Healing Touch Program to the professional modality it has become today. It took a lot of effort, countless meetings, gentle persuasion (and some not) to create our fabulous program. Next time you see her, tell her thanks.

### Interview

*What got you started in energy medicine and, in particular, Healing Touch?*

Back in what '74? I was working at the University of Iowa on faculty, and I got interested in Therapeutic Touch at that point. It really began, you know I'd read Krieger's book. It really began with sharing it with students and with some of the people on faculty. I thought, "Wow, This is great."

I had been involved, a little bit, with some alternative medicine people in Iowa City. We began offering this series of courses, mainly on holistic fear and then we incorporated Therapeutic Touch. We did a little bit of, I'm blocking on the name of it, Polarity. That kind of stuff. And then Greek mythology. None of us were certified, because at that time they didn't even have certification. We just did it.

I was doing that in Iowa City and incorporating it into a course called Holistic Nursing. It was an elective. Students could begin to take that.

Now, when I met Janet, that was at AHNA. We were both asked to sit on the board. We were asked to sit on the board because they had had several people who had resigned, or had been asked to leave, or whatever. I don't know what the circumstances were, because I never really explored that very much.

That was the year she was Holistic Nurse of the Year. At that time, I didn't know her program at all. We became really good friends. We did a lot of stuff, play stuff. We did a retreat for Holistic Nurses at Faraway Ranch which is a thousand acre ranch near Tellurite. That was with Laurie Wrenquist, who was a friend of Charlotte MacGuire. That's kind of how we started.

She began talking about her program. Sometime during that period of the very early days, she was approached by Lynn Stevens, who said, "Why don't you consider using your program as a CE (continuing education) program for AHNA? I mean, run it through AHNA, so that our nurses can be trained in your program."

I still hadn't experienced the program, but I really encouraged her to think about that because, first of all, it was the Holistic Nurses Association and we were both on the board of directors.

I don't know where I was in the office, because we were at the head of the educational board at one point, for what seemed like a long time, probably four or five years. I was treasurer, I think, at one point. Then I went into the line for presidency.

In the meantime, I suggested that she go ahead, if she wants to do that as a CE course. Let's run it as an experiment at the University of Tennessee where I was on faculty at that point. She agreed. Michael Parder, my dean, who was a Rosarian, was very open to it. That's what happened.

We ran the first course at the University of Tennessee in the nursing lab. We had about twenty-five in that class. They were, many of them, instructors, nursing instructors from all across the country. I was just blown away by what she had put together. I think the other people were too.

At that point, I made a decision that I was going to be an instructor in this program, because I loved it. That's kind of the beginning. We were her first class outside of Colorado. She talked about having had it there in Colorado for the previous ten years where she was developing things.

At that point I think it was called Therapeutic Touch or whatever. She had a series of advanced courses where she had the techniques that were in the higher levels of 2 and 3, and they were taught as advanced practice kind of thing at that point. So that's kind of the beginning for me.

*How did it change your life?*

I began devoting everything to it. All my vacation periods went into Healing Touch. She moved us through pretty fast because she needed instructors, especially as there started to be a demand. They went to Gainsville second, and I don't know if they went to

Indiana next or on the west coast. Anyway we could look back in the records and see. It just exploded.

A number of us who were educators already, she moved us through fairly quickly because we were already teachers. I think every single vacation I had, probably for the next twenty years, I would occasionally take another vacation, but most of my time off was spent doing Healing Touch. We were teaching almost every single weekend, just like she was in the early days. That was ridiculous, I'm sure, really, when you think about it. But that's what we did to help her out and to get it going.

That's the beginning for me. It did change my life. I taught it at the University of Iowa and incorporated it into that course called Holistic Nursing and the Level 1 curriculum with Janet's permission. We didn't, at that point, there was no – they were issuing CE's, but the university picked them. as an elective so the students didn't get a course in Healing Touch, they just got a regular three hour elective.

We had it set up so the graduate students could take it as well if they chose to. They had an extra paper to do, essentially. I think they had an additional project to do as well. That's the beginnings for me.

*Do you have a favorite healing story?*

My client was lying on the floor. At that time I didn't have a table in my office. We had a palette for her. She was just thin as a rail. It's like such total love I have never felt as when we were working together, before she died, probably a week or so after that treatment. But we did assist her to have a little more comfort.

I think the biggest thing, and this is what I have noticed across many patients, is that sense of wholeness that they seem to have when we get them balanced and flowing again. She was pretty shut down, if I recall. It's been a long time. My notes are scrapped away somewhere. I just remember how important, incredibly intimate, and loving that whole session was.

You'll have that periodically, but not always with everyone. You love them and we stand there in total presence. But sometimes they'll start a connection that will take your breath away. That's what I remember. The other thing I noticed, in the beginning, especially when I was – I used to chelate really heavily. It was very fast. It's kind of a resignation for that. I noticed that, with that, those sessions cleared all kinds of stuff. It was sometimes very unusual things.

As I have thought since then, I have noticed it's a bunch of junk work. I don't think it's quite as deep. Maybe as deep in different ways, but we're not seeing quite as much of what I would call drama than in those early days, especially when - Level 3 is my favorite, because that's, to me, the deepest course that we offer.

*Do you have any comments or advice for new students?*

Well, I think that they need to understand that it is a life path that will change their relationship. That's the thing that is probably the hardest about it. Because people, many people don't know quite what to do with, I guess, with your knowledge and your understanding. I, of course, learned to be very quiet about it. I mean I was just there. I offered. Many people will accept it. It's much more now than it was. The biggest thing is to me, is it's the missing piece in medicine, because we take care of many things, but the biofield often is neglected. Now, if the biofield is not repaired, it's going to be much harder for them to heal quickly or to heal in a balanced way. To me it's an essential part of healing, an essential part of care.

I think it's interesting, because I was reading Norine's article from AHNA. There was a poll out going over the diagnosis of the certain energy field. The certain energy field diagnosis was been pulled in 2013. I didn't realize that. This brought it to my attention.

They're working very hard to get it back in. It really hurts us within nursing and it hurts us in CAM, you know, the Complimentary Alternative Medicine field of NIH )National Institute of Health).

I'm hoping Norine Frish, of AHNA is working on it very hard with a whole committee of people, some from Iowa, some from different places. I'm getting ready to send her an email on some my observations having done that book on energetic patterns. I think the biggest thing that I noticed is that if you don't repair biofields, people feel off. They feel tilted or unbalanced or unstable or somehow off. I don't know how we quantify that, other than through subjective self-explore. But, to me, it's critical.

Those are some of my passionate thoughts I sense about that.

*What do you see for the future of Healing Touch?*

I'm a little concerned because it feels like our numbers are down right now in classes. I think it's been around long enough that people go, "Oh, ho hum. I don't think I want to do that or whatever." You know what I mean?

I'm not sure how we put a new spin on it or somehow we market it in a way that is going to get it in a bigger presence in the world. I think we do it one chief by one chief, which is what we've always done. Our classes, of course, in the beginning because there was a lot of excitement about it were much bigger. Now, I mean I think we still have classes, but they're certainly much smaller.

Mainly it's the whole business pressing. There is just so much work to be done if we are going to have it the way Janet wanted it in every household as a first aide tool.

I know the oldsters, the first run of people, are at the point where they've gotten tired. They've given and given and given and doing stuff. The youngsters have got come forward. I know they've done a good job getting it into the hospitals, because we pushed the front so that they were able to step in more easily. But, it's been small little pockets.

I think the work is such sacred, light-filled work. I think we just keep plugging away at the research. We keep plugging away offering classes. We do what we can, but I'm not sure. To me it still belongs in every household. Janet was right about that. But how we get it there I'm not sure.

I know I have taught very good classes here in this state mainly because they have a two-tiered CE program and I have to somehow – They rejected our first application. It came from the headquarters, because they thought they didn't want ANCC involved. They wanted just to be a CE people.

So now I have to rewrite it with an addendum that Iowa has a special category and will hand out two certificates: an ANCC certificate and a CE one.

But I have just been dragging my feet on doing that. I've been waiting on this law suit to get done and get through all this stuff that we're trying to clean up. It's dragged our energy down. I feel bad about all that. I know Lisa's getting tired. Chris is getting tired. I am concerned. I am. I talk with them frequently, trying to give them pep talks. I amplify, do whatever I can to help them. But they're wearing out. How long has it been? Since 2005. And here we are, ten years later almost.

I think it is a light-filled, blessed work, over seen by guardian angels and is sacred work. It is our work and it is our job to get it out there, but it just feels like the world is so stressed right now, financially and resource wise and pollution wise. We know all these things. Security is not as secure as it used to be. I think there is a lot that people have to deal with. This feels, I suspect to a number of people, like it's frivolous. It's not. It's essential work. How do we convey that message? I'm not sure. I wish I knew the answer to that.

You're kind of inspiring me to get back on it.

We need articles in popular magazines. We need to get them where they reach the people. I think the people can push this through somehow.

*From what you've talked about it seems like it's a time when it's most needed.*

*Would you tell me about how you brought the Scudder technique to us?*

I went to a conference, Spiritual Frontiers of Minnesota, I don't even remember where. Maybe Rochester, I'm not sure where it was. But it was a great big conference and Reverend Scudder presented this at one of the last things. It was just the most awesome experience for the whole audience and I thought, "Wow. You know, we need to have something like this." At that time, I think I had learned it prior to, even Healing Touch. But anyway, it was at a summer conference.

I asked Janet if we could include something like this and Janet said, "No. We don't need the curriculum changed.

And I said, "Well, to me it's a transition thing, because you are using light touch, loving touch, and you're brushing the meridians, you know, major meridians, not all of them. But you feel the difference. It's a powerful tool so that people can experience that energy makes a difference in their physical body. Finally she agreed to have it as an optional thing in Level 1. Lots of times it didn't get taught. But other times, it did. The people, I think, that have taken to it have really found it a beneficial technique. She never really believed it, but she allowed it.

It was just like the certification. She wasn't interested in that. I said. "It's timely. I'm in a powerful position now with president of AHNA. We either do it or we don't do it. I f you want to add credibility to energy work, we need to do it now. She knew how much work it was going to take, but she agreed, kind of fighting and screaming. (She chuckled.) But she did.

*Who was Reverend Scudder?*

I don't know a lot about him, except that he was real active in Spiritual Frontiers and I really don't. But I wanted him to have credit because it was his technique. I believe that they contacted his foundation later to get the formal kind of permission. I believe that's true. You would have to check with the office on that to make sure.

The other thing I tell the students, if you have a child that you need to quiet, do that. They will allow you to do that. They love it. And they will beg for it, you know, when they're stressed or need a little nurturing. You can put your kids to sleep in a heartbeat, by just doing the scudder when they are going to bed or whatever.

The thing is, and they didn't write this in the curriculum, but I know I've said it as I say it every time I teach it. When you're doing the light touch, very light, it's like a breath. Like an angel wing breath. You are to send love through your fingers, through your fingertips. It's so nurturing.

*Do you have a favorite Janet Mentgen story?*

Oh, my goodness. It's really interesting, because I have a kind of thing about things through all this court stuff. I guess I'll just tell you some funny things.

When we were at Telluride, now this is prior to Healing Touch. I mean prior to it being in AHNA. We were at camp and we had trouble getting water because we had about twenty people in the camp and we would have to go get water. The thousand acre ranch had water for cows, and not for people. We'd have to go to a place where the water was safe. She would get in her jeep, literally, and drive along these ravines. It scared me half to death. I would be looking down to these several thousand feet drops and she was just having the time of her life, scaring me. She liked adventure.

Janet was quite a little scientist. In other words she did a lot with brain waves and stuff, .early in those first ten years. She had machines she would run with brain waves and was very interested in all of that. I think she would have made a practical scientist.

The other thing is, she was an avid gardener. Her daughter has developed a cinder block garden method. She had those all over her place. That was her sanctuary in terms of having a quiet restful place to be.

She would come to my house, loved the chihuahuas. She always would have them come up and visit with her, especially my first little chihuahua. She just thought he was great. He loved her. I could take him to her house. She had great big dogs and three kids and all that. He would get cornered behind the toilet with the great big dog who was chasing him, and be scared half to death and hiding. She'd just laugh. She thought he was great.

She loved to go places like to the Indian Sacred Baths. She did lots of side trips. Lots of hiking in, nature. She always knew where the portals were, where you were to enter and when you asked permission.

Very psychic. Tuned in and very quick to suss people. That was helpful to her a lot. I usually stood as her warrior behind her back. That was my prime role probably, besides helping her to get certification through.

People challenged her at times, because they were envious, I think, of what she was doing. She was a bachelors nurse. She didn't have a master's degree. She was pushing through a fabulous program that she had developed on her own by layering it exquisitely. Her program is exquisitely layered if you follow all the energy. Even though not all the techniques are hers, of course, but she gave good recognition, I thought, to all of the people that developed some of them. She made some modifications and let the people know what those were.

Is that enough?

You know, there are so many stories. If I could – people ask me and I spent a lot of time with her, but it was intermittent because I lived in Texas and she lived in Colorado. Our time together was always good, but it was intermittent.

I would go to her house and stay with her and go to Shadowcliff and all of the various things as much as I could afford to, because I had a family. But I think our bonding was so strong during those two years we ran those camps at Thousand Acre Ranch. That's in our relationship. Plus we were on the board, oh my gosh, I was on that AHNA board for at least eight years. She was too. She stayed on even after I left. She had to as program director, but she was a non-voting member at that point.

I wanted to get off the board and try other things. She put me on the foundation immediately. Then I went on the Healing Touch board after that. I finally said, "Enough."

I really felt Janet appreciated the people who supported her. She's fun. Fun.fun.fun.

Oh, I'll tell you one funny story. It kind of shocked me. I was working on her. We were in Level 4 or maybe 5. I taught a lot of 5's. We had her on the table and I was saying to her, "I don't feel a thing in your field."

She had been stressed and she said to me, "It's because we're the same frequency, Sharon."

I said, "Oh."

She said, "But I do feel better because you worked on me."

I had never thought about that, that if you're the same frequency as your client you won't feel anything. If they are denser than you, then you are going to feel something. That was really, that was like a light bulb came on for me at that point. I really began paying attention to learn about frequencies.

What I found, you see, none of that happens until you get Level 3. You've got to spin out, you've to be higher than your client. Otherwise you're not doing anything. You're just massaging their energy field. You're not curing them. And so when I teach Level 3 now, I expect them to spin up really high.

That was fun. She knew how to get me. It was really interesting too, because Janet – I was always the emotional one, because I'm a psych nurse. I guess that's just my arena. She always hated that part of it. She'd say, "Don't get emotional on me."

And I'd say, "Well, that's my role."

Of course I had developed a course for the University of Iowa. I said to her, "Well, I think this belongs in Healing Touch as one of our electives."

She said, "Oh. Absolutely. And you teach it."

I said, "Okay."

So that's how that one got going. I've been a little bit laggard on it, so we're going to get it reactivated here. Lisa has indicated she wants to buy it and I have about three instructors now. We will be launching that again. I'm dragging my heals on rewriting the manual. It's not because I don't want to do it, it's just that I've had other things I've had to deal with.

And, again, I'm kind of waiting on the court deal to get finished before I take on another project. I know it's going to take little bit of work to get done.

*Do you have anything else you would like to add?*

Well, I do think - I love the work. I mean, it's a passion. I even went through the Healing Touch for Animals course, because that's an eye opener course too. If you haven't, you work with animals and I do. I run that riding stable for special needs kids and normal kids. So do I use Healing Touch on animals a lot? No, I don't. I use it when I need it. It's so good to know.

I think the biofield just needs our attention. Again, I am just a little perplexed on how to make it more mainstream, how to make it common knowledge that this is something important. That it's not, you know, airy-fairy like a lot of people think it is. It's actually a critical piece of us.

Just like the hara line is too. That is one more thing. I have found within our program the one thing that I have pushed, and pushed, and pushed to try to get this in the curriculum. And so far it is not done. Lisa would like to put it in advanced practice. I think it belongs in Level 4. But I don't know that that's ever going to happen. But I think all of the hara work, because that, to me, is the deepest level of everything that we do.

Bless Cathy Sinnett for bringing that forward. I know Mary Jo Bulbrook wrote on that. I know Janna Moll has done some work on that as well. I have followed Cathy Sinnett most in her work, because she was so clear in her psychism and so thorough in her explanation of it in her book. I don't know if you have her book. It's called *Energy Transformation*. You have to buy it from the family now. It's amazing.

All that hara work, if your Level 3 work doesn't hold, that's the level you go to. That will take care of it for you.

I guess that's all I have to say.

# Kathy Sinnett
### RN, HTCP/I
### Elder
### In memorial

The following is taken from the *Energy Magazine* archives. It was lovingly written by Mary Ann Geoffrey and Sharon Scandrett-Hibdon.

A great sense of loss fell upon many as Kathy Sinnett departed earth's plane on the "Wings of the Angels" she loved so dearly. Her last moments were shared with her family as her six amazing daughters sang several songs, including "Amazing Grace". They spoke of a very peaceful transition for Kathy.

For all who knew Kathy, "Amazing Accomplishments" are noted by those whose lives she touched. Kathy studied in-depth with Janet Mentgen and was the sixth certified Practitioner and ninth certified Healing Touch Instructor in this country (1993), as well as, being a cherished member of the Healing Touch Professional Association's Elder Council. Kathy also received certification as a Holistic Nurse through the American Holistic Nurse's Association.

She was a full-time spiritual, energy healer and teacher for over 20 years. She was the author of several self-help books including Energetic Transformations and Insights and was known for her "sense of humor and a delightful writing style". In addition, Kathy wrote a monthly column for Connections, a wholistic news magazine.

A true pioneer in Energy Medicine, Kathy used her remarkable ability to develop a successful business and Healing Touch practice. As a women of great courage, she influenced and paved the way for many students and practitioners to develop sound business practices. She founded the Healing Touch Practice in Farmington, MIchigan as a model clinic, which began in Livonia, Michigan, and is still supporting practitioners in training, as well as, the local community.

Kathy fully believed in holism and self healing - evidenced by her strong will to live and to heal herself. She met her challenges "head on" and dealt with issues with the same regard. She controlled her healing environment when able and made the best possible use of both traditional and complementary therapies. In her daughter's words, "What others saw as obstacles, Mom viewed as challenges to be overcome, and lessons to be learned. When faced with an endless stream of doctors, tests and waiting rooms, Mom decided she must need to learn patience. When her invasive and aggressive treatments stripped her of dignity, she concluded that she must need to learn humility. When her physical limitations made it necessary to rely on the strength of others, she reflected on her need to learn to receive, as well as, to give. Her long recovery period battling the effects of her treatments were for her an opportunity to realize how much her famliy and friends loved her. Mom faced her diagnosis (of Glioblastoma ) with courage, handled her life changes with dignity, and met her physical and mental challenges with humor and grace."

"In 2005, Mom was given less than 6 months to live (only 3-5% of patients live three years). At Mom's quarterly MRIs her neurologist would explain the cancer would return, and Mom always argued saying, 'No, I am healed'. To the doctors amazement and Mom's smug satisfaction, she was always right. An MRI in December of 2011 revealed that she was cancer free."

Kathy applied this same sensitivity when working with others and was very attuned to their needs, always attempting to empower them. Her understanding and gifts of healing were deep and profound. The nurturing Kathy provided healed others. Kathy's legacy includes the role of spouse, mother, grandmother, friend, nurse, healer, author and musician. She was cofounder of the Michigan Holistic Nurse's Association where she served as President for two years. Kathy told her daughter that two things were very important to her -- helping and touching the lives of others in the best way she could and teaching and training others - especially nursing students and other professionals in Michigan.

Included among her many roles was as a "baker". Many are aware of her remarkable ability to bake a few dozen loaves of whole grain bread in one morning, the best carrot cake, rice pudding and oatmeal raisin cookies. Kathy also delighted in "folk lore" music where dozens would gather to sing and play "Irish Tunes". From violins, to washboards and clapping spoons, folks had a great deal of fun as they heartfully shared music that was nurturing and delightful.

Cherished memories and appreciative words are arriving from all over the country to describe this remarkable and spirited woman -- accomplished, determined, loved, caring, compassionate, courageous and a wonderful sense of humor.

In a recent conversation with Kathy, she expressed her great love for her family, friends, children, grandchildren and her work. A true role model, Kathy always put "her best foot forward" as she faced life's many challenges.

She was a true friend to many and her ready laugh, humorous comments and big smile will be greatly missed. May you rest Kathy -- and know that you truly made a difference to those whose lives you touched. For that -- we are grateful.

# Linda Smith
## RN, MS, HTSM-CP/I, CCA
### Elder

**Introduction**

Linda is an early pioneer of Healing Touch. However, she is best known for having founded Healing Touch Spiritual Ministries and the Institute of Spiritual Healing and Aromatherapy. Linda saw a connection between Healing Touch and Christian theology and cleverly brought the two together.

Later, she added aroma therapy. She is one of the leading authorities in aroma therapy. I loved doing her interview, partly because she was so much fun, and partly because I learned a little about aroma therapy, a somewhat new subject for me.

**Interview**

*You were the founder of Healing Touch Spiritual Ministries, is that right?*

Yes. I've been involved with Healing Touch since the very beginning.

*Would you tell me a little bit about Healing Touch Spiritual Ministries and where it is?*

I don't own it any more. You have to go back to the year 1995. I was the administrator for the Healing Touch Program. For a number of years I was somewhere in the country teaching. I began to pick up a pattern of questions that the students would ask me, usually at a break or when they thought no one else was listening. They would say, "Please tell me. How do I talk to my pastor about this?" or "How do I talk to my priest about this?" Or they would say, "How does this stuff fit with my faith?"

At first I would answer from my own experience. Finally, one day I said, "What are you asking me for?"

My student said, "Oh, because you're more spiritual in how you present the work."

I almost fainted. I thought, "Oh my gosh, am I deviating from the curriculum or what? What am I doing that makes people think that I teach it differently from any other teacher?"

It dawned on me that every teacher brings their background with them when they go to teach a class. Part of my background is the fact that I have been a Catholic nun for twenty-seven years, and had moved on from that, about six months before I found Healing Touch. It was like everything I had ever done in ministries prepared me to do this next step called Healing Touch.

I sat down with Janet and I said, "Janet, let me tell you what's happening. How can we tweak the language just a bit? This would go over really well in churches."

She sort of did a double take and said, "No. This is a living, clinical program and has to be taught from a clinical prospective."

Of course, what was I going to say, "But of course, right away. That's what I do. It seeps out in how I present."

Another year goes by. More and more students are asking me to teach them from a Christian perspective. I really, to be honest, didn't want to do that. In fact it was one of my peers, a Healing Touch instructor from Detroit, who sat me down and said, "There's a point here to teach this from a Christian perspective. That's a throwback. You've gone way beyond that. Why do you want to do that?"

That's when I realized, somebody had to turn around and help those behind me come forward. In other words, the work in Healing Touch was too, in that space, too New Age for a lot of the churches and people. They just needed the language changed a bit.

I sat down with Janet again. This time I'm a little firmer in what I want. I said, "Janet, you are missing a whole audience."

Well, she totally shocked me by saying, "You're right. A lot of people have said the same thing to me. Therefore, I've been thinking about it. This is what you're going to do. You're going to leave your position as the administrator of the Healing Touch Program. You're going to move home, and you're going to start a new division of the Colorado Center for Healing Touch. I'm going to call it Healing Touch Spiritual Ministries. Can you live with that?"

Of course, she could have picked me up off the floor at that point. I said, "Okay. You mean, I am going to stop my job and do this?"

She said, "Yes. It's going to take you full time to get this thing off the ground. I'll give you a couple of months to get it rolling. You can use the secretary's desk here at the office. But I won't have room for you. I'll have to replace you. So you'll have to work at home."

I went home and I thought, "Oh my gosh. I just worked myself out of my job." I was in a state of shock. And then I thought, "Pull yourself up. Now you have to produce."

What I did was I put together one eight hour class. You have to understand. I ran Janet's curriculum. I had not developed curriculum myself. This was my first attempt. So I developed this eight hour class and we called it "Introduction to Healing Touch Ministries".

What we did was, we taught that one eight hour class right before teaching a Healing Touch Level 1. People looked and they said, "No, no, no. We've got to have the Level 1 language changed. I went back to Janet and I said, "Okay. Can we tweak the language for Level 1?

She said, "You can do Level 1 and Level 1 only."

I said, "Okay."

I tweaked the language. Janet and I belong to the same Episcopal Church. I went to my pastor and I said, "I need help. I gotta take this class, and I have to change the language. Can you help?"

I taught a Healing Touch Level 1 from a Christian perspective at my church for free. The pastor was in a state of shock, because twenty-five percent of the whole membership showed up for this free class that we taught on four Wednesday nights. What they did was talk about how it was a little different. I would take notes. That's how I developed Healing Touch Spiritual Ministries Level 1.

Then I turned around, and I taught that class in the fall of 1997 times four or five times. We had classes filled with thirty or forty people in each class. Janet called me in, in January of '98 and she said, "You're going to be too big. I don't want to siphon money out of your program to fund my other pet projects. Therefore you're on your own."

Again, you could have picked me up off the floor because you have to understand I did not have an infrastructure. I didn't have a secretary. I didn't have a computer. I didn't have a bank account.

When I looked at my own personal bank account I had exactly $200 to my name. I started calling other Healing Touch instructors, who I know were of the same persuasion, and I convinced them to not only teach Healing Touch, but to come teach for me. That's how we got started.

I hired this lady who supposedly knew bookkeeping, and she didn't know bookkeeping. I am not a bookkeeper. Needless to say, it's a miracle that the program survived the first few years, because I did not know really to get the right kind of a system that I needed, but the program began to flourish.

*How did you, yourself, get started in energy work?*

I was actually director of a hospice in Augusta, Georgia. I belonged to the AHNA. Primarily in name only, I wanted to keep my eyes open, and find out what those weird nurses were doing. I saw that they were going to have a holistic nurses' retreat in the Rockies. Here I am an administrator, and I was putting in over eighty hours a week. I thought I deserved a vacation. But those holistic nurses are really weird. I tell you what, I will go out there, and I will take my own tent and my backpack, and I will camp near them, but not too close.

I ended up getting rained out of my tent within the first four hours. I had to move into the nearest shelter. There were already two ladies in residence there. One of them was Janet Mentgen.

Janet was just getting Healing Touch off the ground. To me that sounded too airy-fairy, too woo-woo. I mean, after all I was an administrator. I paid nurses to touch. I didn't touch. I paid other people to touch. Here we are in Telluride, which is at 8500 feet and it took all day to boil water. Basically we were camped out in these three little buildings: a yurt and two wooden buildings.

I got to know Janet, but I still thought she was a little bit on the weird side. At the end of the week, ten days, she gets assigned to take me to the airport in another town. I forget the name of it. But anyway, she takes me to the airport and she is saying good-by. She said, "You know, I'm going to be teaching one of my classes in Atlanta next weekend, why don't you come?"

I went, "Uh, oh I'm sure after being gone for two weeks there is no way, no way I would be able to get away, again.

She said, "That's all right. But you know, Atlanta is not too far from Augusta."

I said, "Yeah, I don't think so. Thanks, but no thanks."

I went home and I couldn't get the invitation out of my head. By next Wednesday, I had my weekly meeting with my vice president at the hospital.

I said, "You know, there's this workshop this weekend in Atlanta."

He pulled out the form and he said, "Oh, you want to go?" He signed it. He never asked me what the name of it was. I walked out with, "Great, now I've got to go."

I go over to Atlanta. I get there, and Janet is not teaching the Healing Touch class. She's in the next room teaching Level 2. Dorothea Hover-Kramer is teaching Level 1. Well, I had this ah ha experience at the end of which we're gathered in the hotel. Janet found me, and she sat me down and she said, "I want to know what you thought about my work."

These words came flying out of my mouth, "Oh, I saw the next step on my path." As soon as I said it I went, "What!" I looked all around, like who said that. Janet started laughing. She patted me on the knee and she said, "Well, don't worry. You can be one of my instructors." And got up and walked away.

I said, "No, no. I don't do that kind of thing. I'm an administrator, you know. Not that kind of thing."

Over the next four or five months, wherever there was a Healing Touch class in the southeast, I showed up. I never bothered to tell my boss what I was doing. I would just say I needed to take Friday afternoon off and Monday morning off, because I have something else I have to do. I will work extra during the week to make up for it.

After I repeated Level 1 for about five times, I thought I ought to do the next level. Again I asked my boss if I could do a workshop, and again he never asked me the name of it. He just signed the paper. I convinced two other people to take the class with me, and it was Anne Boyle and Jane Hightower. Basically they said at that point, "Well, you're not going to this Healing Touch Program without us. We're going to do it too." So the three of us were the Three Musketeers from Augusta. We went through the whole program together. That's how I really got involved with Healing Touch.

I finished the program in '91. It was in '92, that I went to the AHNA conference that was held in Arkansas that year. I came home with the Holistic Nurse of the Year Award. To be honest, I have no idea of how I got it. Anyway, I got this award. When I brought it home, I had a new boss at that point, and his face fell. I thought, "Oh, I see the handwriting on the wall." He really was going to fire me, because of what they had done when they brought this hot shot MBA in. He demoted five department heads to managers. We were all the outlying programs. I saw the handwriting on the wall, and I thought they're going to rid of all of us, because we make too much money. Before he could fire me, I ended up quitting. I got another job up in Ohio to start a hospice from scratch for the Visiting Nurses Association. They told me up front they only wanted me for a year. I said, "That's fine. You have to understand, I'm a Healing Touch instructor. I will be teaching on weekends."

They said, "We don't care what you do on weekends."

By the time I finished that year, Janet said, "Come out to Colorado. I want you to be my program administrator." That's how that all came about.

*How did Healing Touch change your life?*

Totally, totally changed my life. It took me on a right angle turn and I totally did not expect that at all. My expectation was that Augusta Georgia was going to be my stepping stone to the political level in hospice. I had my sights set on being at the national level in Washington DC. Basically, I walked away from a well-paid job, to one that paid less than half of what I had been making to come to work for Janet. I was willing to it, because I felt this was the work that I was supposed to be doing.

*When did you become a certified practitioner and an instructor?*

It was in the days before certification. I was a practitioner in '91, a teacher in '92 and I think I got my certification in '93. In fact, I really wanted to slow down, because I was an administrator, and I didn't just didn't have the time to do one on one with clients. Janet looked at me and she said, "I need you, and if you don't finish, I will not be able to pull you through, because certification has come."

And I said, "Sign me up."

It was very interesting how I became an instructor, because, bless her heart, Dorothea Hover-Kramer was one of the original four with Janet. But she was, I would have to say, very jealous of me. I had Janet's attention. When I came out to Colorado, Janet moved me into her home, because she couldn't pay me what my salary should have been. In lieu of an adequate salary, I had room and board. So here I am living with Janet, and my very first assignment by Janet to teach, was in California in Dorothea's back yard. That was not a cool thing for Janet to do. Dorothea raised the roof over my quote, unquote lack of experience. I would have to agree with her. I really was not experienced at that point in time. I was barely out of the crib, you know.

Janet, to pacify Dorothea, said, "For the next five workshops, I'm going to have you co-teach with other instructors. At first I was hurt. I thought I did an excellent job. She said, "You did do an excellent job, but because of Dorothea, I have to co-teach you." I got to teach with all my best friends. I taught with Barb Dahl and Susan Lear. I can't remember who else. It was like party time for us to be teaching together. That was how I finally got my certification. That was in '93. I was in the first batch. My original number, let see, even though I was one of the first, they went alphabetical. My instructor was 19 and my practitioner was number 30. Of course, all that changed when I dropped out of HTI.

*Would you like to talk a little bit about Healing Touch Spiritual Ministries and more of what it's about?*

Well, Healing Touch Spiritual Ministries is a certification program. And it's certified through, I'm not sure the name, whoever does the certification for Healing Touch. I'm uncertain of this, because I'm not really involved any more. When the split over HTI and HTP came, HTI, of course, retained the certification, and left a problem for Healing Touch Program. So Sharon Scandrett-Hibdon and Barb Starke were going to put together the certification for Healing Touch Program. It was at an AHNA conference a few years ago, that I sat down with them and I said, "Will there ever be room for certification for Healing Touch Spiritual Ministries?" And they said, "Well, who certifies you now?" And I said, "Nobody. Nobody will touch us with a ten foot pole."

According to the powers that be at HTI, I had done a grave disservice to Healing Touch by teaching it from a Christian perspective. And, of course, the leaders at that time were all Hindu or something. I can't figure out what in the world they were. But they told me I had done a great disservice. That was Diane Wardell.

So, of course, the certification board was out of the question for us. Sharon and Barb looked at each other and said, "We don't know why we can't do certification for you. It'd be different."

I said, "Okay!"

We put together the whole certification packet. Put together the reviewers. The reviewers are a subcommittee of the reviewers for HTP certification. We are now able to certify.

Going back to my story of with Janet, you know she was adamant that I could just rephrase Healing Touch Level 1. The day came when she said, "You can do Healing Touch Level 2. But, no, you can't do Level 3."

Okay. We were teaching three classes then: Introduction to Healing Ministries, Healing Touch Spiritual Ministries Level 1, Healing Touch Spiritual Ministries Level 2. Yet, I knew what most needed to be rephrased, was the work of Healing Touch Level 3. I put together my curriculum, went to Janet, and she said, "Okay." But what she did was, she okayed it without going through the board of directors for Healing Touch International. They were furious. I did not know that Janet had been protecting my program from day one. She had simply approved my program without their input. That's why they were so upset with my program, because they had no input into it.

I was pretty much persona non grata, only because I didn't know what Janet had done. I didn't know that Janet was personally protecting the program, because she really wanted it taught from a Christian perspective. She was very much a Christian, but she realized she could not come across that way to people, because Healing Touch was attracting Buddhists, and Hindus, and people from various different faiths, and some with no faiths at all. She had to appear neutral to all of them. Yet, she would have wanted my program to go forward.

It was probably within the first year of our existence, that I realized that we needed a book. We needed a book to reframe Healing Touch. I kept saying, we need a writer out there to write. I kept saying this over and over. People would say, "Na na, I'm not interested in writing."

I thought, "I'm not a writer." But then I thought, "Well all right. I guess I'll have to take a stab at it."

I started putting together, what I thought should go in a book to really explain Healing Touch as based in the laying on of hands. I got my manuscript done. It was six hundred pages of manuscript. People said, "Well you've got to find an editor."

I said, "Oh yeah. I gotta find an editor." I found this lady in Boulder who was actually a very good book editor. I took her my manuscript. This was in the days when everything was paper. I handed it to her. I was so proud of myself for getting this thing done.

She called me a month later, and said I could come and get it. She sat me down and handed it to me. She said, "Now dearie. We all go through this."

I am going, "Yes, yes. How'd you like it?"

She handed it to me and, honest to God, there was more red ink than black ink on the pages. I started to cry. She said, "Now, now, now. You're going to go home and you're going to rewrite this. And you're going to come back to me, and I'm going to reread it again."

I said, "Okay."

It took me three months to rewrite it. I came back and she went, "Okay, now there's very few changes."

At that point, I'm calling, well I'm going to self-publish it at this point because I don't want to wait two or three years trying to find a publisher who will publish it. But, to get that off, I had to come up with quite a bit of money. Because I wanted the layout of this book so bad, I could put scriptures and references in the columns in between, I had an odd size book. I did realize that an odd size book would triple the cost of the book. I needed to raise $15,000 to print this book for 3000 copies.

Meanwhile, I started the research for teaching Levels 3, 4 and 5 for Healing Touch. I began this class, I forget where it was. It was up north somewhere. I don't know if it was Minnesota or Wisconsin or one of those states. I said to the class, "Now, I'm writing this book. We'll be ending this class about 10 PM and if any of you want me to read one of the chapters of the book, then come back at 10:30 and bring a pillow with a blanket. The whole class showed up. So I read to them the first chapter of the book. The next day one student came to me, and handed me a check for $5000 and said, "I want that book printed."

I said, "But I won't be able to repay you."

She said, "No, no. It's a gift. I want this book printed."

"Okay!"

The next two weekends I'm teaching Spiritual Ministries, one of them was in a big Presbyterian church down in Florida somewhere. I told them I'm writing this book, and when I'm able to raise at least $10,000, I'm $5000 to the good, I'll be able to get this printed. One man came up, and gave me a check for $2000, another person gave me a check for $1000, somebody else gave me a check for a $1000 and I was on my way. That's how my first book got printed, "Called into Healing". It's reclaiming the Judeo-Christian legacy of Healing Touch.

That book has now gone through several printings. It's probably sold, I don't know. I've lost count, at least 12,000 copies. For a self-published book that's unheard of.

It was in the year 2000, we were three years in to the program, that I had a vendor table at the Healing Touch conference for Spiritual Ministries. Marilee Tolen, who was another Healing Touch instructor, had another vendor table. She was talking essential oils. She would come over and look at my table, and she said, "Well, I see you have a book. And you've got student manuals. But I don't think you are doing enough in your program."

I went, "What!? What do you mean? I'm running around the country every weekend teaching this. I've written a book. What else should I be doing?"

She said, "Well, furthermore, if you knew you're scriptures."

I thought, "How dare you. This woman!"

She said, "You should also be anointing."

"For crying out loud," I said. "What has olive oil got to do with healing?"

She said, "Ah, Linda, they were not anointing with cooking oil. And they were not anointing with lamp oil."

I suddenly got, you know, thrown against the wall, because I got caught embarrassed. I knew I was caught embarrassed, but I didn't know where the error was.

I said, "So what were they were anointing with?"

She said, "Well, according to the scriptures, they were anointing with frankincense, and myrrh, and cedarwood, and hyssop."

She just kept going on and on.

I said, "Well, yeah. I recalled reading those words in the scriptures, but those were oils?"

She said, "Go back and read your scriptures."

So, of course, I went over to her table, and she had a kit called "The Twelve Oils of the Ancient Scriptures". Of course, I had to buy it. At that time, in the year 2000, it cost me $95, and I thought, "Oh my gosh, that's a huge expense for me." When I could barely scrape together to pay the bills.

Now I can get a bottle for $300.

So I bought them, and that night I opened every one of them. I didn't like a single one of them. They were all very earthy. I went back the next day and I said, "Well, don't you have any oils that smell good?"

I bought the "Essential Seven" kit. She said to me, "Well, the safest place to put an oil is the soles of the feet."

Okay. At night I put all seven of those oils on the soles of my feet, because I didn't know any better. I didn't have any reference book.

After about six weeks, I noticed that there was something different. What was different was the fact that my blood pressure was now normal. It hadn't been normal in ten years. Even on medication.

I thought, "Hmm. There's nothing new in my life. It's the same amount of stress that I've always been under. The only thing different was I that I'm using these oils, and surely that has nothing to do with it."

I called Marilee and Marilee said, "You know what? We are having a Young Living meeting in Denver, this week and you gotta go."

"Ah, okay. I'll go."

I'm thinking there'll be maybe twenty, thirty people. There were over three hundred people at this meeting. I went, "Oh my gosh!" "What are all these people? What are they in to?"

They had a question and answer period, and my hand went flying up in the air. They called upon me and I said, "So which oil brings down blood pressure? The whole body has turned in the right direction.

One voice said, That's lemon.

Like dodo, That's one of the oils I was using.

The next day I went out to every book store in the city of Denver and I bought every book I could find on aroma therapy. I began to read and read. The more I read the more I realized that Marilee was right. This was the missing piece out of Healing Touch Spiritual Ministries Program. We based all of our work on the laying on of hands. But how were they doing the laying on of hands? It says in the letter to James, "Are any among you sick? You are to call in the elders. The elders are to pray and lay on hands and anoint."

I thought, "That's the missing piece. That's what we're supposed to be doing. It's not two things: pray and touch. It's pray, touch, and anoint."

I put together a twelve hour class called "Center, Heal, and Anoint", which became a sixteen hour class within one month. We taught that class successfully for two years. The students started clamoring, "Teach us more, teach us more." I thought, "I don't know any more."

I got my certification in clinical aroma therapy at the end of which the medical doctor, who taught the class, turned to me and said, "I don't understand why you took this class in the first place."

I said, "Well, what do you mean?"

He said, "You obviously know a lot more about the oils than I do."

I thought to myself, "I'm not really as boring as you are either."

And he said, "You ought to be teaching a certification in a clinical aroma therapy program."

That's when the light bulb went on. And I went, "Yes. That's the next step."

So I said, "Well, what'll I have to do?"

He told me what the rules were. I got it approved at the School of Aroma Therapy.

The course we started out at a $200 course and then a $300 course. We have now certified throughout the United States, Canada,

England, and Australia, probably about three hundred and sixty five people, I think.

That is really the program that financially underwrites the Healing Touch Spiritual Ministries Program, because we never raised the tuition for the Spiritual Ministries Program. It does not begin to pay the bills.

I ran the program for eighteen years. It was about a year ago that I thought, "I'm running myself into the ground. It was taking a toll on me, physically, spiritually. It was like I am exhausted. I am just exhausted.

Margaret Leslie, who was one of the key Spiritual Ministries instructors, had expressed a desire to have the program. She wanted it. I was going to give it to her, but come last January I realized that if she were to have the Spiritual Ministries Program, she would have to have an awful lot of underwriting, because it would never pay for itself. I thought, "Why am I holding on to the Aroma Therapy Program, because I really need to get rid of all the headaches of running a continuing ed program."

I called her up and I said, "Okay. You can have them both,"

She said, "Well, it only makes sense, because I am going to need that aroma therapy program to pay for Spiritual Ministries."

I said, "Yep, you will."

She took it July first. Took the whole program.

I can tell you the whole history of the Colorado Center for Healing Touch. There are so many of us still around that were a part of that. When I first joined Janet, I moved out here in December 1992. I lived in Janet's home. In fact, Janet didn't have much in the way of furniture, so instead of putting my furniture in storage, we used my furniture in her house. When it came to her office, she only had a very small little office. Francina was her girl Friday, who did everything, bless her heart. I think Francina is dead now. Francina was not the most organized person in the world. A lot of things just didn't get done. What I learned was that Janet liked to do everything by hand. Janet did not believe in forms. She didn't want forms ever used. She wanted everything to be done by hand. She wanted her instructors to send in their receipts. Janet, herself, added them up, and then she would write them a check. At that time she would pay each instructor. We were all paid the same amount, $150 to teach a weekend. A Level 1, Level 2, Level 3, whatever, she paid $150.

Her top three instructors, Sharon, Dorothea, and Myra, she paid $200. But Janet did all the bookkeeping herself. She wouldn't let anybody else do that. Everything was all done by hand. A lot of things didn't get done. Here I am the administrator, and yet, she didn't really let me be an administrator. She didn't let me run anything. Basically, the problem was that I left my business. When you leave hospice administration, you cannot get back in. So I thought I had to make the best of this world.

I said, "If we could just have an accounting form, that we could put in a file and say, okay. This is where it occurred. This is who taught it. This is how many students. This is how much money came in. This is how much expenses. In one form. It took me six months to get approval from her, so that I could have one form. Each time we would want to add something to it, to make it more accountable, it was like pulling teeth.

She had a bookkeeper, a part time bookkeeper, who did not know how to use a computer. Everything was done with a calculator. She did everything by hand the whole five years I was there. Because Janet liked her. Janet didn't like to fire anybody. She liked her. She didn't want to rock any boats. That gal was still there years after I left. Still doing everything by hand with a hand calculator.

Janet was a visionary. She was great as an inspiring person, but, this is my opinion, she was a terrible business person. She kept everything pretty close to her chest. Even though I was the administrator, there were only certain things I was allowed to know.

When she told me to start my own program, it was actually kind of a relief. It took me, oh gosh, the first four or five years were an absolute struggle, because every person who I would hire, turned out to be not who they presented themselves to be. One person, basically, stole money out of my checking account and took off. Yes, she embezzled the money. I had somebody else who only lasted two weeks. I had somebody who lasted seven months, but she brought me the person who would stay with me for fifteen years. My assistant, Pat, has just retired a month ago, and I am losing my mind trying to do the finance thing. At least I am not running the continuing ed program.

*What do you see for the future of Healing Touch?*

I have to be honest, I'm just not real involved any more. I don't know how things are going. I was at conference. I was actually with Sharon Robbins the night before she died. We had spent the whole evening drinking at the bar, catching up, and just having a great time. When she died, I was in such a state of shock that I pretty much lost it all, because I gave up my program the month before the convention. Therefore I wasn't privy to anything that was going on, because now it passed to Margaret Leslie. I just had to forget that.

*Did you ever use social media, Facebook and things like that?*

I use Facebook all the time. I use it, not for Spiritual Ministries or Aroma Therapy Program now, I use it for my Essential Oil Coaching Program. I have a newsletter, weekly newsletter, but I'm thinking of changing the format of the weekly newsletter to a private Facebook page. I've got to think all that through

After the latest of the FDA coming down so hard on supplements and essential oil companies, I have to be extremely careful of what I can say. I cannot tell you how the essential oils work anymore. I can't even quote to you the research on how these oils work, because it implies a medical point now. How can I educate, how can I tell you to look at the chemistry, so you can figure out how this oil works, unless I'm allowed to do that?

Actually what had happened was one of the diamonds in Young Living gets my weekly newsletter, and she called me on the carpet for actually telling you how pine oil works. It was like, okay, well then I've got to figure out another way to be able to communicate to people, so that its private, and you have to be accepted in order to get this information out.

In my coaching program, I have individual coaching in aroma therapy. I also have individual coaching for people in my company down line. That's basically my income now, my Young Living down line.

*Anything else you would like to add to things?*

Well, let's see. The thing with Healing Touch is, that once you become a practitioner of that work, even though you may not have, like I don't have a client load at this point, because I am phasing so much out, and I'm selling my home. I hopefully will be retiring to some place warmer than Colorado.

It becomes part of who you are. I can't imagine not ever doing this work. But, it may not be in a formal way in the future for me.

*Do you have any comments or advice for new or potential students?*

Know your goals. What is it that you want to accomplish? What is it that you want to do in life? Figure out a way to get there, because you can't just fall into this work. You can't just go through the program, get your education, get your certification, and then look around and say, "So where are the clients?" You have to learn how to let people know about your services. What they want. What I tell people is you gotta be in Facebook, or LinkedIn, or any of the other social media.

But, you know, young people today don't even like to talk on the phone. They all text. Texting would be a great way of getting the message out to potential people of what you can do.

The days of sending out brochures are past. Yes, you need a business card, but that day is going to end soon. It will be past too. This is the day of networking. It's all electronic now. I would say that to bring in people you'd best to learn how to let other people know about your services. And yet, this work is word of mouth, but word of mouth is not so much about speaking anymore. It's about typing, and that stuff. Texting.

Those of us who are over fifty, for me, seventy, that's not how we learned. We like to have that piece of paper in our hands. We like to have that brochure. We like to have that business card. We like to have that face-to-face, and that's not how young people communicate. If you want to attract young people, you have to know what it is that they do, in order to communicate.

The other piece of advice is, don't hang your hat on one modality. You'll never make it financially. You've gotta have three, four, or five different modalities so that as a healing practitioner, you can draw upon whether it's Healing Touch, aroma therapy, Reiki, Polarity Therapy, massage, reflexology, or whatever your modalities are. The whole thing is to assess the individual in front of you and be able to address their needs: physically, mentally, emotionally and spiritually. It may need a combination of several different modalities.

*Have you explored other modalities?*

Of course. I never offer any, in my practice, just Healing Touch. In their training, you offer them certification in Healing Touch. Not in aroma therapy, not in reflexology. Not in massage. In your training, you want to be pure with Healing Touch. In your healing practice, no. You would do your clients a disservice if you say, "Oh. I'm sorry, but I'm only going to offer you Healing Touch. Next time I will only offer you aroma therapy. No, no."

No matter how you slice it, Healing Touch is spiritual healing. So these people who say it is only clinical, I have to laugh at them. Like, who are you trying to kid?

*Do you have a favorite Janet Mentgen story before I let you go?*

I have lots of healing stories with Janet. Some them, though, I don't want to tell so that's why I hesitate. Janet would easily go into an altered state. I didn't know that, until the two of us were on this group thing in Yosemite, and I had brought my drum along. The two of us went off together by this, I don't know, creek or whatever. Janet picked up my drum and she said, "Play your drum for me."

I used to belong to a women's circle in Augusta, Georgia. We did all these drumming songs. I started drumming and singing these songs. She goes into an altered state. She's stuck. She can't remember who she is. This scared me. I finally had to take her by the hand, and take her back to where our group was.

I got read the riot act for getting Janet into an altered state. I said, "Well, just ground her." It wasn't that easy. She, literally, would trip out.

*Do you have a favorite healing story regarding Healing Touch?*

I have a funny one. One of the first times that we would teach classes in Hawaii, Janet had brought me over to Hawaii to teach a

Level 2 with her. She was going to be coming from Australia to Hawaii, and we were going to "co-teach" the class together. The only reason I can think of that we were doing that, was because we had a class of sixty people. She arrived from Australia with bronchitis and no voice. She had to sit in the front of the class, and I had to teach the entire class in front of Janet by myself.

The next class I'm going to go over to Hawaii, we needed another Level 1 teacher. Ann Day was going to be over there teaching Advanced Classes. Janet was going to be teaching Advanced Classes. I was going to be teaching Advanced Classes, so we needed another Level 1 teacher. Janet said, "Well, who would you recommend?"

I said, "Let's get somebody from California. We don't want to bring somebody from the east coast. Let's pick Clara Mae Webber.

Janet said, "Good choice."

Where did we go? We were in California, and we were going to have to teach Clara Mae how to teach Level 1, because at that point she had not really taught a class all by herself. She was going to be a brand new teacher going over there to teach a Level 1 class. The problem was, she could never remember where to put her hands for chakra connection. We had Janet on the table, and I'm trying to talk Clara Mae through how to teach the students how to do chakra connection. It was hysterical. Finally Janet looked at me and she said, "Well, this is going to be interesting."

We get over to Hawaii. We were running two Level 1's in the same city on two completely opposite ends of Honolulu. I am teaching one Level 1. Clara Mae had to teach the other Level 1 at the totally different place. Come to find out, she had to teach outside, under, it looked like a park area with all these picnic tables. She had people working on picnic tables and she's having to teach this class out there in the sunshine for her very first class. She did fine.

I have another funny story. This was actually the Spiritual Ministries Program. Clara Mae was my best friend. She stuck with me in the Spiritual Ministries Program from the very beginning. I think this was in Cincinnati. We would bring her in, and I was training her to teach Healing Touch Spiritual Ministries Level 2, which is pretty much the same as Level 2 in Healing Touch. Only we go in for some different languaging.

We get to magnetic clearing. She puts some music on. I am standing back, and mind you, this is in a hospital. I got thirty massage tables. We got sixty students. There is a sea of tables in this huge auditorium. She puts on music that's like the "Right of the Valkeries", It's not that but it felt that. I'm standing there looking at these sixty students going, "Dah ta duh ta dah, dah ta duh ta dah!"

I said to Clara Mae, "What do you observe here?"

She said, "They're going awfully fast."

I said, "Do you think the music might have anything to do with it?"

She went, "Oh, that can't be anything."

I said, "From now on, no music. No music on that one."

I want to back up on my story. I was in Augusta Georgia in the very beginning. But as I came back from that Level 1, my first Level 1 class, I had belonged to, like I said, this women's circle. Two of my friends, Anne Boyd and Jane Hightower, said, "Oh by the way, what did you learn in that class you went to a few weeks ago?"

I whipped out a little pendulum and said, "Let me show you."

I started showing them. I put one of them on the table and I showed them some of the things, and they went, "Hah. We've got to learn this."

When I started coordinating Healing Touch classes in Augusta, they both participated, and that's when they said, "You're not going to go through this program alone. We're going through it with you."

Of course, both of them are elders in the program now.

# Barbara Ann Starke
## RN, MSN, FNP-BC, HTCP/I

### Introduction

Barbara Starke is one of the gems in Healing Touch. I always know where I stand with her. She has a quick wit making conversation with her a lot of fun. She's highly intelligent, speaks her mind, and her honesty is refreshing.

She is one of our tireless promoters of Healing Touch. She has done much to help smooth out the certification process, and at the same time, built it into the respected institution that it has become.

She is also one of our busy instructors. Her class schedule is always busy. She works hard at building both the frequency of her classes and student participation. She encourages all practitioners and instrutors to do introductory classes as a way of promoting Healing Touch. I think she is right. It's that one on one discussion that encourages people to sign up for classes, be it in an intro class or jsut talking on the phone.

### Interview

*What is your position In Healing Touch?*
I am a Level 4 instructor and the chair of certification.

*What does the chair of certification do?*

Oversees the process of certifying practitioners and instructors, as well as their renewal, and helping maintain the standards of certification.

*Have you held other positions in Healing Touch?*

I have been a reviewer for the certification process.

*What does a reviewer do?*

The reviewer looks at the packet applications sent in and evaluates them for their quality and safety of the practitioner, and makes sure they have met all of the qualifications to be certified.

*What attracted you to energy medicine?*

I got started in the 80's realizing there was more to nursing than just medicine and whatever we were trained to do. I went to a Seventh Day Adventist nursing school, so I had a holistic upbringing as a student nurse and as a baby nurse. When I went into community health, it was probably because of my holistic nursing education. I felt that it made more sense to help people be well and stay well than to fix broken bodies once they were in the hospital. I have always been interested in wellness and wholeness and self-promotion.

As the years moved on, I got more interested in the concept of healing and what did that really mean. How I found energy medicine was through Therapeutic Touch and Delores Krieger and Dora Kunz. And then I found the Holistic Nurses Association and found Healing Touch.

*So how did you find them?*

A friend of mine was doing workshops for healthcare providers and helping. He was a physician, Dr. John Travis. He was one of the first preventative medicine physicians. He felt that most healthcare people had issues of codependence and wounded warrior or wounded healer archetype. He said that we need to look at ourselves, not fix our deficiencies, but at least look at our deficiencies and see what it was that drove us into healthcare to begin with.

As I was doing those workshops with him, I was getting more and more frustrated with healthcare. And he said, "Well, you know you should find out what's missing in healthcare. I think you call it the AHNA. You'll find likeminded nurses. "

I found AHNA and that led me to Healing Touch.

*Was Janet your first instructor?*

Actually Janet was not my first instructor. Pat Burger from Denver was.

Yeah. It was in 1991, I think, maybe '90. I got the brochure from AHNA when I joined. They had a flyer in there for a Level 1 Healing Touch class. I read it, saw the word chakra and didn't know what it meant. All I knew, and that I could think of, was to check this out. I started traveling to Healing Touch workshops and I went all over the country. I went to Memphis, and Baltimore, and Louisville, and Canada for 4 and 5. It wasn't easy.

*When did you become certified as an instructor and what made you decide to be certified?*

I've always felt like I'm a very leaderful kind of person. I'm also a person who, if I do something, I want to do the best I can. I felt that certification made sense. I wanted that, probably for my own acknowledgement, and for my own sense of satisfaction. I wanted to keep lifting up nursing, I guess.

I was getting my masters at the same time. I remember thinking this is really tough and stupid to do both. I wanted to get my nursing masters. I did it because I wanted to find out what's going on in nursing, and either I'd fall back in love with nursing, or get out.

I started doing blacksmithing with my husband, Jeff. This helped me find my artistic side. I realized it was the alchemy I was loving: making something out of nothing, or transforming, or transmuting something. I still feel like that's what you do in healing with humanity. There is always the process of transmuting yourself, and re-forming, and transcending. When I went to do my masters I told them this is what I want to do, but I want to do this from an energy medicine, holistic perspective. They said fine. We don't know what that means, but go ahead.

As I was working on my masters, I was studying energy therapy, and doing my Healing Touch workshops, writing, and getting my stuff ready for certification. When I had to write a paper for school, it would be on the holistic nursing theorist. I fell in love with Florence Nightingale and Martha Rogers.

When I got done with my masters I realized that it was really Healing Touch that had pulled me along all this time.

*How has Healing Touch changed your life?*

It probably has given me more of my authentic self, if anything. It's given me permission to be who I came to be, who I would prefer to be. Growing up I always felt like I don't belong here. I don't belong in this dysfunctional, cruel family and all the sarcasm, the alcoholism. Not the dishonesty, but the hiding behind veils. I could see all of the sad ways that people are not authentic. Not honest with one another while trying to sustain a societal mold that not's healthy. I think Healing Touch has helped me be, or helped me see beyond medical models. It's helped me see, of course, we are more than bones and blood and guts and body parts. And that's what kept me going. Believing that we are so much more than what we've been brought up to believe.

That was the angle when we first started our conversation and I told you my father's death has been very interesting to me. I went through a period of being really angry with him, because as a physician I believed everything he said. He was my God and he was my father and I looked up to him with enormous respect. He and I were very close. I came to realize in my adulthood that I don't believe half the stuff I learned from him. It's not true. People do heal a lot of illnesses. Too much of what he believed, I have come to see as not so.

*Do you have a particularly meaning story in your Healing Touch practice you would like to share?*

I don't know. I would have to think about it. I noticed in my growth and development as a Healing Touch practitioner, my clients have been the ones that have shown me the way. When I was an HIV/AIDs nurse, when I was a public health nurse, it wasn't Healing Touch so much as working with HIV people that helped me appreciate that it isn't really what the body is doing, it's the attitude that carries one day to day. It was my AIDs patients that helped me see how we can transcend a situation on the earth and still be very, very happy. That they were able to forgive themselves, and come home to the love of themselves. That's being at peace with yourself. I think that being able to help people be happy with themselves, that's what Healing Touch does for me.

*Have you explored other healing modalities?*

Oh yeah. I explored nutrition a lot. I explored food and the energy of food. I explored and now do acupuncture, five point NADA (National Acupuncture Detoxification Association) ear acupuncture. Because it' so comprehensive and possible. I have taught teenagers to do it. It's wonderful to do for PTSD (post-traumatic stress disorder), for addictions and pursuing the issues we have in our culture, because we are an addictive culture and we promote addicting people.

*Why do you stay with Healing Touch?*

It's so possible. It's so gratifying to help people see that they are way much more than our conventional model of who we are. I have stayed with Healing Touch because I think the curriculum is inspiring: how it takes people from beginner to expert. It's inspiring. I think the curriculum is very beautiful. Actually, I'm wanting to integrate a program from England, Clean Learning, into HTP. Clean Learning techniques help people to tell their story for their own healing. And that's what I want more than anything at this point in my life. I want to help Healing Touch practitioners let clients do their own healing. And help us get out of the way so we can honestly be facilitators and not fixers.

*Do you have a Facebook page or use social media as a way of promoting your classes?*

Sometimes. Not too often.

*Does it work for you?*

Not too often. If I were proficient at it, I could post my classes on a web site. When I think about it I put it on my Facebook page. But I'm not as competent with social media as I am with computers and I haven't done that. I guess I could. I don't have a web site. People can Google me and find me. People can go to Healing Touch and find me. People who are really savvy with the Internet can find me. Part of me says I don't want to be that busy. My concern is that if I had the web site, I would be traveling more than I want to. I'm quite happy right now. I would rather spend the effort to get classes in my own neighborhood. That's my goal.

*Do you have comments or advice for new or potential students?*

Use this work for yourself. Don't worry about doing it for others. Probably because it was so empowering for me to learn this work and to continue to study it as long as I have, it's been a very liberating education. The conventional system seems so hell bent on promoting fear and lack of empowerment. I think it's very important for young people to understand how much more they are, than what we think they are. What we've taught them.

*What do you see for the future of Healing Touch?*

We need to become more diversified. I want more men in Healing Touch. More people of color in Healing Touch. I want younger women but I am not sure, developmentally, younger women will necessarily be easy to get. You have to be in a place of readiness in your own development. Most of us who came to Healing Touch were in our 30's, 40's typically. We needed to do this because we realized something was missing. I was about thirty something when I realized something was missing. Unless people have in-sight to realize something is missing they are not going to seek something as alternative as or progressive as Healing Touch. I wish we were starting at a little bit younger age. I think it would be helpful overall to educate people and invite awareness of our unifying aspects, younger and younger.

*Do you have a favorite Janet Mentgen story?*

No. What I loved about Janet was her pragmatism. The model that we use "Just do the work". I think Janet was one who did that. I admired her strengths. People criticized for years her lack of emotional element. I rather admired it. I do wish she had taken better care of herself. But I think we all have our blind spots. She was a busy woman: mother, a business person, a teacher. It is what it is. No I don't have a favorite story about Janet.

What I loved about Janet was in all the classes I had done with her, she always made it look so easy. I admired her acceptance, her – I guess the confidence that she exuded in doing the work. I hope I do that with students. For many years I was quite skeptical about all of this. And I still am. There are still times where I am amazed how it works. Like a headache will go. I am amazed at the ease in shifting someone's pattern. The migraine will go and won't come back. And they had migraines everyday of their life before Healing Touch.

Why is healing so simple? That's where I get confounded. How can this be so simple? How possible it is to be well?

# Linnie Thomas
## HTCP/I, QM, MLW

I can't really call my chapter an interview as I can only write it and, while a few people offered to interview me, when it came time to do it, no one was available. I hadn't planned on being in the book, as I don't consider myself an elder or a prominent leader in Healing Touch. I do occasionally write or compile books. Cynthia and Lisa insisted I be included. Humble as they are, here are some of my stories.

I am a Healing Touch Level 1 Instructor and a Qualified Mentor. I took my first Level 1 class in October of 1997 in Hillsboro, Oregon. Barb Dahl was my instructor and, to my delight, has become one of my dearest friends. But my story doesn't begin there.

Back in January of 1978, I took a human potential workshop put on by PSI World. It's a four day class and is still being taught. By the way, if you get a chance to take one of their classes, I highly recommend them. But I digress.

The first day of class, someone had put a sign on the back wall that read, "To Think Is to Create." In my loftiness, I thought, "Well, if you have a problem, and you think on it for a while, you may get an answer. I've got this class nailed." Ahem.

The next day a new sign appeared on the wall that read, "Thoughts Are Things." I could really get me teeth into that, as the word *thought* is a noun, therefore it is a *thing*. Again I thought I had this class nailed. You may laugh at this point.

The following day, a new sign showed up. This one said, "If You Don't Like Where You're at, Change Your Thinking." I realized I didn't have a clue in the closet as to what this class was all about. I kept asking myself questions like, "How can I change my thinking? It just happens." I was too embarrassed to ask about it out loud.

It became a lifelong quest. I wanted to know just how my thoughts created my universe. Could I actually influence the outcome of an event or even a meeting with someone. Could I change my life around just with thinking about it in a different way?

We were given a number of tools, including positive thinking, workshop of the mind, and affirmations. But the thing that fascinated me most, was an exercise to show just how powerful the human mind can be. We paired up. One student gave the name, age or approximate age, and location of a person they knew with a health problem. That is all that could be said. The other student would go into their workshop of the mind and bring the person with the problem into their workshop of the mind. From there, the person would ascertain what the health problem was and visualize that person as whole and healthy. Some students got good at describing what the person looked like. Amazing healings were reported after these classes by people who didn't even know their friend was in a class. That caught my interest big time.

We formed phone trees. This was years before cell phones and computers. When someone was ill or had an injury, we'd start up the phone tree and everyone would go into their workshop of the mind and see the person healed and whole. It worked.

About sixteen years later, I was working as a bridal alteration specialist in the alteration department of a local drycleaners. One of the women working there had a nineteen year old daughter who was in a car accident and broke two vertebrae in her neck. She was paralyzed from the neck down. I kept thinking that if to think is to create really works, this little gal could walk again. It bothered me. For three months thoughts of her walking again went through my mind. It became an obsession. Finally, I couldn't stand it any longer. Their insurance had run out, and the gal was living in the downstairs family room. I asked if I could come work on her.

Her mother was all for it. They had hired a shaman to come out and see what he could do. My friend told me he was smelly and nothing happened. At least, the daughter would see a friendly face when I showed up.

My goal was that this girl would walk again. I went over after work. As I started to get out of the car, I noticed a tennis ball on the floor of the car. I picked it up on a hunch and went inside. The gal was residing in a hospital bed. She was quite talkative, but obviously depressed about her condition. As she talked, I thought about what I could do for her using the positive affirmations I had learned. It came to me to use the tennis ball.

For those of you who have not met someone who is paralyzed, their hands stay flat. The fingers do not curl at rest like a healthy person's does. I put the tennis ball in her hand, and with my fingers holding hers in place, I had her close her eyes and remember what it felt like to hold a tennis ball. Once she had that picture in her mind, I had her open her eyes and look at the ball in her hand. Then I had her close her eyes once again, and imagine what it would be like to hold a tennis ball now. Once she had that firmly in mind, I told her to open her eyes, and I let go of her hand. The four fingers stayed in place.

Tennis balls have friction which helped with the next step. It took a little work, but we managed to get the thumb to stay in place, and she held the tennis ball all by herself. The family went ballistic. I was invited back. I started working with her once a week and soon it became twice a week. Later our time together became three times a week. Each session, I would go into the workshop of my mind and ask what to do that session. Sometimes she came up with suggestions and we did them.

At the end of a year, she had full use of her arms. Some of her fingers are still a little numb, but she can feed herself, use a computer, comb her hair, and put on make-up. During one session I had her make chocolate chip cookies. The only thing she could not do was open a box of brown sugar. Her fingers didn't have the stability needed to open the box. Otherwise she did it all by herself.

Towards the end of the year, to my delight, I could feel a slight twitching in her leg muscles when I asked her to think about moving her feet. I thought my goal of her walking was now possible. But another lesson occurred for me. The time I had available for these visits, coincided with Days of Our Lives, her favorite soap opera. She also had a little girl who was sent to be with Grandma during our sessions. She didn't like being denied access to her mother.

One day I came, and learned I had been fired. Here comes the lesson: the difference between cure and healing. You see, this gal walking again was my goal, not hers. We had not really discussed long term goals. She had reached a point in her healing where she was ready to continue on with her life, and no longer felt the need of a therapist. She was healed.

Cure is the absence of symptoms. Healing is just where this little gal was at. She had come to a place in her life where she felt she could cope with life in spite of her physical handicaps, and do the things she wanted to do.

Most paraplegics die within ten years of their injuries. It has been over twenty-two years and this little gal is still going strong. I still see her occasionally as a friend. I have not been invited back as a therapist.

About that time, I had a love affair go wrong. I was wondering what to do with myself. A friend, Jody Stevenson, was starting a ministerial school. I talked to her about being a student. She thought that would be a good idea. It was close to the date when the classes started. I had four days to fill out a long questionnaire, get references and a recommendation, have a formal picture taken, and a bunch of other stuff. I also had to write about what I had been doing recently that had significance to me, and what I would like to be doing five and ten years from that point. Of course, I told the story of this little gal and I working together, and how I would like to do more of that kind of work.

I completed the requirements and turned it in the day before classes started. The next morning Jody called me into her office. She told me the board had met the night before and prayed about my application. She prayed much of the night and the decision made was to turn me down. I thought I had flunked out of ministerial school before I even got in the door. What Jody said next totally changed my life.

After we picked up my teeth from off the floor, she said, "The world is full of ministers. We badly need healers. Your application is full of healing work and we would like to offer you a scholarship to the healing school of your choice."

Wow.

I began the quest of finding a healing school. I was, of course, looking for schools that taught positive thinking and affirmations. I couldn't find any schools that worked that way. I looked at Reiki. It was way too woo-woo for me at that time. My college major was nuclear engineering with the goal of becoming a nuclear physicist. It sounded good when I was young. However, I had a little bit of a bother with the math needed. I got married instead, and never finished my degree.

But this woo-woo thing with Reiki didn't ring my chimes. I was used to working with reason and logic. My dad and his father were civil engineers and designed railroad bridges. My mother's father was a lawyer. Woo-woo just didn't enter into our lives.

I looked at Barbara Brennan's classes. Her background in physics and engineering had a big appeal. But $30,000 a year in class expenses didn't, even with a scholarship. I knew the scholarship wasn't that big.

After some time spent searching the web, we had a meeting at Jody's office. She remembered she had a friend in Seattle, who had just completed Healing Touch Level 3. She called her and put me on the phone. I liked what the friend had to say. I love the synchronicity of what followed. The gal in Seattle gave me the number of the Colorado Center for Healing Touch. I called them, and they told me a class was being taught in Hillsboro, a nearby suburb of Portland, in three weeks. I signed up.

Half an hour after introductions had been done, and we started to get into the meat of the class, I knew I was home. It didn't make any sense, but I loved every minute of it.

We had a lot of unofficial rules at that time. The current trend was to wait a whole year before taking Level 2. That was all right with me as it gave me time to save up for the tuition.

In the meantime, five of us formed a practice group. We met almost every Friday night for a little over three years. My first glimpse of what Healing Touch can do in real life came at one of those practice sessions. We met, in the beginning, at the hospital where the class had been held. One of the gals worked as a nurse there.

At one of the sessions she came to practice with four blisters on her fingers. She had accidentally touched the broiler in her oven not knowing it was still on. Her thought was that, if anyone can help ease the pain of the burns, our practice group would.

She placed a frozen blue bag over her fingers. We couldn't see the burns, because of it. For forty-five minutes we took turns working on her fingers alternating between pain drain and hands in motion. At the end of that time, the blue bag had warmed up. When she removed it, half the blisters had disappeared and she reported the pain was much less. She got a new blue bag from the freezer, and, encouraged, we continued to work. At the end of the practice session, she had one tiny bit of blister on one finger. The rest were completely gone. She was pain free. When she got home, she showed her husband. He said he didn't understand it, and that it was a little scary, but he wanted her to continue the work and take more classes.

At the end of a year, three of us from the practice group took Level 2, and almost a year later, we took Level 3. Two of us took a local class and one of us took Level 3 somewhere else. We continued with our practice group for a long time after that. Two of us are now instructors and one became the first person in our area (she was a social worker, not a nurse), to be hired to do Healing Touch in a pain control clinic. She had the courage to offer a session to her boss. He was so impressed, he offered her the job.

I took Level 4 soon after in Denver, as I had a daughter living in Longmont and it meant I could visit her and her family, before and after class. I met Janna Moll at the Level 4 and asked her to be my mentor. Away we went.

Because I was a non-nurse, as was Janna, I asked Anne Day, who was a nurse, to oversee the mentorship. Both women were fabulous mentors. When it came time for Anne to submit her letter for certification about our mentorship, she recommended I go to Level 6 and become an instructor. That was a surprise. A few weeks after I got my certification, I was off to Level 6. I got to see a lot of my daughter and family during all that time. A double delight.

In spite of all of this support, I still had trouble believing Healing Touch worked. I could definitely feel something when I put my hands on people. They would report great things. I even had a client come out of a coma brought on by a stroke. She regained the use of her right side, which had been paralyzed by the stroke, and was back at work four weeks later. I just thought I had been at the right place at the right time.

It took a major incident to finally convince me this wasn't all hocus-pocus. I loved the work. Don't get me wrong. I was too embarrassed about my doubts to discuss them with others. I had an office and had set up a regular practice. It wasn't enough to quell those deeper misgivings.

Bringing the office into existence was a miracle in itself. My ministerial friend had found an office building where the top floor was being remodeled. She had picked out a room and took me to see it. I found a space I liked. I didn't have the money for a five hundred dollar deposit. I kept going over to look at the room every night after work It started as nothing but two-by-fours,. I watched it take shape and would pace back and forth, while imagining myself doing the healing work in the room. Two days before the room was ready for me to move in, the money appeared. I had appointments for clients, and a friend gave me a massage table she didn't want. I was ready to go.

I split my work hours between working as a bridal alteration specialist and my healing practice. It took me three months to do my hundred healings. I was disappointed that I didn't make enough to support myself doing just Healing Touch.

One day, I decided to sell a commercial sewing machine to my boss at the cleaners. A friend came over to help me load the thing into the back of his pickup and deliver the machine to my work place. I never made it. At one point, the sewing machine came loose from its connections to the table it rested on. It fell and landed on my foot. It also bounced off my shin on the way down. We managed to get it off my foot and into the truck. I knew I was in trouble.

With his help, I hobbled into the apartment where I lived and I stayed on the couch for several days. My friend and I sang in our church choir. Another choir member was a chiropractor. He x-rayed my foot and sure enough, I had broken the fourth metatarsal in my left foot. I had no money to go to a hospital for a cast, much less the surgery to put in the pin the chiropractor recommended.

I called my wusband (Yes, that is what I call him), who is a Reiki master and had studied a number of other healing modalities. He came right over. I lay on my back with my foot up on the arm of the sofa. He placed one hand on one side of my foot and the other hand on the other side of my foot. He did still hands for about thirty-five minutes. I know the time, because there was a cuckoo clock behind him, and I would look at it trying to take my mind off what he was doing.

All I can say is the guides came in big time. I could feel them massaging the broken bone back together. It was quite painful. At times they would stop for a minute to let me catch my breath. The experience reminded me of being in labor. At the end of the treatment, I was looking up at the ceiling wondering if it was ever going to end, when I felt someone pull on my big toe.

I asked my wusband why he was pulling on my big toe. He hadn't moved his hands from either side of my foot. I looked at my toe and so did he. We both watched it stretch out and then the guide let go. The toe went back into place and I got the message that the toe had been dislocated and needed to be moved back into its socket.

It was a tough lesson. It worked. I still have doubts from time to time, and enjoy and appreciate validation of the work. I once asked

Janet Mentgen if she liked to be validated after all her years of experience. Her answer was, "Yup."

My appreciation for Healing Touch grew through the years. I became a Level 1 instructor. I am a charter member of HTPA. I went to conferences and took every class I could find for a long time. To cover expenses, I coordinated most of the classes. I would bring instructors in from other parts of the country. I loved it. They would stay at my house. That way I got one on one time with a lot of brilliant people, including Janet Mentgen.

I brought her out for Advanced Practices I and II. She stayed in my very humble apartment for four days. The first day of class, one of the more affluent people in the community asked Janet if she would like to come stay with her. Janet told her she was quite comfortable staying with me. I was delighted. Janet and I chatted about all kinds of things to and from class. On the day she was to fly home, I took her to Multnomah Falls for brunch. We chatted all the while until we got in the car to drive to the airport. She got very quiet and I teased her about her mind being back at the office. She admitted to that and we rode in silence the rest of the way.

After listening to all these interviews I have pondered on what I would like to see in the future for Healing Touch Program. I am so proud of all the work that has been done. At first, I saw the accreditation work as just another bit of nonsense required to be a part of our society. However, I wanted to be supportive and even got involved in writing questions for the test. Now I see the importance of all that effort, especially when working with the healthcare community. Because of it I have had times, as a non-nurse, when I have been allowed in the recovery room to work on a client. I am grateful for that. I can see we have more prestige in the healthcare community. This is a good thing.

In my not so humble opinion, the emphasis on ethics mentioned in all the classes, on documentation, and other clinical stuff has run its course. It is time to get back to doing the work. It is great to say we have not one, but two accreditations. However, I find I get far better response, when I simply offer a treatment and they get off the table saying how much better they feel.

Social media, web sites, texting are all good means of communication today. But it is that face to face contact that convinces people what we are doing has value. If we really want to spread the word at a grass roots level, we have to talk to people. It is much easier to say no, via email or text, than it is face to face, and even more difficult to say no once a treatment has been received.

Which brings up another point I would like to see change. No more giving treatments away. I know a lot of people believe this work should be free. Much of that thinking stems from religious beliefs. But do doctors, physical therapists, massage therapists, and chiropractors give away their work? Is it any less important than what we are doing? Of course not!

I am all for doing healing work for free at military stand downs. All healthcare providers come to offer their services for free at such events. That can be said for health fairs and other informative events. But, giving away your work in the hopes that people will find value in it, doesn't work. If you don't value it, how can you expect someone else to value it?

I like to think of our work as the Rolls Royce of energy work and charge accordingly. I still do a lot of pro bono work, but mostly I charge between $75 and $150 a session, depending upon the type of work I do and how long the session goes.

I do have advice for new students and for people working towards certification. First, join or form a practice group. Don't think of it as just practicing the techniques. Actually do the work. Set intentions. You'll be surprised at the unexpected results.

We had been practicing for almost two years when I took Level 3. The class took place at a hotel down at the beach. It was a fairly large class. People like to go to the beach for classes and were willing to pay a little more for the privilege.

Someone brought a basket of MacIntosh apples. I had been suffering from irritated bowel syndrome for many of my adult years. Apples were one of the foods that set it off. I dearly love apples. I got thinking, I could eat a small one and if my colon acted up, I would be in the right place and the class could ease the discomfort. This was on the first day of class. Nothing happened. No colon problems arose.

The second day I got brave enough to try a second apple. No problems. It dawned on me I hadn't had an episode in quite a while. All those times of being on the table had healed the colon. I hadn't mentioned the problem to my practice group. It has been eighteen years and I have had only two episodes of colon distress, both during times of extreme personal stress. I don't eat apples during very stressful times any more, just to be on the safe side. I enjoy them when I am at rest. I can eat ice cream with no problems to my delight.

The point of all of this is that no one knew about the colon problem. But the energy went where it was needed. My body knew, even if I consciously didn't. If it weren't for the practice group meeting every Friday night, I would probably still have the problem. Those meetings are a lot more important than just to practice.

The other thing I would like to say is to tell people about what you are doing. Let your enthusiasm shine. It takes courage to do that. Be careful of your language though. I have found it is much better to speak in scientific terms, using the term *human energy field* instead of *aura*, for example, will make what you have to say a lot more acceptable.

I once went to a celebration of life. A lot of the people there were very professional, lawyers and such. When someone asked me what I did, I replied, "I am a biofield therapist. I work with the human energy field."

The response I got delighted me. They had no idea what I was talking about. But they all agreed that was a fascinating field and gave me an opening to talk about it further. Some of them took an interest. I was very careful to use scientific terminology and went home with a couple of new clients to schedule. If I had said I am a hands-on healer and work with auras and chakras, I doubt very much if anyone would have spoken to me after that.

If we want to have Healing Touch in every hospital, clinic, home and office, we have to talk about it. Find a small radio station that features local talk shows . They are hungry for interesting and controversial topics. It's not that hard. You can even do that by email if you feel uncomfortable making a cold call.

Once I became an instructor, I had students ask me if Healing Touch was the right modality for them to study. With so many available, students wondered how to find the right one. Of course, the first thing I say when asked that, now, is that of all the modalities I have studied, Healing Touch Program is best entry level course I can find. The techniques work and it also allows freedom to explore the world of energy medicine. I have yet to find a better entry level set of courses with a better science background.

However, to answer their question, I got to thinking a book on the subject is needed. As a former software technical writer, it one day occurred to me, I have the skills to do just that. It took four years and *The Encyclopedia of Energy Medicine* got published.

The subject of ethics and knowing your state's laws concerning touch and counseling came up. So I compiled *Laws Governing Energy Medicine Practitioners*. During a Level 6 which I audited as a way of making sure I was up to date on the latest changes, the need for a who's who in Healing Touch came up. You are reading the result of that.

Healing Touch can take you into new places. I began working with hospice patients and dying family members. I saw a lot of people make their final transition. This led me to write *There Is No Hell* to bring comfort to those going through the process and to friends and family there to support them.

You don't have to be a writer to spread the word about Healing Touch Program. You do need to communicate, using whatever media you like. Keeping all the wonders of it to yourself may feel good to you, but your neighbors, friends and family members aren't going to know about it. You would be surprised at how many people want to know what you do and what you can do for them.

And lastly I would say:
Just do the work.
And tell others about it.
You'll be glad you did.

# Amelia Vogler
## MS, HTCP/I

### Introduction

Amelia is the Executive Director of the Healing Touch Professional Association. Amelia is also a power house running the professional association and all the other things she does. She is one of those amazing people who sails through obstacles and problems and comes out smelling like a rose once the work is done.

    She is infectious. Her enthusiasm for Healing Touch is catching. I love being around her. When I am feeling down or discouraged, all I have to do is talk to Amelia and I am immediately back on my feet again. I don't even have to tell her I have a problem; she's an intuitive after all. She's just great to have in your space.

### Interview

*You babbled on about how you got into Healing Touch at the instructor's gathering. I would like you to babble on again. Start at your own beginning and go from there.*

    I didn't really know about energy medicine or anything Healing Touch, or anything like that when I first started. Except that my father has been a funeral director, in the same funeral home as seven generations of my family. That's two hundred and fifty years of the family holding space for people during the time of loss and grieving.

When I was a little girl, I would go to my dad's funeral home after school. He would pick us up. He had stuff to finish up. We would put our roller skates on and we would roller skate through the funeral home, because it was nine thousand square feet of rooms with big doors and pathways that could hold either a gurney or a casket stand. We had a lot of leverage around this big funeral home. He would say, "Don't go in that room. Don't go in that room. That one's empty. Don't go in that one."

We went in all the rooms we weren't supposed to go in. We didn't bother in the ones that were empty. It was kind of like, "Well, who's in there? Oh! She's got a pretty dress on." We were checking out what dead people looked like. As a little kid, I was always curious about that, because when you look at a lot of dead people, what you don't see is the light in their eyes. What you don't see, is whatever it is that comes into our body and our skin that makes us alive, which I now know of as the human spirit, the energy. I had a lifelong curiosity about what is that thing that lights up our eyes. What is that thing that gives warmth to our skin and I don't mean temperature. I mean warmth as in life. There was that, but I didn't know what it was.

I hated the grocery stores when I was a little girl. It was my least favorite place everywhere. You could take me anywhere but the grocery store. My mom would stick me in a little grocery cart, and push me around, and leave me over there at the oranges while she went over here to get the broccoli and the carrots. Somebody would walk by me and I would know whether their knee hurt, because my knee would hurt. Somebody over there was really sad, and somebody over there who's mom was dying.

I didn't have words for all this, but I was a little empath. And I still am. I hated the grocery store. It was like getting a little flip book of horrible experiences that weren't mine. Or wonderful ones, like a good bit about - I don't know. I was living out these people's lives for one second at a time in the grocery store and I didn't want to do that. It pissed me off. I would go home crying and my parents would say I was too sensitive.

Then I learned, like many sensitive people, that that wasn't going to help me in my life. My mom and dad, bless their hearts, said, "You're too sensitive." They know how to do life because they were my parents. So I bottled all that stuff up.

At the same time, while I was growing up I watched my dad with his clients. I remember this one day when there were these two African American sisters with these beautiful Sunday purple hats on, and these beautiful purple dresses on. It was actually a suit top and skirt and stockings and these adorable shoes. They looked like twins. I don't know if they were twins, but they looked like twins. Same height, same hat, same shoes and dress. And the same grief in the same moment.

My dad came up in between them and he put one hand on each of the gals' backs, right around the back of the heart. I watched him hold these two women for a moment. I saw his heart stream light around the three of them. He said to them, "I'm going to get you through this. I don't know how we're going to do it, but I'm going to get you through this day." I watched them soften and relax in a way that I'll never forget. Because I watched him hold them in his heart.

Every time I tell that story, I can feel the same quality of caring, heart-centered caring, that I did for the first time in that moment. I knew that there was something to being with someone. Just standing with them, being with them.

You keep those experiences, and just shove them to the side as if they're, I don't know, an introduction to a story and then you start it on page one. Page one started because I was a normal kid for a long time. I set all that sensitive stuff aside and let it simmer somewhere deep in my body. I never forgot it.

I went to boarding school, which I loved. I begged to go because there was creativity there. I felt cramped in my mom and dad's home; I think a little because I'm a big dreamer and a little because you have to look really sharp when you leave the house if you are the child of a funeral director.

Every time I left the house I had to have a collared shirt on. I had to look really put together. Put together is something that I look like about thirty percent of the time (and usually only when somebody needs me to). Put together is something that always was irrelevant to my spirit

My family was amazing and my mom a woman who tap danced in the kitchen and she grew plants and created hybrid rhododendrons and created new plants. She was a woman who cultivated life and watched it grow. My dad was a man that care-taked over the dead and the grieving. In my life I saw a lot of life from beginning to end. I just had to make my own way with it.

We drove together: my mom and dad and myself eight hundred and sixty miles north to Pomfret, Connecticut to the boarding school. My dad dropped me off with my mom, at what I would call the next door step for the rest of my life. He gave me over to new parents, my dorm parents. My dad looked at me and cried and said, "I am not ready to let you go, but I love you so much and I just know it's the right thing to do."

I think that they knew that my spirit was bigger than that little house with all the flowers and the phone calls in the middle of the night. They called in that their mom has died or that my daughter's died. We would listen to those calls. Death was all right there and always a present part of my childhood.

I had a normal life. I played varsity field hockey and varsity tennis. Let me share that if it makes it into the book because I'm not really an athlete, so that's a good thing to have in writing, or least have recorded on the video so that this unnatural achievement can be recorded as part of my public history.

I went to college, studied English literature and social psychology. I fooled around in Boston for a while until I realized I needed to get my shit together. I moved home. I started teaching special ed. I went back for a master's and was completely duped when I went to select my master's. Because I was an English major I went to the English department and I said to the graduate school dean, "What does someone do with an English major?" And they said, "Go do technical writing. It's engineering for writers."

I went, "Is it creative?"

He said, "Yes."

I said, "I'm in."

He lied to me. I found my way to IBM, a Fortune 500 company. I was working straight through my master's. I was making a shit load of money as a technical writer intern. I mean it like quadrupled my salary from teaching. Along with the money came back my migraines. Big time.

Migraines I had had ever since I was little. I would get them four times a year when the season changed. They put me in the hospital. I'd vomit all night. They'd fix me on drugs and then I'd be back to my life.

I got these migraines more frequently and I went to an acquaintance, who is sharing now with a massage friend of mine, and he said, "Why don't you go see this lady?"

I said, "What does she do?"

He said, "I don't know. I don't know what she does. She's going to wave her hands around you and hold your feet and put rocks on you. I just think you should go see her."

I went to go see this woman who nobody knows what she does, who puts rocks on you, and waves her hands over you and holds your feet. Her name was Sally Nyholt. I love Sally Nyholt! She's one of the most important people of my entire history. Like for me, there's my mother. There's my father. And there is Sally Nyholt.

That very first day she gave me some forms, like a medical intake form. She gave me also a form with a body drawn in, like the silhouette of a body, and she said, "Fill it in if you have pain or discomfort. Draw it in."

While I knew I was going for headaches, I put a little star over my heart in red. That was all I drew on the form. The day I went to see Sally, I dropped my forms. We talked for a while and she put me on the massage table, fully clothed. I never really liked massage because I don't really like people touching me. That was like amazing, that I didn't have to be touched and still get on a massage table.

Then I heard her breathing. I'll never forget the way Sally breathes, because it's like the mother of the earth taking each breath through all the trees. She placed little rocks down me and she breathed. She sat at my feet and she held my feet. I now know she grounded me. It was like I remembered being in the grocery store being able to feel all that which I could not see, or knew the things I wasn't supposed to know, or feel things in way that could teach me more about the world. I was so relaxed. I was so comforted. I felt I had found my way home through Sally in that day.

She was so gracious with her time, because I had, then, about a thousand questions about what is this thing? What did she do? Was it the rocks? Even though I rather knew it wasn't the rocks. Something in the way she was holding my feet and waving her hands over me in a very soft and kind and loving way.

I started to see Sally. I was an addict. I became a Sally addict. Every two weeks I would make an appointment and just run to the table. I mean, I sped more in my life trying to get to Sally Nyholt's office than I sped at any other time in my life. I never got a ticket so that was divine intervention, I believe.

At IBM I had quite a job. I was working like eighty hours a week. It was ridiculous how much I was working at IBM. It was no wonder that my headaches were returning because I was all in my head doing writing and it was up, up, up and running, running, running. I had been an intern and then they hired me. And then they hired me to be a team lead. And then they hired me into the management of a team. I had a team of five. I was twenty-eight years old and I was managing a team of writers on a really successful project.

We had an engineer who was an aerospace engineer. He used to work for NASA. The guy was just brilliant. My boss said to me one day, "I'm moving him to another team."

And I said, "I'm screwed. My team was screwed. I'm screwed. You can't do that. He's the best."

He said, "Amelia. You can figure it out. You can do it."

I am not an aerospace engineer. I love NASA, but I am not an aerospace engineer. So I went to Sally that day, and I was like, "Sally, I'm screwed!"

She gave me a session. At the end of the session she said, "I want you to go online and look for a job at SAS." SAS was a company in our area. It was voted one of the best companies in the world to work for.

I said, "Well, um. I've applied there about six times. They don't even answer my phone calls."

She said, "Just try it."

When I got home, it was like five o'clock. I looked at SAS's website and they had posted a job at three PM for the type of work that I do. I applied straight away. When I interviewed for the job, a man came down the steps and I said, "Bret?"

And he said, "Amelia?"

I said, "What are you doing?"

And he's like, "I'm interviewing you."

I thought, "Oh my God." I had written some research for him in graduate school.

He walked me up the stairs saying, "We use your research all the time. We use your metrics all the time. It's so great to see you."

I was thinking, "This is good."

I got the job. It's a thirty-five hour work week. Suddenly half of my life opened back up. A little bit after that Sally said to me, "I am no longer going to treat you until you go and take the first class of Healing Touch."

I was like, "What the heck? I thought you liked me." I didn't like that agreement at all, because I really liked paying Sally to help me relax and I could do my life and then everything would be fine. But I think there were other plans for me.

I told Sally, "I'm never going to do this work. I don't want to do this work. This is ridiculous, like I'm your client. I'm so like not even that. I'm a lofty client who just wants to pay you and do my life. Gross."

She told me that there were two different programs and she said, "Why don't you research the two programs and see which one calls you." She was so amazing. She didn't give me a lot of guidance. She just said to follow your heart.

I found that Healing Touch Program had the accreditation and it just seemed more grounded. I looked for a class. There were some classes in North Carolina, but I wasn't drawn to the instructors, which was like asinine, because I wasn't even drawn to doing the class.

But yet, I called Ines Hoster in Atlanta, six and a half hours away, and I said, "I saw you have a class. Do you mind if I come down for it?"

She said, "Sure."

I registered. I drove my ass six and one half hours south to Atlanta to take a class with some lady named Ines. I don't know why I was there. There were four or five other people in the class. I took the first day. I freaking hated it. I absolutely hated it. I felt sick as a dog. All I wanted to do was drink like three gallons of orange juice and go to bed.

I called Sally from the hotel room and I was like, "You were wrong. This is awful. I hate Healing Touch. I hate this class."

She said, "Hmm. Sounds like maybe the people in the class weren't as grounded as I am. But I've had a lot of experience, so your body might be going through a little something. Like trying to figure it out how to be with this other type energy work that the people are just learning. Why don't you go to Ines's house a little bit before class. Let her know you're not feeling well and finish up the course. Then we'll see what happens when you get home."

At seven in the morning I went to Ines's house and she met me at the front door with her bathrobe on, looking at me like I had about fifteen heads coming out of my neck. She looked horrible. She was still half asleep. I know I woke her up and she's like, "Who the hell's at my front door? Oh. it's one of my students."

You know, maybe that's why you should teach at a different facility than your house. But that's a side comment. I told Ines that I felt like crap after the class and I needed her. My mentor or my practitioner told me to come over. She put me on her back porch facing her labyrinth and a fountain. She gave me some water and held my shoulders. She breathed a little. I started feeling better.

I finished up the class and then I had my six and a half hour trip to drive back from Atlanta to home. It was like seven at night when I left. I don't know. It was like really late in the morning when I finally got home. What I noticed after that first class was that I was driving and every single leaf was a brighter green than I'd ever seen in my life. Every flower was a brighter color. I was awake in way that I hadn't ever been awake. And clear in a way that I had never been clearer. I was so empowered with these new tools. Like the twelve methods that you learn in Level 1.

I went back to SAS the next day and said to some of my friends on my team, "What's going on in your body these days?"

They're like, "What?"

"Yeah. Like what are you getting? Headaches? Backaches? Like anything going on - any knee things? Anything cracking, aching? What a ya got?" I got a laundry list of common irritations and I said, "Why don't you come to my house? I learned something."

I would invite people to my home. I had a massage table that I got at Sam's Club for like a hundred bucks. You know, I just did the work. I fell in love with the work.

I put a tip jar out. "Take me to Level 2." People would toss money in there. Like I made so much money on tips. It was amazing as a Level 1. Cause I had to go back to Atlanta and pay for gas, and get a hotel room, pay for the course. I did Level 2 and then I did Level 3 and then I did Level 4 and then I did Level 5. And that was it. I was lost at Level 1 in the work. There is no turning back.

I even worked on my boss. I was like, "Oh, you look tired. Your back hurts. Let me do the thing." People became aware that Amelia in this office could do this thing and so just go see her.

Which sort of brings me to the question of describe a nice experience of Healing Touch? One day when I was in my town house and I should mention by this time I had the cutest town house. It was an open floor plan. It was so great. You could see all the way through. My husband at the time, who I later found was not the perfect husband. It's funny how Healing Touch happens and unfolds in our lives. He loved to drink these fancy beers and they were aligned up in the kitchen.

I thought, "Oh my God. My clients are not going to like to see beer bottles." So I hung up a full curtain in the middle of my open floor plan. No one could see back there. It was quite something for somebody who loves their house as much as I do to hang up a big heavy curtain to block the energy of everything back there.

A woman called me named Karen. She said, "I heard you do a thing."

And I said, "Yeah. I do a thing."

She said, "Well, how do I get the thing?"

I said, "Well, come to my house. "It sounded like a drug deal really."

She said, "All right." She came in and Karen was awesome. She was bubbly, expressive, an amazing woman.

She said, "I just got a terminal diagnosis." And she smiled.

I thought, "Uh oh." I kind of held back because I was just Level 3. I didn't know what to do.

She said, "Well, right now, my knee just hurts. So maybe you could just work on my knee."

I worked on her knee. Her knee didn't hurt when she got off the table. She said, "I'm coming back."

I saw Karen every two weeks for five and a half years. I saw Karen through ten surgeries, and experimental treatments. I saw Karen through experimental drugs, clinical trials - I think three of them. I saw Karen through one back surgery that was just - I think it was twelve vertebras that they tried to scrape tumors off of. I saw Karen through the joy of living and the joy of dying. I saw Karen more, well the day before she died, than I saw her that first day she came into my office and her knee hurt. I saw Karen through migraines and I saw Karen through stomach aches, and losing her hair and growing her hair back.

One day, my biggest regret in my whole life, was that Karen told me she was speaking to a group of her Alcoholics Anonymous community, because she had been sober for twenty-five years. She had bought a pink dress and a pink hat and she said, "Amelia, can you come?"

I was busy that day doing something and so I didn't go. I asked her the next time I saw her how was it. "How was it, Karen? How was your speech?"

She said, "I stood up there and I told two hundred and fifty people that I was dying and I still didn't want to have another drink. And I did it in my pink hat and my pink dress."

So my biggest life regret is that I didn't get to see her say that. I got to feel the pride and the power and the love when she shared it with me. I felt honored that she did share it with me.

Karen was my case study. Sally was my mentor. Ines Hoster was my QM, my Qualified Mentor. Those three women were my team that brought me into this work. I never thought that I would do the work full time until I moved around in the company a little bit. One day I found myself in a counselor's office and I said, "You know what Sharon? I feel like I'm wasting my time in this company."

She said, "I think that's really important."

I was like, "I got this other thing. I love to do it and maybe I should just try it."

She said, "Maybe you should listen to yourself."

I got depressed and I went to the doctor. The company I worked for, they had a doctor there. Like a really nice one. A two full service labs kind of doctor. I said, "Dr. Baskett, I'm really sad."

She said, "Amelia, I've treated you for like seven years and I've watched you just kind of dull out. Maybe you need some time to think about it."

She is what a doctor, to me, really is. She wrote me a prescription for ten days off of work to pray. short term medical leave, fully paid for so I could go home and pray about what it is that was making me dull and what it was that might make me feel better. She said, "I can't tell you to quit your job, because I work here. But I can give you some time to think about it and what that means for your health."

After those ten days off I told my boss, "I'm giving my one hundred and eight day notice."

He said, "I've never had anyone quit before. I've worked here twenty-eight years and I don't even know what to do."

I said, "You know what? Let's call HR and figure it out."

We did and for a hundred and eight days I prayed about what it would look like to be on the other side of corporate America. I realized about three weeks in that I was praying wrong, because I was praying for things like courage, strength and fortitude. My life got so freaking hard. I started being asked to show up in courage and show up with more strength. I called my counselor. I was like, "What is going on? This is hard. I thought this was going to be easy. I'm just praying."

She said, "What are you praying for?"

I told her and she's like, "Why don't you pray for things like easiness? Happiness? Clarity?"

Duh. So then I learned to pray 'right' and life got a lot easier. By that time I already had an office and was already seeing clients part time. I had been doing that since- gosh - Level 3 really. I wanted to get that curtain out of my house, 'cause I'm a Taurus and I really, really love home decor and that just wasn't doing it for me.

I actually shared an office with Sally. She gave me a few days of the week. It was wonderful there. It was right near my office, so it was quite easy.

After I quit my job, my boy friend asked me to marry him. My life changed a hundred and fifty percent. Everything changed. Absolutely everything changed after that moment. I just did the work.

My dad, rightly so, was a little curious about this decision. He was like, "You just quit your job with the best company in the world to work for, to do work that's invisible?"

"Yup. I did Dad.'"

All the while I've been on the table receiving work and working with Sally doing my hundred sessions. I became certified and I just kept on. I love this work.

At some point, you know the woman who thought she would just pay someone to do Healing Touch so she didn't have her migraines. Oh, that's another part. My migraines went away forever. It was like six months after seeing Sally I realized, "Oh my God, I haven't had a migraine." It was quarterly. So that was kind of my first quarter where I realized I didn't have to go to the hospital. Then a year went by. Then a year and a half and then two years. It's now been thirteen and a half years and I haven't had a migraine. Because of Healing Touch. Because I learned to ground myself. Because I learned the dynamics of the energy system and I learned to listen to myself.

That's what made me know that Healing Touch was something tangible even though my spirit knew very well that something intangible was quite more important than the tangible.

Because I had a strong background in business, along the way I went to Level 6 with Cynthia for teaching because I thought I would never do the work and I never thought I'd have a practice. I definitely thought I'd never be teaching it. So I went to Level 6. I've been two times already. I loved it so much I took it again a few years later.

I signed up for Level 6, and called Cynthia, and said I don't really have a place to stay.

She said, "You can stay with me. It's thirty dollars a night."

I said, "Okay."

Cynthia and I realized we were like sisters from a long time ago. maybe she's sisters with everybody. She seems to have a very large soul family. But at any rate, I am happy to be counted among them.

In that Level 6 we had discussion about my business background. Sharon had died a few years before that or a year before that. There was an absence at this thing called the Healing Touch Professional Association. I said, "What is that?"

She said, "Sharon used to run it and she really dreamed and envisioned the professional association helping our practitioners be more professional.

I said, "That sounds lovely. A few years went by and I was teaching. Cynthia tapped me and said, "I really think it's time we do something with the professional association. Lisa and Chris are thinking of hiring somebody. Would you apply?"

I said, "No. I don't want to do that. Just like I didn't want to do the work and I didn't want to teach and I didn't want to do the professional association." I asked why I spent a really long time working on my resume` when I was in California at Disneyland or World. Whichever one is in California. I was at a conference for burn survivors that I go to. I was taking a break and I was like I gotta do my resume` for this job application for a job that I don't want to apply for. Spirit can literally move a pen. I know it. Water a line, move mountains, move pens. I believe it. Here we go.

I applied and I thought, "What am I doing? "

Lisa said, "This is cool. Great. You're amazing. You've done so much."

I was like, "Oh. This is looking promising." I said, "Yeah. I would love to join your team," when they offered me the position. It was like, "Okay. This is just like all the other things I didn't want to do this work and suddenly I'm signing up for something else." The one thing that I asked for was that I keep my practice part time, because I will always, ALWAYS have a practice and always do the work.

What I love about the professional association is that it gave me an opportunity to do more healing in a different way. The professional association's mission is to support practitioners through advanced education, business support, internal community development, like our Healing Touch community, and external community development, like the larger community of energy medicine: the energy psychologists, the intuitives, the energetic nutritionists. You know like the larger communities: ACEP and ION's and I am sure I can think of more as soon as we hang up. You know what I mean.

What I love about this work is that every day along the way I realized that what was moving me each day is to bring healing to this planet, to support healing of the planet, support healing of the people that I share my life with on this planet. People like Karen, people like Sally, and all us people at work who have headaches and all those people who are sad because they lost somebody. All those people in the oncology department and the children who are having nightmares. And the young gentleman from the middle east who was on a train running away with his little brother to God knows where. Just getting out of their home state because there was war.

You know there are stories that people bring in that just makes you realize that this human life we live is not small and is something to be honored. Every day I want to honor it the best way that I can and helping the practitioners learn more, be together, expand their practices. That's what keeps me in this role. Because it's more healing to the planet. One practitioner at a time.

I don't know what I don't want to do next, but we'll have to see. That's my story.

.

Pioneers in Healing Touch

# Dawn Warnaca
## HTCP/I

### Introduction

Dawn's devotion to Healing Touch leaves me in awe. Dawn is not an elder, but she isn't a newbie either. I wanted her in the book because she has been such a passionate leader and an avid supporter of Healing Touch. Her interview was short, but I learned more about her that increased my admiration and gratitude we have her as part of our organization.

She was secretary for Healing Touch Worldwide Foundation for two years.

Dawn has been a huge support to HTPA (Healing Touch Professional Association) and has been instrumental in the development and administration of the *Community Connections* network. She helped support Healing Touch Professional Association as Sharon Robbin's assistant for a number of years. When Sharon died, she took over as Acting Executive Director for eighteen months and is now supporting Amelia Vogler.

Dawn just finished her Level 2 advancement instructor training. She teaches several Level 1 classes each year. She is a Qualified Mentor and an instructor for the Healing Touch Qualified Mentor Training class.

She was Master of Ceremonies at the last two worldwide conferences and will be again this year. She wrote an article for

Energy Magazine entitled "Discussion on Healing Crisis.," and also an article on the pros and cons of Third Party Reimbursement.

She has been a huge support for local, meaning the Pacific Northwest, students and practitioners. She coordinated at least five Level 4/5 classes in the greater Seattle area, with the help of Meg Haggerty led the committee for the Seattle Regional Conference, and continues to mentor Healing Touch students. I have found her to be a valuable friend. She is not afraid to kick me in the rump when I need it.

Right now, her focus is on building a sustainable private practice. Along with everything else mentioned.

The following comes from another article Dawn had written in December of 2011.

*"You will never be well – as long as you live – but your condition can be managed with medication." I wonder if those words, from my doctor, are what touched me, deep enough to spur me beyond my comfort level. This trusted professional loved me, cared for my welfare, but had no hope and offered me no hope of healing.*

*The high wire I stepped out onto included changing doctors, beginning body work (a form of massage), and I began to work with an energy medicine therapist. I loved all three – oh, don't get me wrong - each of these practitioners could share with you my initial fear and trepidations. I didn't even give the massage therapist my real name! Oh, how I wanted to hide from what I was facing.*

*I acknowledge that Energy Work chose me, for I did not enter into it intentionally – or rather my intention was just to explore it from a student perspective, instead of a client.*

*I attended my first full time college class, which just happened to be the first day that I was completely medication free. I had been granted a one year leave of absence from my office assistant position in the local elementary school where I had worked for 14 years. I loved my job, I loved the staff, and I loved the children – both those that presented as child and parent. I was fully supported by those who loved me to try my hand at higher education. It also appealed to me to learn more than academics. As I embraced, instead of resisted, what I jokingly referred to as my mid-life crisis, the earth itself seemed to rise up and become a safety net. Stepping out, did not mean stepping off.*

*That fall a Level 1 Healing Touch class was offered in Seattle, and it gave a $100 discount for full time college students! I maturely arrived as a curious skeptic, my ignorance about energy work profoundly revealed when the discussion soon turned to the chakra system. What the heck was a chakra? As I was currently a model college student, I asked questions, lots of questions, I listened, and I participated. Healing Touch classes are only part lecture. The real lessons come in the hands-on practicing of the techniques taught.*

*My skepticism was tempered by my enthusiasm to try these techniques out – on just about anyone that would sit still. It was the feedback from these family, friends, and the occasional fellow student that complained about a sore shoulder or twisted ankle – that peaked my curiosity. My hands felt cool, but they reported them as warm. They felt vibration at the same physical location that I felt vibration. Pain, stress, and depression were measurably changed. I was able to help them – but I knew it wasn't really me; it had to be the techniques, the energy work, but the question remained – how did this work?*

*My husband, Mike, was vocal and supportive from the beginning. He willingly submitted to my experimentations – with the text book on his stomach, or the middle of his back. He wasn't lying, and was as surprised as I when the pain level in his back was reduced by 80 or 90%. He deals with chronic back pain from a high school trampoline injury. He told me that he preferred HT to massage. "Massage hurts" he said, while Healing Touch allowed his body to relax. He soon offered to pay for my Level 2 class... level 3, level 4 and more, oh so much more! Reiki, Thai massage, and aromatherapy classes have also broadened my field of study.*

*I graduated from Pierce College having perhaps the unique opportunity to combine my interest in Healing Touch with basic studies. I prepared an ethnography on a Healing Touch Practitioner for Anthropology, studied the healers in Shakespeare, researched Healing Touch for English, wrote a business plan in Marketing, and compared the ethics standards of the American Psychologist Association, American Anthropology Association and Healing Touch Program in Linguistic Anthropology. The more I learned the simpler and more profound the mystery became. I came to appreciate my passion, and the passionate teachers that have walked with me.*

*I have completed the 5 levels of training with the Healing Touch Program, which included a one year mentorship. I applied for and was granted certification in March of 2010. Complementing my current status, I recently completed a qualified mentorship course; I am one of three practitioners in the State of Washington up to date on the current standards and requirements in the Healing Touch Program. More recently I have completed Level 6 – the Instructor level and will soon be a Certified Healing Touch Level 1 Instructor.*

*My 'condition' no longer requires medication management, yet I continue doctoring. I see it as self-care or preventative maintenance; healing for me is much more than managing symptoms, healing means getting out of the circus, a stop to the performances, juggling acts and clowns. It means embracing my human condition, whatever that may be, for as long as I live.*

## Dawn's Interview

*What attracted you to energy medicine and why did you choose Healing Touch?*

I came into Healing Touch sick, because Western medicine told me I would never get well again. I was very sick. It doesn't really matter what I was sick with. My wonderful team of doctors said that they would help control my situation for the rest of my life. What one doctor actually said to me was, "We'll help you. We'll control you."

I have resisted control most of my life.

At that point I started looking around. I found a body worker. I changed doctors, because my former doctor told me, basically, I wasn't going to get well. I figured why continue with that doctor. I went to a book store and I ran my hand across a bunch of books trying to decide what to buy in this metaphysical arena that I had never heard anything about until I had a body work massage. When she put her hands on me, she would feel underneath where I couldn't relax. She would ask me if there was a reason why I couldn't relax there. I was so out of touch with my body that I didn't even know I wasn't relaxed.

She told me to go to the book store and just run your hands across the books and see which one falls out. It was a book on healing energy. I didn't know metaphysics. I didn't even know that word. I ran my hand across a book, by Echo Bodine, called *Hands That Heal*. It's a very simple, small book. I read it before I went to bed that night.

I went to work the next day; I was an elementary school secretary. A little boy came in crying. He had something really hurt. He was trying to tell me what was going on. I walked him into the nurse's room. I was the nurse. I wasn't a nurse, but it was my job. I said, "I learned something last night."

It was similar to what we call pain drain. I asked him if I could put my hand on him and see if it would stop hurting. He knew me and he trusted me. It was fine. I put my hand on him. I didn't feel a thing and I was looking around me, hoping nobody was watching while I was doing it.

Within about two seconds the little boy said, "I feel better. Let's go to breakfast."

I was so amazed and considerably frightened that I could do this after reading one book. Of course, I didn't do it again for months. I needed to know more.

I soon started seeing an energy practitioner. I didn't know that's what she was. My girlfriend had said to me, "I go to see this lady when I am at the end of my rope. I don't really know what she does, but I'm better when I leave." I too felt better after a session.

I started seeing this person once a month. Sometimes it seemed like it was guided imagery. Sometimes I sat in a chair, and sometimes I would lie on her treatment table and she would touch me. It was in her house. So I didn't know what it was. She never gave me her card. I knew she was a licensed social worker before she did this. We had talked about being able to use insurance, but then she would get to diagnose me and I was sick of diagnoses. I was sick of having to look up what I was in a code. So we didn't.

I was probably five or six months into seeing her, when I typed into the Google, Healing Touch. It went to a web site that I had never heard of. I went to the practitioner list and she was in there. She was a Healing Touch Certified Practitioner.

She also does all kinds of other things as well, her training is vast. Her name is Dale Golden. She is in Tacoma. She is amazing, simply amazing. Then when I was seeing her, I really started asking her what she was doing when she was doing it, and about the energy work.

The following school year I took a year's leave of absence in order to go to college. I was nine years old the first time I applied for college. I was forty-nine when I got to go to college for the first time. I decided that since I was just opening up to whatever was out here, and doing what I wanted to do, I would see if there wasn't something else.

I typed in Healing Touch again, into the World Wide Web and low and behold, there was a class in late September in nearby Seattle. I thought, well, here's my chance. I got a hundred dollar discount as a full-time student.

I went to my first Level 1 class. At that point I had moved out into the apartment we have in the barn. I needed to be alone. I needed to heal. I couldn't do that with the roles I was playing as wife. So I lived in the barn and my husband lived in the house.

We had bought a massage table in order to touch each other without any other reasons for touching, but to just be kind to one another. So I had a massage table that was up in our house when I went to Level 1 in Healing Touch.

I came back home from that and I said to my husband, "I don't know what I just did this weekend, but get on the table and let me show you."

I had a great big Level 1 Notebook. I put it on his stomach, right there while doing the chakra connection. I completed the chakra connection and he said, "I don't know what either, but I will pay for your next class."

That was how I really got started. He was so supportive of what I did. It was amazing work that we did with each other that helped him. He said it was better than massage because it doesn't hurt and he feels better.

There were people in that first class that totally scared me to death. One woman, her name was Rainbow something or other. She knew so much more about energy than anybody else in that room. I didn't even know what a chakra was.

*Why do you stay in Healing Touch?*

So why did I stay? I think the reason I stayed, more than anything else, was because of how well it worked. I never planned this journey. In fact, Level 2 wasn't even a thought until my husband suggested it. After Level 2, and again working on Mike most every chance I got, he decided that he wanted to learn at least L1, so he could also give back to me. I took L3 the same weekend he took L1. He has now taken up to L4, and we have a table up and ready in our home to work on one another.

Another reason I stayed, is that most of my life I was in situations where I couldn't do anything. Now I have something I can do. Whether my mother-in-law was having open-heart surgery, or whether my husband was having his toenail removed, I had a skill that I could use and I could use it for myself as well. I started doing self-chakra connection very early. The spiral meditation was fantastic to me, when I learned that one. That's why I got started and that's why I stayed. It gives me something to do.

*What is your favorite healing story?*

One of my favorite stories is my first "cancer" client. She had metastasized breast cancer, yet I had noticed congestion over her hip area during my initial hand scan. After a full body technique, I began doing Magnetic Passes-Hands In Motion over her hip. As I visually scanned her body, I noticed she was very quietly crying. "How did you know where my cancer started?" I most honestly could say, that I had no clue that was where her cancer began! It was a moment in our work together where things shifted, into a deeper trust of what Janet taught – "Just Follow The Energy". Her cancer had started as Ovarian Cancer, but my hands had noticed something not nearly that specific – but for my client, it was important.

*What do you see for the future of Healing Touch, or what would you like to see in the future for Healing Touch?*

I really long for the day when – instead of drive through coffee stands – we have Drive Up Energy Work Studios! On the way to work, or on the way back – sort of like a Barber Shop. Two or three practitioners always there, No appointment necessary, but you might have to sit a bit to wait your turn. I see a time when public knowledge around Energy Work is common and fully accepted as an option in Self Care and focused care supporting whatever condition common to humanity. Wouldn't it be great if after a fender bender, the car insurance company referred you to a Healing Touch Certified Practitioner?

I would really like to see an outreach to the younger generations. I'd like young men and women to learn about Healing Touch in childhood, as a way of life and loving, and then for those that are so called, to move into the business of caring for others using Healing Touch as their training and business model. Healing Touch IS enough – to offer the public.

*What advice do you have for new or potential students?*

I have found my students almost impervious to advice. I say that with loving laughter. It seems that when the Healing Touch bug bites --- well, there is nothing I can do to slow them down. And, that would be my advice, slow down, learn the techniques one level at a time. Practice, practice, then practice some more! Practice on healthy people! Practice on all ages, stages, and keep your eyes and ears open. Seek to notice the verbal and the non-verbal energetics that show up.

Ask questions, create community, and understand that the more you understand, the less you have to understand. Then begin again at the practice, practice, and practice part.

Final words of advice: Healing Touch is enough! Healing Touch is amazing. Digging deep into Healing Touch: the Techniques, the Concepts and Principals, adhering to the Code of Ethics and Scope of Practice are enough.

Made in the USA
San Bernardino, CA
18 January 2019